The Bible as Literature

This book introduces the Bible as one of the greatest works of world literature. Luke Ferretter provides a comprehensive history of the field, alongside detailed readings of the texts of the Bible and the most influential theories in the area.

The Bible as Literature: A New Introduction is divided into groups of texts in the Bible by genre – the Pentateuch; the histories; the poetry; the Wisdom literature; prophecy; the Gospels; the letters; and apocalyptic writing – reflecting the majority of courses. Organized into three sections, each chapter begins with a clear introduction to current theories around who wrote and edited each Biblical book. Ferretter then offers detailed and original literary criticism of that book, encouraging readers to pursue similar literary criticism of the Bible themselves. The final section in each chapter discusses a text related to each Biblical book. These texts include visual, musical, poetic, fictional, philosophical, theological, and psychological works. Throughout the guidebook, there are also useful text boxes and discussion questions, which contextualize examples and enrich students' understanding.

This engaging and accessible introduction reveals the Bible's significance both as literature and for literary study in light of current Biblical scholarship. It is essential reading for students and scholars of literature, Biblical studies, and cultural studies.

Luke Ferretter is Professor of English at Baylor University, USA, where he teaches twentieth- and twenty-first-century British and American literature and theory, and the Bible as literature. He is the author of *The Glyph and the Gramophone: D. H. Lawrence's Religion* (2013); *Sylvia Plath's Fiction: A Critical Study* (2010); *Louis Althusser* (2006); and *Towards a Christian Literary Theory* (2003).

The Bible as Literature
A New Introduction

Luke Ferretter

LONDON AND NEW YORK

Designed cover image: Shir ha-shirim, 1794, ink on vellum. General Collection, Beinecke Rare Book and Manuscript Library, Yale University

First published 2025
by Routledge
4 Park Square, Milton Park, Abingdon, Oxon OX14 4RN

and by Routledge
605 Third Avenue, New York, NY 10158

Routledge is an imprint of the Taylor & Francis Group, an informa business

© 2025 Luke Ferretter

The right of Luke Ferretter to be identified as author of this work has been asserted in accordance with sections 77 and 78 of the Copyright, Designs and Patents Act 1988.

All rights reserved. No part of this book may be reprinted or reproduced or utilised in any form or by any electronic, mechanical, or other means, now known or hereafter invented, including photocopying and recording, or in any information storage or retrieval system, without permission in writing from the publishers.

Trademark notice: Product or corporate names may be trademarks or registered trademarks, and are used only for identification and explanation without intent to infringe.

British Library Cataloguing-in-Publication Data
A catalogue record for this book is available from the British Library

Library of Congress Cataloging-in-Publication Data
Names: Ferretter, Luke, 1970– author.
Title: The Bible as literature : a new introduction / Luke Ferretter.
Description: London ; New York : Routledge, 2025. |
Includes bibliographical references and index. |
Identifiers: LCCN 2024045724 (print) | LCCN 2024045725 (ebook) |
ISBN 9781138806634 (hardback) | ISBN 9781138806665 (paperback) |
ISBN 9781315751566 (ebook)
Subjects: LCSH: Bible as literature.
Classification: LCC BS535 .F46 2025 (print) | LCC BS535 (ebook) |
DDC 809/.93522–dc23/eng/20241021
LC record available at https://lccn.loc.gov/2024045724
LC ebook record available at https://lccn.loc.gov/2024045725

ISBN: 978-1-138-80663-4 (hbk)
ISBN: 978-1-138-80666-5 (pbk)
ISBN: 978-1-315-75156-6 (ebk)

DOI: 10.4324/9781315751566

Typeset in Times New Roman
by Newgen Publishing UK

For Sam

τῶν γὰρ τοιούτων ἐστὶν ἡ βασιλεία τῶν οὐρανῶν

Contents

Acknowledgments	*xii*
Introduction	1
The Bible 1	
Literature 3	
The Bible as Literature 4	
1 The Pentateuch, Part I: Genesis	6
The Composition of the Pentateuch 6	
The Documentary Hypothesis 7	
Beyond the Documentary Hypothesis 8	
The Creation Stories 10	
The First Creation Account 10	
The Second Creation Account 11	
A Gender Community 12	
An Ecological Community 13	
Text for Discussion: Enuma Elish *15*	
Abraham 17	
Hagar and Ishmael 17	
Text for Discussion: Søren Kierkegaard, Fear and Trembling *19*	
Jacob 21	
Jacob and the Struggle for Existence 22	
Esau and the Face of God 23	
2 The Pentateuch, Part II: Exodus-Deuteronomy	26
Exodus 26	
The Divine Name 26	
The Passover 27	
Text for Discussion: St. Augustine, On Christian Teaching *29*	
The Ten Commandments 31	

viii   *Contents*

Leviticus 34
  Purity and Horror 34
  The Logic of Purity 36
Numbers 39
  Murmuring in the Wilderness 39
  What Did Moses Do? 41
Deuteronomy 43
  The Deuteronomists 43
  The End of the Torah 44
  An Endless Call 45
  Text for Discussion: Michelangelo, Moses *47*

3 The Histories   51
  The Deuteronomistic History 51
  Joshua 52
  Text for Discussion: The Ethics of the Conquest Narratives 52
  Samson 54
    Israel's Worst Nazirite 54
    Sex and Violence 56
  Ruth 57
    Introduction 57
    A Moral Story 58
    A Love Story 59
  David 61
    Introduction 61
    David as an Artist 62
    David, Bathsheba, and Uriah 63
    Text for Discussion: Rembrandt, David and Uriah *66*
  Esther 68
    Introduction 68
    Vashti's Refusal 69
    The Sex Contest 71
    The Slaughter of the Enemies 72
    Text for Discussion: The Greek Additions to Esther 73

4 Biblical Poetry   77
  The Psalms 77
    Introduction 77
    Intimacy 78
    Anguish 80
    Enemies 81
    The Wicked 83

Contents ix

The King 84
Praise 85
Text for Discussion: Psalm 1: Hebrew Poetry 86
The Song of Songs 89
Introduction 89
Ancient Near Eastern Love Poetry 90
The Eros of the Senses 91
The Songs of Description 92
Searching in the Night 94
David and Solomon 97
Text for Discussion: St. Bernard of Clairvaux, On the Song of Songs *99*

5 Wisdom Literature   102
Job 102
Introduction 102
Yahweh and the Satan 103
Job and His Companions 105
Job and Yahweh 107
Text for Discussion: C. G. Jung, Answer to Job *109*
Proverbs 111
Introduction 111
Madam Wisdom 112
The Woman of Strength 114
Text for Discussion: Lucy Newlyn, Diary of a Bipolar Explorer *116*
Ecclesiastes 117
Introduction 117
Qohelet 118
Vanity 119
Hedonism 120
Pessimism 121
Fearing God 121
Not-Knowing 122
Text for Discussion: Ernest Hemingway, The Sun Also Rises *123*

6 The Prophets   126
Isaiah 126
Introduction 126
History and Theology in Isaiah 1–39 127
The Highway through the Desert 129
The Servant Songs 132
The Non-ending of Isaiah 56–66 133
Text for Discussion: from Georg Friedrich Handel, Messiah *134*

x *Contents*

Jeremiah 135
   Introduction 135
   The Siege of Jerusalem 136
   Prophecies of Judgement 137
   Prophecies of Consolation 138
   Text for Discussion: Gerard Manley Hopkins, "Thou art indeed just,
      Lord, if I contend" 141
Ezekiel 142
   Introduction 142
   Ezekiel's Call 143
   Ezekiel's Sign-Acts 146
   The Valley of Dry Bones 147
   The River of Life 148
   Text for Discussion: William Blake, The Marriage of Heaven
      and Hell *149*

7 The Gospels   153
   The Synoptic Gospels 153
   Matthew 156
   Introduction 156
   Jesus's Parables 156
      The Theory of Parables 157
      The Laborers in the Vineyard 160
      Text for Discussion: The Infancy Gospel of Thomas *161*
   Luke 163
   Introduction 163
   The Annunciation 164
   The Crucifixion 167
   Texts for Discussion: The Alexamenos Graffito; *George Herbert,*
      "Easter Wings" *169*
   John 171
   Introduction 171
   In the Beginning Was the Word 172
      The Word Made Flesh 175
      Text for Discussion: William Holman Hunt, *The Light of the*
      World 175

8 Paul's Letters   179
   Introduction 179
   Paul's Life 179
   Undisputed and Disputed Letters 180
   Adam and Christ 182
   Text for Discussion: The Correspondence between Paul and Seneca 185

Contents   xi

9 Revelation   189
Introduction 189
The Two Beasts 191
    The Beast from the Sea 191
    The Beast from the Earth 193
    The Number of the Name 194
The New Jerusalem 196
Text for Discussion: Albrecht Dürer, The Four Horsemen, *from*
    "The Apocalypse" *199*

Index   *203*

Acknowledgments

I am grateful to the College of Arts and Sciences at Baylor University for the award of a Research Leave in Spring 2024, which enabled me to complete this book. My thanks to the Dean of the College, and to the chair and members of its Research Leave Committee, for this award. My thanks also to Baylor's Academy for Teaching and Learning for the award of an Undergraduate Teaching Development Grant to attend the Society for Biblical Literature conference in San Diego in 2019. I owe a great deal to my department chair of English at Baylor, Dr. Kevin J. Gardner, who constantly supported this project, even and especially during a period in which I recovered from serious illness. It has always been a joy to research and teach under his leadership. I owe a great debt of thanks to my research assistant, Lydia Martin, whose intelligence, diligence, resourcefulness, and competence in every aspect of the work I have done on this book have been invaluable. My thanks to Dr. Gardner for making her assistance available to me during summer 2024 with a Jimmie McKain Scholarship. My thanks too to her successor Annie Roufs. Baylor's English department is a wonderful place to research and teach in, and my colleagues and students, particularly in our courses on The Bible as Literature, have all contributed to the culture of intellectual excellence and charity in which this book grew. My editorial team at Routledge, in particular Karen Raith, have been professional and supportive throughout the project. My greatest debt of all, too great even to begin speaking of here, is to my beloved wife, Jen. This book is dedicated to my son, Sam.

I am grateful to the following for permission to reproduce texts and images:

Cover image. *Shir ha-shirim*, 1794, ink on vellum. General Collection, Beinecke Rare Book and Manuscript Library, Yale University.

The Scripture quotations contained herein are from the New Revised Standard Version Bible, copyright © 1989, Division of Christian Education of the National Council of Churches of Christ in the USA. Used by permission. All rights reserved.

A Diagram of the Documentary Hypothesis. Michael D. Coogan and Cynthia R. Chapman, *The Old Testament: A Historical and Literary Introduction to the Hebrew Scriptures*, 4th ed. © 2018 by Oxford University Press. Reproduced with permission of the Licensor through PLSclear.

"The Babylonian Creation Epic"; "The Babylonian Theodicy." Benjamin R. Foster, *Before the Muses: An Anthology of Akkadian Literature*, CDL Press, 1993. Used with permission of Pennsylvania State University Press; permission conveyed through Copyright Clearance Center, Inc.

Søren Kierkegaard, *Fear and Trembling/Repetition*, translated by Howard V. Hong and Edna H. Hong, Princeton UP, 1983. Used with permission of Princeton University Press; permission conveyed through Copyright Clearance Center, Inc.

Saint Augustine, *On Christian Teaching*, translated by R. P. H. Green © 1997 by Oxford University Press. Reproduced with permission of the Licensor through PLSclear.

One of the Possible Routes of the Exodus. *Exodus of Israel from Egypt and Entry into Canaan*. Credit: Leandro Perin Pissolato / Alamy Stock Vector. Image ID: 2A89PPA

Michelangelo Buonarroti, *Moses*, c. 1513–15, marble, San Pietro in Vincoli, Rome. Credit: Classic Image / Alamy Stock Photo. Image ID: E1FKJE.

Rembrandt van Rijn, *Haman Recognizes His Fate (David and Uriah)*, 1665, oil on canvas. The State Hermitage Museum, St. Petersburg, Russia. Credit: Heritage Image Partnership / Alamy Stock Photo. Image ID: DE0J7X.

"Happy the Man: Psalm 1." Ernesto Cardenal, *The Psalms of Struggle and Liberation*, translated by Emile G. McAnany, Herder, 1971. Used by kind permission of Emile G. McAnany, Professor Emeritus, Santa Clara University.

Biblia Hebraica Stuttgartensia, edited by Karl Elliger and Wilhelm Rudolph, Fifth Revised Edition, edited by Adrian Schenker, © 1977 and 1997 Deutsche Bibelgesellschaft, Stuttgart. Used by permission.

From *The Song of Songs and the Ancient Egyptian Love Songs* by Michael V. Fox © 1985 by the Board of Regents of the University of Wisconsin System. Reprinted by permission of the University of Wisconsin Press.

The Works of Bernard of Clairvaux. Vol 3, On the Song of Songs II, translated by Kilian Walsh OCSO, Cistercian Publications, 1983. Used with permission of Liturgical Press (MN) Books; permission conveyed through Copyright Clearance Center, Inc.

C. G. Jung, *Answer to Job*, translated by R. F. C. Hull, Princeton UP, 1983. Used with permission of Princeton University Press; permission conveyed through Copyright Clearance Center, Inc.

"The Route of the Exile to Babylonia." Credit: biblemapper.com. https://biblemapper.com/blog/

Lucy Newlyn, *Diary of a Bipolar Explorer*, Signal Books, 2018. Used by kind permission of Lucy Newlyn and Signal Books, Oxford.

"The Instruction of Amen-em-Opet"; "The Epic of Gilgamesh." *Ancient Near Eastern Texts Relating to the Old Testament*, edited by James B. Pritchard, 3rd ed., Princeton UP, 1969. Used with permission of Princeton University Press; permission conveyed through Copyright Clearance Center, Inc.

The Sun Also Rises by Ernest Hemingway. Copyright © 1926 by Charles Scribner's Sons; copyright renewed 1954 by Ernest Hemingway. Reprinted

xiv *Acknowledgments*

with the permission of Scribner, an imprint of Simon & Schuster LLC. All rights reserved.

"The Infancy Gospel of Thomas." *The Apocryphal Gospels: Texts and Translations*, ed. Bart D. Ehrman and Zlatko Pleše © 2011 by Oxford University Press. Reproduced with permission of the Licensor through PLSclear.

The Alexamenos Graffito, c. 200 CE, plaster, Palatine Museum, Rome. Credit: Zev Radovan / Alamy Stock Photo. Image ID: DGYB0G.

William Holman Hunt, *The Light of the World*, c. 1851–53, Keble College, Oxford. Used by kind permission of the Warden, Fellows, and Scholars of Keble College, Oxford / Bridgeman Images.

"The Correspondence between Paul and Seneca." *The Apocryphal New Testament*, edited by J. K. Elliott © 1993 by Oxford University Press. Reproduced with permission of the Licensor through PLSclear.

Albrecht Dürer, *The Four Horsemen, from "The Apocalypse"*, 1498, woodcut. The Metropolitan Museum of Art, New York. Gift of Junius Spencer Morgan, 1919.

Introduction

Whatever else it may be, the Bible is a powerful and moving literary work. St. Jerome described it as the *bibliotheca divina*, the "divine library," and this is a good description. The Bible is a collection of the most diverse works, written by hundreds of authors and editors, over a period of hundreds of years, in a wide variety of times and places, from Babylon to Greece, and with a wide variety of styles and concerns. It is most comparable in genre to an anthology. Just as one could find an Anglo-Saxon lament, Chaucer's *Wife of Bath's Tale*, a bawdy lyric by the Earl of Rochester, a Shakespearean sonnet, and fiction from Charlotte Brontë or Salman Rushdie next to each other in an anthology of English literature, so one finds a similarly wide diversity of texts between the covers of the Bible. Indeed, the very word "Bible" speaks to the simultaneous diversity and unity of the collection. The Old and New Testament canon came to be known in the early centuries of the church by the Greek neuter plural noun *ta biblia*, "the books," but in the Latin Middle Ages, the word *biblia* came to be understood as a Latin feminine singular noun, "the Book" or "the Bible." It contains an astonishing array of different kinds of texts, including creation stories, national epics, theophany, law, ritual, narratives of all kinds, poetry of all kinds, history, comedy, theodicy, songs of all kinds, wisdom writing, proverbs, philosophy, erotic literature, prophecy, lament, apocalyptic writing, visions, Gospels, parables, biography, letters, theology, oratory, and many more. It also has a broad unity in that these diverse texts are ultimately forms of expression by the Jewish people (in the Old Testament) and then the Jewish sect that would become called Christianity (in the New Testament) of how they thought and felt about every aspect of the greatness and wretchedness of human experience. It is this astonishingly broad, deep, and aesthetically powerful book, the cornerstone of Western literature, that we will read as literary critics in this book.

We will begin with some working definitions:

The Bible

There are many Bibles. In this book, we will be reading the Protestant Bible. This is because the Protestant Bible has been most influential in the British and American literary history with which the readers for whom this book is written will be most

DOI: 10.4324/9781315751566-1

2 *The Bible as Literature*

familiar. One could equally well write about the Jewish Bible, the Roman Catholic Bible, or the Eastern Orthodox Bible as literature. Indeed, the Latin Vulgate Bible, which was the major European Bible for over a millennium, could be said to have had a longer and wider influence on Western culture. But since it is necessary to choose one of the many biblical canons, this is the logic of our reading the Protestant canon. It is the text that has most influenced the authors of British and American literature from the sixteenth century on; and, in the form of the Authorized or King James version (1611) in particular, has often been considered a major work in the canon of English literature.

The Protestant Bible contains 39 books in the Old Testament and 27 in the New Testament. Its Old Testament contains the same books as the Jewish Bible, but in a different order and in different groupings. The Hebrew Bible was finally canonized about the time of the Roman destruction of the Temple in Jerusalem in 70 CE. Its books are in three groups, the Law (*torah*); the Prophets (*nevi'im*); and the Writings (*ketuvim*). The Prophets are subdivided into (a) The Former Prophets: Joshua, Judges, Samuel 1 and 2, and Kings 1 and 2; and (b) The Latter Prophets: Isaiah, Jeremiah, Ezekiel, and The Twelve (Hosea–Malachi). The Writings, the third section of the Hebrew Bible, contains:

Psalms
Proverbs
Job
The Five Scrolls:
    Song of Solomon
    Ruth
    Lamentations
    Ecclesiastes
    Esther
Daniel
Ezra–Nehemiah
Chronicles 1 and 2

So, although the Hebrew Bible contains the same 39 books as the Protestant Old Testament, they are in a different order and are associated differently with each other. The reason for this difference is that, during the Reformation, Protestant scholars followed the order not of the Jewish Bible but of the Septuagint.

The Septuagint (LXX) is the Greek translation and expansion of the Hebrew Bible begun in Alexandria in the third century BCE. It is so called because of a legend that 70 (in Latin, *septuaginta*) or 72 translators worked on it (in the latter case, six for each of the 12 tribes of Israel). Intended for Greek-speaking Jews of the Diaspora, it also became the Bible used by the early Christian communities. Its books are divided into four sections – the Torah; the histories; the poetic and Wisdom books; and the prophets. It includes many more books than the Hebrew Bible, which are retained in the Roman Catholic and Eastern

Orthodox Bibles. When St. Jerome was authorized by Pope Damasus in 382 CE to create a new Latin translation of the Bible, the text now known as the Vulgate (or "commonly used") Bible, he separated these extra books, which existed only in Greek, from the 39 texts for which he had Hebrew originals, putting them at the end of the Old Testament. As a result, Roman Catholic Bibles include the following books, translated from the LXX original, which are not found in the Hebrew Bible:

Histories
   Tobit
   Judith
   1 and 2 Maccabees
Poetic / Wisdom Books
   Wisdom of Solomon
   Sirach
Prophets
   Baruch

The Roman Catholic Bible's books of Esther and Daniel also contain additions to the Hebrew text contained in the LXX. Eastern Orthodox Bibles (which vary from one tradition to another) also include some the following texts, which exist only in Greek:

1 and 2 Esdras
Prayer of Manasseh
Psalm 151
3 Maccabees
4 Maccabees (in an appendix)

At the Reformation, Protestant scholars kept only the texts with Hebrew originals in the canon, translating into the vernacular languages of Europe the Masoretic Text (MT) of the Hebrew Bible. The MT is the edition of the Hebrew Bible developed from the fifth to tenth centuries CE by Jewish scholars known as Masoretes, the name deriving from a Hebrew word for "tradition." This is the base text for the Hebrew books in the Jewish, Protestant, and modern Roman Catholic Bibles. Eastern Orthodox Bibles use the LXX. The New Testament contains the same 27 books in the Protestant, Roman Catholic, and Eastern Orthodox Bibles.

Literature

Literature is a large, amorphous, and changing concept. Loosely speaking, the word denotes writing considered valuable. As Terry Eagleton points out in his chapter on "What is Literature?," the concept has a history but not an essence (11–14). That is,

4   *The Bible as Literature*

literature is writing considered valuable, but what is considered valuable changes throughout history and throughout the world. Jonathan Culler observes that there is an institutional definition of literature – it is what those considered experts in the subject say it is – and a textual definition – there are elements in the texts that are the reasons for which experts consider them literary. There is a constantly shifting tension between institutions and texts that at any given time and place produces a loosely defined idea of good writing (28). For our purpose here, as we think about reading the Bible as literature, we can say first that, in our time and place, the Bible contains all kinds of writing that can be considered good or valuable by literary critics. Second, we will make the following observation about literature: it is not written by God. In the nebulous system of written and unwritten ideas about what constitutes literature and the study of it by literary critics, although almost every definition can be questioned, almost everyone would agree that the concept refers only to texts produced by human beings. This may seem obvious, but it matters for our understanding of what it is to read the Bible as literature.

The Bible as Literature

In Christian doctrine, each book of the Bible has two authors, God, and the person (or persons) who wrote it. Since literature is by definition written by people, to read the Bible as literature is to read it as the work of people. Many of the Romantic and post-Romantic writers who developed the concept the Bible as literature consciously intended it to mean that the Bible was literature produced by human beings rather than a book inspired by God. But it does not have to mean that. David Norton's magisterial work *A History of the Bible as Literature* makes clear that reading the Bible as a literary text is practiced both by those who do and those do not believe that the Bible is inspired by God. In this book, we will mean the following in speaking of the Bible as literature. Reading the Bible as literature means bracketing from consideration the belief, held by Jews and Christians, that the Bible is written by God. We will neither affirm nor deny that belief. To do so would be to enter another discourse than literary criticism, that of religious studies or theology. We will be reading the Bible as the product of the human beings who wrote it, just as we would read any other literary work. Readers of this book may or may not believe that it is also written by God, but all will agree that it is written by people. For Jewish and Christian readers, it is written both by people and by God; for readers who do not hold those systems of belief, it is written only by people. In either case, it is the product, and the aesthetically brilliant product, of human beings. That is how we will read this great text in this book.

This book is organized as follows. We will discuss all the main groups of texts in the Protestant Bible – the Pentateuch; the histories; the poetry; the Wisdom literature; the prophecy; the Gospels; the letters; and apocalyptic writing. Each chapter will deal with several biblical texts, usually individual books but sometimes groups of texts (like the Abraham stories or the David stories). Each book will be discussed in the following three-part form. First, I give an introduction to the theories of composition of the book. Literary scholars and students may initially be surprised at

Introduction   5

how few facts there are to give about who wrote each book, when, where, and why. Almost all such facts, particularly for the Old Testament books, are lost to history. So, biblical scholars build hypotheses out of the internal evidence of the texts themselves and the related ancient Near Eastern texts and artifacts that exist. In my introduction to each book (or group of texts), I give an overview of the dominant patterns of hypothesis and consensus at present. Second, the main body of the section is my literary criticism of the text. This is presented, like all literary criticism, as my best attempt to speak truly about the text in the light of previous scholarship on it. As with all literary criticism, subsequent critics (including the readers of this book) will be able to agree with, disagree with, or develop my views as they see best. Finally, each section concludes with a text related to the biblical book we have been discussing. This may be a literary, visual, theological, philosophical, or musical text. It is marked "Text for Discussion," and is followed by a series of questions on the text to guide the reader in thinking about its relationships to the Bible. These questions can be used individually or in a classroom setting.

This book is intended for all scholars and students of literature who are interested in the Bible. It can be used in teaching and studying in courses on the Bible as literature, both undergraduate and graduate. I have used the material in this book, in this three-part format, in both kinds of course, and indeed have refined the material in it as I have refined those courses. This book is also intended as an introduction to the Bible for literature scholars and students who want a single, clear volume on the Bible's significance both as literature and for literary study in the light of current biblical scholarship.

Works Cited

Culler, Jonathan. *Literary Theory: A Very Short Introduction.* Oxford UP, 1997.
Eagleton, Terry. *Literary Theory: An Introduction*, 2nd ed., U Minnesota P, 1996.
Norton, David. *A History of the Bible as Literature,* vol. 2, Cambridge UP, 1993.

1 The Pentateuch, Part I: Genesis

Genesis is the first book both of the Bible and of the first group of five books in the Bible. This group, from Genesis to Deuteronomy, is known as the "Torah" in Jewish tradition and the "Pentateuch" in Christian tradition. The word "Torah" means "Instruction" or "Law," and the word "Pentateuch" means "Five Scrolls."

The Composition of the Pentateuch

Literary critics are used to facts. The texts we study in British, American, and European literary traditions, from the present day as far back as the late Middle Ages, come to us as it were swimming in facts, about their authors' lives, thought, works, social, historical, and intellectual contexts. This is not the case with almost any of the biblical texts. It is certainly not the case with the Pentateuch. Indeed, the history of scholarly thought on the question of who wrote the Pentateuch, how, when, where, and in what contexts is almost as rich and fascinating a narrative as that of the Pentateuch itself. What we have, as we begin to think about the Pentateuch as a literary work, in terms of knowledge of the conditions of its production, are almost no facts, but a narrative, a changing history of scholarly hypotheses and shifting balances of consensus, which continues to change to the present day.

We will begin with two statements that can be described as facts concerning the authorship of the Pentateuch:

1. The Pentateuch gives abundant evidence, in almost every passage, of having been put together, in a complex and multiple process, out of pieces of other texts.
2. There is no agreement among scholars as to exactly what that process has been.

As David Carr puts it, "Source-critical studies have established the high probability *that* the Pentateuch/Hexateuch contains multiple sources, but clarity on *what* those sources are has not been achieved" ("Source Criticism" 321, emphasis in original). Here we will focus on two major elements of the history of scholarly thought on the question, first, the "documentary hypothesis," which achieved widespread consensus for about a hundred years (approximately the 1870s to the 1970s), and second, what has come after the documentary hypothesis since the collapse of that consensus.

DOI: 10.4324/9781315751566-2

The Pentateuch, Part I   7

The Documentary Hypothesis

The documentary hypothesis was first formulated as such by Julius Wellhausen in his *History of Ancient Israel* (1878). In 1805, the biblical scholar Wilhelm de Wette had argued that the Book of Deuteronomy was recognizably by a different author than those whose work can be seen in the books of Genesis through Numbers, based on its unique style and theological concerns. He also argued that it was reasonable to believe that Deuteronomy was the "book of the Law" found in the Temple in Jerusalem during the reign of King Josiah (640–609 BCE), as described in the book of Kings:

> The high priest Hilkiah said to Shaphan the secretary, "I have found the book of the law in the house of the LORD. When the king heard the words of the book of the law, he tore his clothes, [saying] […] "Great is the wrath of the LORD that is kindled against us because our ancestors did not obey the words of this book."
>
> (2 Kings 22:8, 11, 13)

By the time Wellhausen writes, this has become one of the "results that can be regarded as settled" of criticism of the Pentateuch, that "Deuteronomy, as an essentially independent law book, admits of being separated most easily" as an originally independent source of the Pentateuch (6). The next most easily separated source was called by scholars the *Grundschrift*, or "basic text," of the Pentateuch. As Wellhausen says, "its basis is the book of Leviticus and the allied portions of the adjoining books – Exod. 25–40, with the exception of chaps. 32–34, and Num. 1–10, 15–19, 25–36." Wellhausen argues that, because of its concerns and its authors, it is "entitled to be called the Priestly Code" (8). Pentateuchal scholars would come to call Deuteronomy and the Priestly source D and P respectively. What remains in the Pentateuch when D and P are separated out, for Wellhausen, is the "Jehovistic history book," which, by contrast with D and P, is "essentially of a narrative character, and sets forth with full sympathy and enjoyment the materials handed down by tradition" (7). Wellhausen dates this source to the eighth century BCE, to "the period of the kings and prophets which preceded the dissolution of the two Israelite kingdoms by the Assyrians" (9). He calls the document JE, by which he means that it is a combination of two earlier sources, J and E. "J" stands for the "Yahwist" source (spelled with an initial "J" in German), and "E" stands for the "Elohist" source.

Since the eighteenth century, Bible scholars had argued that, since the divine name Yahweh is used in some of the stories in the Pentateuch, and the Hebrew word *elohim*, "God," is used in others, these stories can be separated out into two originally independent documents. One of the first such critics, Jean Astruc, had argued that these were the documents Moses had used in assembling the Pentateuch. He called them the A and B sources (and also identifying C and D sources), and published an edition of Genesis with the text separated into these four sources. Subsequent scholars would call Astruc's A and B sources J and E, often dating J to the tenth or ninth centuries BCE and E to the ninth or eighth centuries BCE.

8 *The Bible as Literature*

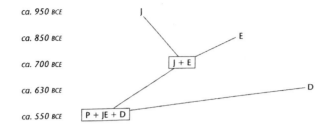

Figure 1.1 A Diagram of the Documentary Hypothesis. Michael D. Coogan and Cynthia R. Chapman, *The Old Testament: A Historical and Literary Introduction to the Hebrew Scriptures*, 4th ed. © 2018 by Oxford University Press. Reproduced with permission of the Licensor through PLSclear.

Wellhausen's particular contribution to the documentary hypothesis is that the Priestly Code is not the earliest or foundational text in the Pentateuch, as most previous scholars had believed, but rather the last. He argues that it dates from after the Babylonian exile, from which the people of Judah began to return in 538 BCE. So, in Wellhausen's formulation, the sources of the Pentateuch are put together like this: the J source was a history written in the southern kingdom of Judah; the E source a later history written in the northern kingdom of Israel. Both sources, and their combination into the JE document, date from between the ninth and eighth centuries BCE. The E source has come down to us "only in extracts" incorporated into JE (8), whereas J is a relatively continuous narrative. The D source dates from King Josiah's reformation in the late seventh century BCE, and P from the postexilic period, no later than the mid-fifth century BCE. P was also the final editor of the already existing sources. The J and E sources were combined, perhaps after the northern kingdom was destroyed by the Assyrians in 722 BCE, and refugees from the north had brought E to Jerusalem. After the Babylonian exile, P combined JE, D, and his own traditions and documents into the Pentateuch. See Figure 1.1.

Beyond the Documentary Hypothesis

The consensus achieved by the documentary hypothesis until it began to be seriously criticized by several leading scholars in the 1970s was always a consensus only on its broadest outlines. There were always tensions within individual accounts of the theory, and between other methods of research on the Pentateuch and the documentary hypothesis. The E source was often recognized to be so fragmentary as scarcely to constitute a source at all. The J source was quickly split into multiple sources, designated by symbols such as J^1 and J^2. Other scholars hypothesized other aspects or origins of these sources, such as a lay source L, a nomadic source N, or a Seir source S. The nature of J's thought and text differed greatly too among individual scholars.

Once criticisms of the documentary hypothesis began to be taken seriously, even this broad consensus began to collapse, and what has emerged in its place is, as

David Carr puts it, "a debate surrounding virtually every aspect in it" ("Changes" 434). As John Van Seters writes, "there is no consensus, or even a majority viewpoint" on the composition of the Pentateuch in current scholarship (52). Here we will mention just one influential move beyond the documentary hypothesis, that of the contributors to the volume *A Farewell to the Yahwist?* (2006). The general thesis of this volume is argued by Konrad Schmid, that the different narrative parts of the Pentateuch – the primeval history, the patriarchal stories, and the Exodus story – stand more or less on their own. They seem to be much more autonomous literary units in their original form than parts of a long story from the creation to the conquest of the land (29).

If this case can be proved, that the Pentateuch is composed of individual narrative sections with a history independent of each other, rather than of three long narratives (J, E, and P) dealing with the same subjects, then the documentary hypothesis is wrong. As Schmid poses the question, "One may ask: Did the older sources, J and E, really exist?" (29). His answer, like that of all the contributors to the main body of the volume, is "No." Schmid focuses on the connection between Genesis and Exodus, that is, between the stories of the ancestors of Israel and the story of the Exodus. He argues that the text of the Pentateuch shows "discontinuity" in its connection of these two sets of stories (31); and that there is evidence to show that it was P that joined them for the first time. He concludes that "a Pre-Priestly connection between Genesis and Exodus cannot be proven and does not seem likely" (48), which means that the patriarchal stories and the Exodus story were composed from two separate "blocks of tradition" that existed "next to each other as two competing concepts containing two traditions of the origin of Israel" (49). They were not composed, as the documentary hypothesis posits, from a series of continuous and parallel source texts. These texts, at least J and E, simply do not exist.

So, what can we say about the composition of the Pentateuch – who wrote it, where, and when, and how it has been put together – in terms of certain facts, on the basis of which we can begin to understand and interpret it as a literary text? There is broad consensus among scholars, and I share this view, that there are three recognizable sets of authors' work in the Pentateuch. There is the material that constitutes much of the Book of Deuteronomy, which has a characteristic set of rhetorical styles and theological concerns. There is the Priestly material, of which there is a large continuous block from Exodus 25 through Numbers 10:10 (with the exception of Exod. 32–34), and which can also be found throughout Genesis and Exodus, for example in the first creation account (Gen. 1:1–2:4a), with its account of the divine sabbath, or the second account of the covenant with Abraham (Gen. 17:1–27), with its concern for the rite of circumcision. It is reasonable to call this material Priestly, because of its "strong concern for all matters that have to do with priests, the sacrificial cult and formal regulations of worship" (Van Seters 9). Then there is the non-Priestly material which remains. Much of this material consists of lively, earthy stories. It is unthinkable that behind each of the written works of these three strata of the Pentateuch there is not a long tradition of oral and written

10   *The Bible as Literature*

discourse. In the case of D and P, it seems most likely that there are multiple writers who have contributed to each stratum, so in discussing P, we will speak of Priestly writers rather than a Priestly writer. The D writers we will discuss in the introduction to the section on Deuteronomy in Chapter 2. The non-Priestly material clearly comprises the work of multiple lay authors. There has been much discussion in recent decades on the nature and role of the redactors of the Pentateuch, and I will assume here that it is unlikely that a redactor would not have an agenda, a set of reasons and concerns for which he is editing the text, and which he is attempting to express through that editorial work. Concerning dating, there are only hypotheses.

The Creation Stories

The First Creation Account

Perhaps the most striking thing about the beginning of the Bible is that, from its very first word, it is ambiguous. This word is *be-reshit*, "in the beginning." In Hebrew, nouns can take either the "absolute" or the "construct" form. The absolute simply means the noun; the construct (loosely) means the noun, plus the word "of." So, the absolute form *torah* means "law"; the construct form *torat* means "law of." If you want to say, "the law of God" in Hebrew, you use the construct form, "*torat* (law of) *elohim* (God)." Now, to complicate things a little, some nouns look the same in both the absolute and the construct form. The noun *reshit*, "beginning," is one of these. *Reshit* can mean "beginning" or "beginning of." The Bible's first word, *be-reshit*, "in the beginning," can mean "in the beginning" or "in the beginning of." So the first sentence of Genesis can be construed either as:

> In the beginning, God created the heavens and the earth.

or:

> In the beginning of God's creating the heavens and the earth, the earth was a formless void.

So, with respect to the metaphysical and theological question "Did God create *ex nihilo*?", the text of Genesis 1, from its very first word, is ambiguous. If that word is in the absolute form, the implication is yes, God created out of nothing; if it is in the construct form, the implication is no, God did not create out of nothing, but rather out of something already there.

The significance of this ambiguity is that the text is interested in other questions than the metaphysical and theological one about the nature of the divine creation of the world. As Terence Fretheim puts it, the origins of what may have been already existent at the creation "are of no apparent interest" to the authors of the Priestly creation account ("Genesis" 342). The text is not interested in authoritatively teaching its readers about the nature of the divine creation of the world. It is not primarily a philosophical or even a scientific text, although it is interested in both kinds of inquiry. Rather it is above all a reverent text, a text that expresses wonder, awe, and even joy at the marvel, the miracle of the divine creation in which its authors deeply and passionately believe. Despite its long history in Western culture as such, especially in debates from the nineteenth century to the present day on creation versus evolution, religion versus science, the text of the Priestly creation account does not seek to be an authority. Quite the contrary, it clearly and deliberately signifies its lack of authority, its lack of knowledge with respect to the God in whom its authors believe. It does not attempt to master God, as it were, with its theology, its metaphysics, or its science. Rather, it is content and even joyful to be mastered by God, to acknowledge that it does not and even cannot know the nature of the wonder of the divine creation of the world. It does not clearly know how God created the world, and says so; rather, it loves the fact that God has created the world, and expresses amazement beyond description that he has done so.

Let us be clear, as we think about beginning to read the Bible as literature. From the very beginning, the Bible is literature, and clearly signifies as much. By "literature" here, I mean that the first creation account is deliberately, clearly, and beautifully formed language, language part of whose purpose, meaning, and effect is that it is consciously formed into more beautiful patterns of sound and sense than more ordinary or everyday or practical uses of language tend to be. To put it more simply, it is poetry. Although not laid out in the Masoretic Text as poetry, and although not in fact poetry in the ordinary sense of Hebrew poetry, the first creation account is highly poetic. Kathleen O'Connor calls the first account a "poetic narrative," describing its language as "poetic like a hymn of praise" (27). As Fretheim points out, with its "rhythmic cadences" and "doxological character," it may have grown out of the liturgy of the exilic or postexilic community in which it was primarily formed ("Genesis" 341). Genesis 1:1–2:4a makes clear, first of all, that poetry is the most proper response to the divine creation of the world. Not science, not philosophy, not a master-discourse of any kind, but poetry. As Walter Brueggemann puts it, "The creature's proper mode of speech about the creation is not description but lyric, not argumentation but poetry" (27–28). To read the Bible "as literature," it turns out, from the very first chapter, is not to read it in a special, artificial, or contrived way; "literature" is, in fact, the very first point it makes. Poetry, language transformed into beauty, is the very first thing the Bible does, in Genesis 1:1–2:4a, as the first and most proper response to the awesome mystery of divine creation.

The Second Creation Account

Halfway through Genesis 2:4, the text cleverly and beautifully modulates from the Priestly creation account into a second, non-Priestly, creation account. In Hebrew, this modulation has a clearly crafted chiastic structure:

elleh toledot ha-shamayim ve-ha-arets be-hibbar'am
These [are the] generations-of the-heavens and-the-earth when-they-were-created

be-yom asot YHWH elohim erets ve-shamayim
in-the-day he-made the-LORD God earth and-heavens.

12   *The Bible as Literature*

In the first half of the verse, we hear about "the heavens and the earth"; in the second half about "the earth and the heavens." In the first half of the verse, the verb *bara* is used, a Hebrew word that means to "create" but can only be used with God as its subject. In the second half of the verse, the very common verb *asah*, to "do" or to "make," is used, which can be used with anyone as its subject. The first half of the verse, that is, neatly sums up and uses the heavenly, transcendental language and ideas that have been emphasized in the first creation account; the second half the earthly, immanent language and ideas that will be emphasized in the second.

Commentators disagree about the relationship between the two creation accounts, and indeed it is difficult to describe the relationship simply. I think that Fretheim is right to emphasize two things at once – both that the Priestly editors of the text incorporated a very different, non-Priestly account into the text, and also that they made careful efforts to create a coherent single text out of their account and the one they incorporated ("Genesis" 341). Two kinds of discourse on creation have been thoughtfully and aesthetically molded into a single, complex text. The best way to describe the complexity of this relationship is one of perspective. The first creation account emphasizes the heavens, while the second emphasizes the earth. The first emphasizes God's transcendent greatness with respect to humankind and our experience; the second God's immanent closeness to us. The first uses poetry, the language of the ultimate; the second uses story, the language of daily human life. The final, canonical text of Genesis contains and joins both perspectives. The two fused creation accounts say that the God of whom they write is both transcendent and immanent, both very far above human experience and intimately close to it. Its men and women, as a result, are the same – above all liminal beings, heavenly and earthly, great and humble, spirit and dust, all at once.

A Gender Community

Both creation accounts strongly emphasize the equality, the complementarity, of men and women in divine creation. Indeed, they do so to a surprising degree, given the patriarchal culture in which they were produced. As O'Connor puts it, it is "against ancient cultural expectations of male dominance" that Genesis portrays that "male and female form equal parts of creation" (38). In Genesis 2:18, we read, "It is not good that the man should be alone; I will make him a helper as his partner" (NRSV); "I will make him a help meet for him" (KJV). The Hebrew word for "helper" or "help" here, *ezer*, is frequently used of God in the Hebrew Bible, for example in Psalm 121:

> I lift up my eyes to the hills –
> from where will my help [*ezri*] come?
> My help [*ezri*] comes from the LORD,
> who made heaven and earth.
> > (Psalm 121:1–2; cf.
> > Psalm 33:20; Isa. 41:10)

As Nahum Sarna puts it, the term "cannot be demeaning" in its use in Genesis 2:18 in the light of its wide use in this and similar contexts, in which God is said to be the

The Pentateuch, Part I   13

ezer, the "help," of human beings (21). As O'Connor puts it, the term rather places the woman in relation to the man in the creation account "in a similar role to God" (52). The relationship between men and women, according to Genesis 2:18, is one of equality, mutual assistance, and respect.

This relationship is also one of intimacy – "bone of my bone, flesh of my flesh; this one shall be called Woman [*ishshah*], for out of Man [*ish*] this one was taken" (2:23). The text associates the relationship between the Hebrew words for man and woman, *ish* and *ishshah*, with the close relationship between the referents of these words, men and women themselves. This relationship has already been given a theological significance in the first creation account:

> So God created humankind [*ha-adam*] in his image,
>   in the image of God he created them [*oto*];
>   male and female [*zachar u-neqevah*] he created them [*otam*].
> (Gen. 1:27)

In no other ancient Near Eastern creation account is the creation of woman narrated separately from that of man, as in Genesis. The theological burden here is that men and women bear the image (*tselem*) of God. As many commentators point out, the cultural background for this idea is that of the ancient Near Eastern king, who represents God to his people, who is the image of God to his people. As Sarna puts it, this idea is "democratized" in Genesis (21). It is not only the king but rather all human beings who represent God in and to the human and non-human world. And we need to emphasize that the image of God exists in human beings only together, according to Genesis 1:27. As Brueggemann observes, "Humankind is a community, male and female. And none is the full image of God alone. Only in community of humankind is God reflected" (34). It is only in the relationship between men and women that their creation in the image of God comes into being. It is only together that human beings participate, in whatever mysterious sense that Genesis means that we do, in the life of the deity.

An Ecological Community

A similarly communal view is expressed by both creation accounts with respect to the natural world and human beings. The non-Priestly account emphasizes the essential relationship between humankind and the earth through its association of the Hebrew words *adam* ("mankind") and *adamah* ("earth"): "Then the LORD God formed man [*adam*] from the dust of the ground [*adamah*]" (Gen. 2:7). *adam* means "humankind"; *adamah* means "ground, land, earth." There are other Hebrew words that cover the latter semantic range, especially *erets*, "earth, land," which the first creation account uses 22 times. But the author of the second creation account deliberately emphasizes the relationship between *adam* and *adamah*, because he believes that the relationship between the words indicates a relationship in being. As Carol Newsom puts it, "For the Yahwist [...] there is no more telling indication of the intrinsic relatedness of things than the similarity of words. So to call the

14 *The Bible as Literature*

creature *adam* is to recognize its solidarity with Earth" (63). Hence she translates the term as "Earth creature" (64). William Brown uses "groundling" (80). The relationship is also emphasized in the content of the second creation account: "The LORD God formed the man from the dust of the ground, and breathed into his nostrils the breath of life, and the man became a living being" (Gen. 2:7). The author strongly emphasizes the physical relationship between human beings and the earth. We are made out of it, he says, and from the most intimate cellular level out are related to it and a part of it.

"The LORD God took the man and put him in the garden of Eden to till [*abad*] it and keep [*shamar*] it" (Gen. 2:15). The verbs here are significant. The NSRV translates them as "till" and "keep"; the KJV as "dress" and "keep." The first verb, *abad*, means to both to "work" and to "serve." It is also used in Genesis 2:5, "there was no-one to till (or "serve") the ground." As Norman Habel points out, since the "garden" (*gan*) of Eden is described as more like a forest than a field, "the specific rendering 'till' is unlikely" (49). Furthermore, along with *shamar*, to "keep, watch over, preserve," the sense seems to be something like "to serve and preserve." This is the relationship God intends, according to the second creation account, between human beings and the earth. Human beings are to serve and preserve the earth out of which they are made and in which God has placed them. As Habel puts it, "*adam* is *adamah*'s keeper" (52). In the ecosystem of Eden, this relationship is mutual. The garden provides sustenance for creation. A river flows out of Eden to "water the garden" (Gen. 2:10) and becomes four branches that water the whole world. The word "Eden" means "luxury" or "delight," a cornucopia. The second creation account envisages a mutually sustaining relationship between the created world and human beings who are a part of it. As Brown puts it, "God bestows upon [the *'ādām*] the commission to preserve the garden that nourishes him. The garden exists for the groundling and the groundling for the garden" (82).

The first creation account also contains the commands that human beings should "have dominion over" (*radah*) all the other creatures of the earth, and that they should "subdue" (*kabash*) the earth (Gen. 1:26, 28). In an early ecocritical work, Lynn White argued that these texts have given rise to "modern technology with its ruthlessness towards nature" (42). Although the object of White's critique is Western Christianity rather than Genesis, many subsequent commentators have criticized his implicit interpretation of the text, as I would myself. As we have seen, the Priestly account of creation in the image of God democratizes the contemporary ancient Near Eastern idea that kings were the earthly image of the god they served. All human beings, in Genesis 1:26–27, become the representatives of God on the earth, exercising dominion in his image. As Fretheim puts it, "Every human being […] is to relate to non-human creatures as God would" ("Ecology" 690–691). In the Priestly account, this means primarily a creative appreciation of the goodness in themselves (without relationship to human beings) of these creatures. God looks at each thing he has created, and "sees that it is good" (Gen. 1:10; cf. 1:12, 18, 21, 25). *Kabash* ("subdue") is a more violent term, but Fretheim is right to point out that "while the verb may involve coercion in interhuman relationships […] no enemies are in view here" ("Ecology" 690). In the context of God's blessing of human beings (Gen. 1:28), and in the context of

Eden, in which God envisages both humans and animals being vegetarians rather than predators (Gen. 1:29–30), the word means something more like "tame," "bring under control," or "cultivate." As John Rogerson comments, "Whatever they mean in other contexts, in Genesis 1 [*kabash* and *radah*] occur in the context of a non-violent world" (26). Above all, as we read the Bible as literary critics, the two accounts demand to be read in the light of each other, so that having dominion and subduing are to be understood as a kind of serving and preserving, and vice versa.

TEXT FOR DISCUSSION

Enuma Elish

The Akkadian poem Enuma Elish *(named after its first words, "When on high") is sometimes called the Babylonian Epic of Creation. Dating to the latter half of the second millennium BCE, it was recited or enacted each year on the fourth day of the New Year Festival in Babylon. The Judean exiles in Babylonia in the sixth century BCE may have heard some version of it. These are three extracts from the 1,100-line poem:*

> When on high no name was given to heaven,
> Nor below was the netherworld called by name,
> Primeval Apsu, their progenitor,
> And matrix-Tiamat, who bore them all,[1]
> Were mingling their waters together,
> No cane brake was intertwined nor thicket matted close.
> When no gods at all had been brought forth,
> None called by names, no destinies ordained,
> Then were the gods formed within these two [...]

> [*From within Apsu and Tiamat emerge four generations of gods. They annoy Apsu with their playing, and he wants to kill them. But Ea, his great-grandson, kills him first and begets Marduk. Tiamat declares war on the gods, and only Marduk can save them by fighting her and her army. He wins.*]

> The Lord [Marduk] trampled upon the frame of Tiamat,
> With his merciless mace he crushed her skull.
> He cut open the arteries of her blood,
> He let the North Wind bear it away as glad tidings [...]
> He calmed down. Then the Lord was inspecting her carcass,
> That he might divide the monstrous lump and fashion artful things.
> He split her in two, like a fish for drying,
> Half of her he set up and made as a cover, like heaven.
> He stretched out the hide and assigned watchmen,
> And ordered them not to let her waters escape [...]

16   *The Bible as Literature*

[*Marduk creates the world, including a sanctuary for himself in Babylon. The gods proclaim him their king.*]

When Marduk heard the speech of the gods,
He was resolving to make artful things:
He would tell his idea to Ea,[2]
What he thought of in his heart he proposes,
   "I shall compact blood, I shall cause bones to be,
   I shall make stand a human being, let 'Man' be its name,
   I shall create humankind.
   They shall bear the gods' burden that those may rest" […]
Ea answered him, saying these words […]
   "Let one, their brother, be given to me,
   Let him be destroyed so that people can be fashioned.
   Let the great gods convene in assembly,
   Let the guilty one be given up that they may abide."
Marduk convened the great gods in assembly,
He spoke to them magnanimously as he gave the command […]
   "Let him be given over to me, the one who made war,
   I shall make him bear his punishment, you shall be released."
The Igigi,[3] the great gods answered him […]
   "It was Qingu[4] who made war,
   Suborned Tiamat and drew up for battle."
They bound and held him before Ea,
They imposed the punishment on him and shed his blood.
From his blood he made mankind,
He imposed the burden of the gods and exempted the gods.

QUESTIONS

1. The primal beings in *Enuma Elish* are not the God (*elohim*) or LORD God (*YHWH elohim*) of Genesis, but rather Apsu and Tiamat, the fresh water and the sea. What is the significance of this different conception of who or what precedes the created world?
2. *Enuma Elish* begins with a theogony, in which several generations of gods are born. Most ancient Near Eastern creation stories do the same, as do those of the Greeks and Romans. Why does Genesis not do this?
3. *Enuma Elish* also features a theomachy, a struggle between the gods. The Hebrew word translated as "deep" (NRSV, KJV) in Genesis 1:2, *tehom*, is thought by some to be cognate with the Akkadian *tiamat*, both meaning "sea." There are passages throughout the Hebrew Bible that seem to refer to a story in which God created the world by defeating a sea monster

representing the forces of chaos (Job 26:12–13; Psalm 89:9–10; Isa. 27:1). To what extent does the Bible use or reject the story of Marduk creating the world out of the vanquished Sea?

4. Marduk creates the waters above the earth and the waters on the earth out of Tiamat's body. This is very reminiscent of God's creation of the waters above and below the "dome" of the sky in Genesis 1:6. What is the most likely relationship between these features of the two creation stories?

5. Ea, the god of wisdom, creates humankind in order to make a race of workers for the gods, so that work previously done by the gods can be done by men and women. No such idea appears in Genesis. Why not?

6. Ea creates humankind out of the dead body of one of the gods who sided with Tiamat in her attempt to kill all her children. Qingu is killed for this crime, and out of his blood Ea creates humankind. This is very different to Genesis, in which men and women are first created in God's image, and second out of dust and the breath of life. What is the significance of these differences?

Abraham

The cycle of stories about Abraham are heterogeneous, complex, often repeated, and the logic of the way in which they have been edited together is not always clear. The heart of the cycle, however, is the covenant (*berit*), God's series of promises to Abraham and his "seed" (KJV) or "offspring" (NRSV) (Gen. 13:16). These terms translate the Hebrew *zera*, which means both. In this covenant, God promises Abraham that he will become the progenitor of a great nation (12:2), that his offspring will be so numerous that they cannot be counted (13:16; 15:5; 17:2; 22:17), and that God will give Abraham's offspring the land of Canaan (12:7; 13:14–15; 15:18–21; 17:8), which they will possess forever. Indeed, Abraham will be the father of a "multitude of nations [*hamon goyim*]" (17:4), and God changes his name from Abram to Abraham to signify precisely this. The word *hamon* means a crowd (or the noise made by a crowd); the name Abraham (*avraham*) is derived here from the words for "father" (*av*) and *ham(on)*, "large crowd," and so means "father of a multitude." God promises Abraham that his wife Sarah will bear a son, although she is 90 and Abraham is 100 (17:15, 17; 18:10–15; 21:1–2), and that he will "establish his covenant" with this son Isaac "as an everlasting covenant for his offspring after him" (17:19). The sign of the covenant is circumcision (17:10–14).

Hagar and Ishmael

Perhaps the most striking thing about the story of God's covenant with Abraham is its dual, indeed ultimately universal, nature. On the one hand, God makes his covenant with Abraham, and through him with his son Isaac, and through him with all the people of Israel. As Sarna puts it, "God elects Israel to be his special people"

18 *The Bible as Literature*

(124). But, as we have already seen, it is a part of that very covenant that Abraham will be a father of "a multitude of nations" (Gen. 17:5), not only the single nation of Israel; and that all peoples will be blessed (or bless themselves) by Abraham's offspring (Gen. 12:3). As Fretheim puts it, "God's choice of Abraham serves as an initially exclusive move for the sake of a maximally inclusive end" ("Genesis" 424). This tension (or perhaps harmony) is expressed most clearly in the stories of Hagar and Ishmael.

There are two extended stories of Hagar and Ishmael (Gen. 16:1–16; 21:8–20), and they are both primarily non-Priestly material. Fretheim rightly points out that "through this 'doubling', Hagar and Ishmael become more prominent figures in the story of Abraham, receiving almost as much attention as Isaac" ("Genesis" 487–488). Both stories are remarkable for their emphasis on the way in which God treats Hagar and Ishmael as if they were members of his covenant people. In both, Hagar is compared to the people of Israel. She is an Egyptian slave, calling to mind the slavery the Israelites will endure in Egypt. When she "looks with contempt" on Sarah after she has conceived, Sarah "dealt harshly [*anah*]" with her (Gen. 16:6). The verb *anah* means to "afflict," and it is the verb used of the harsh treatment of the Israelites when they are slaves in Egypt (Exod. 1:11, 12; Deut. 26:6). Hagar is as oppressed by Sarah as the people of Israel are by the Egyptians. As a result she runs away, wandering in the desert near the Egyptian border in the first story (16:7), and in the desert south of Canaan in the second (21:14). This means that in both versions of the story, Hagar wanders in the very wilderness that the people of Israel will wander in for 40 years on their way to the promised land. God even miraculously provides water for her in this wilderness (21:19), just as he does for the people of Israel (Exod. 17:17; Num. 20:1–13).

God's promises to Hagar and Ishmael are precisely the same as those he makes to Abraham and Isaac. He promises Hagar, "I will so greatly multiply your offspring that they cannot be counted for multitude" (16:10), just as he promises Abraham (13:16; 15:5; 17:2; 22:17). He says that he will make a *goy gadol*, a "great nation," out of Ishmael (17:20; cf. 21:18, 13), just as he says of Abraham (12:2). Indeed God says of Ishmael, "I will bless him and make him fruitful and exceedingly numerous; he shall be the father of twelve princes, and I will make him a great nation" (17:20). Not only will Ishmael be blessed as Abraham is, and have numerous offspring as Abraham will, but he will also be the father of 12 princes, just as Isaac's son Jacob will be the father of 12 sons, the ancestors of the 12 tribes of Israel. Indeed, the sons of Ishmael are called "twelve princes according to their tribes" (25:16), just as are the people of Israel (Num. 2:1–31). Ishmael is circumcised, which is "the sign of the covenant" (17:11), making him "integrally related," as Fretheim puts it, to the chosen line ("Genesis" 461). Finally, the stories make it clear that not only is Hagar blessed by God as much as any of the patriarchs of Israel, but in one sense she has an even closer relationship to him than any of them. She gives God a name, the only person in the Hebrew Bible to do so. "She named the LORD who spoke to her, 'You are El-roi' [the God who sees me]; for she said, 'Have I really seen God and remained alive after seeing him?'" (16:13).

The Pentateuch, Part I 19

Indeed, not only does she name God, but she names him for precisely the unusually close relationship God has allowed her to have with him.

So the stories about Abraham, Sarah, and Isaac, and the stories about Abraham, Hagar, and Ishmael exist in a very unusual relationship with one another. Both the Priestly and the non-Priestly material contain explicit attempts to resolve the tension between them, but the stories as a group insist upon it. In Genesis 17 (which is Priestly), God says, "As for Ishmael, I have heard you; I will bless him and make him fruitful and exceedingly numerous [...] and I will make him a great nation; but my covenant I will establish with Isaac" (17:20–21). Isaac is distinguished as the only son with whom God establishes his covenant. But Ishmael, as we have seen, is promised all the blessings of the covenant too. Fretheim is exactly right to say that God's promises to Ishmael "amount to a covenant" ("Genesis" 459), although that word is not used. The single difference between the promises to Isaac and Ishmael is the land of Canaan, which is promised only to Abraham's descendants through Isaac. But in terms of the stories themselves in the Abraham cycle, they end with the sons of Ishmael settling "from Havilah to Shur" (25:18) and with Isaac settling at Beer Lahai Roi (25:11). Although only Isaac's descendants are promised Canaan, the Abraham stories end with Isaac and Ishmael both living in a place that they can call their own. In Genesis 21:13 (which is non-Priestly), God tells Abraham, "It is through Isaac that that offspring shall be named for you. As for the son of the slave woman, I will make a nation of him also." Indeed God will "make a nation of [Ishmael], because he is [Abraham's] offspring" (21:13), terms that could be precisely applied to the nation of Israel (cf. 12:2). Despite the apparent attempts by both Priestly and non-Priestly writers in the Abraham cycle to restrict the covenant to the descendants of Isaac and Jacob, they in fact clearly say two things at once in the stories they collect, write, and edit. On the one hand, the people of Israel, the descendants of Abraham, Isaac, and Jacob, are God's chosen people, the people with whom he makes his covenant. On the other hand, so is everyone else. The Abraham cycle tells the story of God's covenant as it were on both a treble and a bass clef, telling two stories concurrently. In the foreground is the story of God choosing Israel; in the background, and only just in the background, is the story in which God chooses everyone else as well.

TEXT FOR DISCUSSION

Søren Kierkegaard, *Fear and Trembling*

In Fear and Trembling *(1843), the Danish philosopher Søren Kierkegaard meditates on the radical nature of faith, which he argues cannot be considered in any way inferior to or a mere step on the way to reason. In the text below, he begins by imagining a man who thinks deeply about the story of Abraham's trial, in which God tells him to sacrifice his son Isaac (Gen. 22:1–19). The man imagines several versions of the story, including these three:*

20   *The Bible as Literature*

I

Abraham lifted the boy up and walked on, holding his hand [...] Then Abraham turned away from him for a moment, but when Isaac saw Abraham's face again, it had changed: his gaze was wild, his whole being was sheer terror. He seized Isaac by the chest, threw him to the ground, and said, "Stupid boy, do you think I am your father? I am an idolater. Do you think it is God's command? No, it is my desire." Then Isaac trembled and cried out in his anguish: "God in heaven, have mercy on me, God of Abraham, have mercy on me; if I have no father on earth, then you be my father!" But Abraham said softly to himself, "Lord God in heaven, I thank you; it is better that he believes me a monster than that he should lose faith in you." [...]

II

[Abraham] looked up and saw Mount Moriah far away, but once again he turned his eyes toward the ground. Silently he arranged the firewood and bound Isaac; silently he drew the knife – then he saw the ram that God had selected. This he sacrificed and went home. – From that day henceforth, Abraham was old; he could not forget that God had ordered him to do this. Isaac flourished as before, but Abraham's eyes were darkened and he saw joy no more [...]

IV

Abraham made everything ready for the sacrifice, calmly and gently, but when he turned away and drew the knife, Isaac saw that Abraham's left hand was clenched in despair, that a shudder went through his whole body – but Abraham drew the knife. Then they returned home again, and Sarah hurried to meet them, but Isaac had lost the faith. Not a word is ever said of this in the world, and Isaac never talked to anyone about what he had seen, and Abraham did not suspect that anyone had seen it [...]

Thus, and in many similar ways did the man of whom we speak ponder this event. Every time he returned from a pilgrimage to Mount Moriah, he sank down wearily, folded his hands, and said, "No one was as great as Abraham. Who was able to understand him?"

QUESTIONS

Read Genesis 22:1–19, the story of God's command to Abraham to sacrifice Isaac. Kierkegaard reflects deeply on this story as a portrayal of faith.

1. In the first version of Kierkegaard's imaginative revision of the story, Abraham pretends to Isaac that the sacrifice is his idea, not God's, so that

Isaac does not lose faith in a God who would ask for something so terrible. In the biblical story, Abraham does not do this (Gen. 22:9–10). What is the difference between Kierkegaard's Abraham and the Abraham of the biblical story? Why has Kierkegaard created this difference? (I would suggest that Kierkegaard is creating a more understandable, more ordinarily human character to emphasize the extraordinary nature of the faith exemplified by the biblical character. Would you agree, or not?)

2. In the second imaginative reconstruction, Abraham loses all joy in his relation to God, because the God who could ask this is a cruel God. Why has Kierkegaard created this difference between his Abraham and the Bible's? (I would suggest that he is imagining how easy it would be for an ordinary, fallible human being to feel this way, and therefore how extraordinary the faith of the biblical Abraham is. Would you agree or not?)

3. In the final reconstruction, Abraham betrays his horror at the God who asks for this sacrifice as he draws the knife. Isaac sees this on his face, and quietly abandons faith in such a God. What is the significance of these differences from the biblical characters?

4. None of the understandable or expected human emotions are narrated in the biblical story. As O'Connor puts it, "Missing are sounds, shouts, struggles, gasps of fear, cries of sorrow, screams of resistance" (313). Why is this? What is the effect of this detached, objective style of narration?

5. Enlightenment philosopher Immanuel Kant thinks very differently about the story than Kierkegaard. He writes:

> In some cases man can be sure that the voice he hears is not God's; for if the voice commands him to do something contrary to the moral law, then [...] he must consider it an illusion. We can use, as an example, the myth of the sacrifice that Abraham was going to make by butchering and burning his only son at God's command [...] Abraham should have replied to this supposedly divine voice, "That I ought not to kill my good son is quite certain. But that you, this apparition, are God – of that I am not certain, and never can be, not even if this voice rings down to me from (visible) heaven."
>
> (115)

Who interprets the biblical story better, Kierkegaard or Kant?

Jacob

Perhaps the first question that strikes the reader of the cycle of stories about Jacob is the question of the morality of the stories. Jacob is God's chosen son, to whom God continues to make the promises of the covenant he made with Abraham and Isaac (Gen. 28:11–17; 35:9–15). He is the eponymous ancestor of the nation of Israel. But throughout the cycle of stories about him, he behaves in a morally

22   *The Bible as Literature*

questionable, often contemptible, way. He lies to his father and cheats his brother. He schemes against his uncle, apparently with God's help, and is portrayed neither as a good husband nor father. He breaks the precepts of the Torah, in marrying two sisters (Lev. 18:18), and in deceiving a blind person (Deut. 27:18). His mother urges him to lie and cheat. The questions strongly arise for the reader of these stories, What is the good, according to these stories? Who is God and how does he want men and women to behave?

Jacob and the Struggle for Existence

The stories are clear about Jacob's character in the names he is given and their meanings. The name Jacob, *ya'aqov*, is explained twice. When he is born, his twin, Esau, is born first, and "afterward Jacob came out, with his hand gripping Esau's heel [*aqev*]; so he was named Jacob [*ya'aqov*]" (Gen. 25:26). The text derives Jacob's name from the Hebrew word for "heel." The cognate verb *aqav* means literally to "follow at the heel" and so figuratively to "attack insidiously," to sneak up from behind on someone. Jacob's very name means he is tricky, deceitful, someone who will take advantage of others as and where he can, sneaking up and attacking them from behind rather than honestly facing them. This indicates his character from birth. The meaning of his name is emphasized again after he cheats Esau out of the blessing of their father. When Esau discovers the trick Jacob has played, he says, "Is he not rightly named Jacob [*ya'aqov*]? For he has supplanted [*aqav*] me these two times" (Gen. 27:36), over Esau's birthright (25:29–34) and his blessing (27:1–40). Here Esau uses the verb *aqav*, to sneak up from behind and take advantage of someone, literally to attack from the heel. Jacob's name indicates his character throughout the stories – he is a "heel," a sneaky son of a gun, someone who gets ahead in the world by deceit and trickery rather than honesty, integrity, or plain dealing.

This does not change when Jacob is given a new name. When he wrestles with the divine man at Peniel, the latter tells him, "You shall no longer be called Jacob [*ya'aqov*], but Israel [*yisra'el*], for you have striven [*sarita*] with God [*elohim*] and with humans, and have prevailed" (Gen. 32:28). Jacob has wrestled with the divine man all night, and he renames Jacob *yisra'el* because he has "struggled" (from the verb *sarah*) with "God," *elohim*. The new name Israel, very surprisingly for a symbolic new name in this story of a dramatic encounter with God, does not mean anything radically different from Jacob's old name. When he was called *ya'aqov*, he was named for struggle; now he is called *yisra'el*, he is still named for struggle. The first name indicates a tricky, deceitful mode of struggle, and the second a more honest, direct, face-to-face struggle. But in both cases he is named for the fact that he is a battler, a fighter, someone determined to come out on top in the competition for resources that he finds life to be. As Fretheim puts it, "Struggle so characterizes Jacob that it will shape his relationship with everyone" ("Genesis" 573). This is true. Jacob does not markedly improve throughout the cycle of the stories about him. Sarna writes that Jacob's new name "signifies a final purging of the unsavory traits with which the name *ya'aqov* has come to be associated" (227), but it is difficult to see that such a purging occurs. Jacob's life remains as characterized by self-interest after he is renamed as it was before.

In the very next story, that of his reunion with Esau, although Esau graciously forgives Jacob his crimes against him, Jacob nevertheless ends the story by deceiving Esau. He tells Esau he will meet him in Seir, Esau's country, and although Esau is presumably expecting a continuation of their reconciliation in Seir, Jacob does not meet him there as he said he would. Rather, he settles in Succoth, much farther north – indeed, he builds *sukkot*, "shelters," there for his herds. Even as Esau forgives him for his past deceptions, Jacob continues to deceive him. Nor does Jacob seem to display any kind of moral improvement in the next story, that of the rape of his daughter Dinah. He offers no guidance nor takes any action throughout the episode. As Sarna puts it, "His passivity throughout the entire incident is remarkable" (234). Jacob shows no concern for the well-being of his daughter, nor for the murder of the many innocent citizens of Shechem committed by his sons. He says to them only, "You have brought trouble on me by making me odious to the inhabitants of the land [...] my numbers are few, and if they gather themselves against me and attack me, I shall be destroyed" (Gen. 34:30). As O'Connor puts it, he is "more interested in peace with the neighbors and his own safety than in the fate of his only daughter" (120). He remains as characterized by shrewdness and self-interest after he is named Israel as when he was named Jacob.

Esau and the Face of God

So what kind of ethics do the Jacob stories express? In my view, the moral center of the Jacob stories is Esau. Jacob is not a model of the good life nor of a life lived according to God's will. But Esau is. Or rather, he becomes such as the stories develop. After Jacob tricks him out of their father's blessing, Esau wants to kill Jacob. As a result Jacob flees Beer-sheba for Haran, some 500 miles to the northeast. When he returns to the land of Canaan, Jacob knows he will have to meet Esau again, and is afraid that his brother will kill him. As Jacob goes south, Esau comes north to meet him with 400 men. But Esau does not kill him. On the contrary, despite Jacob's crimes against him, he overflows with love for his unjust brother: "Esau ran to meet him, and embraced him, and fell on his neck, and kissed him, and they wept" (Gen. 33:4). As Sarna puts it, Esau is "genuinely moved" by Jacob's gestures of humility as he approaches his brother (229).

Most importantly, in his forgiveness of and overflowing love for Jacob, Esau behaves as God does. The stories have been carefully edited to emphasize this. The powerful story of Jacob wrestling with God at Peniel (Gen. 32:22–32) has been interpolated into the middle of the story of Jacob's return to Esau. The narrator carefully links the two stories by emphasizing the concept of the "face" in both. The word "face" (*panim*) can mean "presence" in Hebrew. So when Jacob thinks of trying to appease Esau as he returns to Canaan with extravagant gifts, he thinks:

> "I may appease him [*panayv*, lit. "his face"] with the present that goes ahead of me [*panai*, lit. "my face"], and afterwards I shall see his face [*panayv*, lit. "his

24 *The Bible as Literature*

face"]; perhaps he will accept me [*panai*, lit. "my face"]." So the present passed on ahead of him [*panayv*, lit. "his face"].

(Gen. 32:20–21)

These are the last two verses before the story of Jacob wrestling with God at Peniel begins. In that story, the concept of the face of God is also emphasized. After the struggle is over, "Jacob called the place Peniel [*peni'el*, "the face of God"], saying, 'For I have seen God face to face [*panim el-panim*], and yet my life is preserved'" (Gen. 32:30). Finally, as the story of Jacob's reunion with Esau continues, after this dramatic interpolation, Jacob responds to Esau's forgiving love by saying, "Truly to see your face [*panecha*] is like seeing the face of God [*penei elohim*] – since you have received me with such favor" (Gen. 33:10). The two stories are clearly and deliberately linked by the concept of the face emphasized in both of them.

The nature of the link is made clear by Genesis 33:10, "To see your face is like seeing the face of God." When Jacob sees that Esau forgives his injustices toward him, and that Esau overflows with love for him, what Jacob sees in these actions is the face of God. It has been difficult thus far in reading the Jacob cycle for the reader to work out what God wants. But finally, it is clear. God wants, indeed God is, the kind of forgiveness and love that Jacob hoped against hope to find in Esau, although he knew all too well that he could not expect it (Gen. 32:5; 33:8). To be in the presence of Esau's love and forgiveness for a person who does not deserve these things is to be in the presence of God.

The Jacob cycle therefore has an unusual moral structure. The hero is not the locus of the moral value of the stories. Rather, the apparent antagonist exemplifies how to behave, and this occurs quietly and subtly, in the background of the far more dramatic stories of the Jacob cycle. What is the effect, the significance of this moral structure? In my view, it is a question of the place of moral values within a realistic portrayal of social life. Brueggemann writes of the story of Jacob's cheating Esau out of their father's blessing, "The narrative exemplifies what is generally true of Genesis. This is not a spiritual treatise on morality. It is, rather, a memory of how faith moves in the rawness of experience" (229). This is exactly right. Like the Book of Genesis as a whole, the Jacob cycle constitutes an honest, realistic picture of the many horrors of which human beings are capable toward one another. Society emerges in the Jacob stories, quite accurately, as a ruthless competition, as a constant struggle of each against all. The fact that Jacob/Israel himself, the eponymous ancestor of the people of Israel for whom these stories are written, is constantly involved in this process of competition suggests that the stories' intended readers are all too familiar with this world. But, in the background of this world of constant struggle, quietly but unmistakably there exists God, who teaches human beings to behave better than this, according to his will, which in these stories is shown to be forgiveness and love. The Jacob cycle, with its very striking moral structure, says that this remains true at the time and place of reading, as it was in the time and place in which the stories are set. A person can choose, the stories suggest, between the competition for the world's resources by which society is primarily characterized, and the will of God who quietly but really exists behind the dramatic phenomena of society, and calls men and women, Israelite and non-Israelite, to the good.

Notes

1 Apsu is the name of fresh water personified as a primal divinity; Tiamat the name of the sea so personified.
2 God of wisdom, Marduk's father.
3 The younger generation of gods.
4 Tiamat's lover and leader of her army.

Works Cited

Brown, William P. *The Seven Pillars of Creation: The Bible, Science, and the Ecology of Wonder*. Oxford UP, 2010.

Brueggemann, Walter. *Genesis*. Westminster John Knox Press, 1982.

Carr, David M. "Changes in Pentateuchal Criticism." *Hebrew Bible/Old Testament: The History of Its Interpretation, Vol. III, Part 2: The Twentieth Century – From Modernism to Postmodernism*, edited by Magne Sæbø, Vandenhoeck and Ruprecht, 2015, pp. 433–66.

———. "Source Criticism." *The Oxford Encyclopedia of Biblical Interpretation*, vol. 2, edited by Steven L. McKenzie, Oxford UP, 2013, pp. 318–26.

Dozeman, Thomas B. *The Pentateuch: Introducing the Torah*. Fortress Press, 2017.

Fretheim, Terence E. "Genesis." *The New Interpreter's Bible*, vol. 1, edited by Leander Keck et al., Abingdon Press, 1994, pp. 319–674.

———. "Genesis and Ecology," *The Book of Genesis: Composition, Reception, and Interpretation*, edited by Craig A. Evans, Joel N. Lohr, and David L. Petersen, Brill, 2012, pp. 683–706.

Habel, Norman. *The Birth, The Curse and the Greening of Earth: An Ecological Reading of Genesis 1-11*. Sheffield Phoenix Press, 2011.

Kant, Immanuel. *The Conflict of the Faculties*, translated by Mary J. Gregor, U Nebraska P, 1992.

Newsom, Carol A. "Common Ground: An Ecological Reading of Genesis 2-3," *The Earth Story in Genesis*, edited by Norman C. Habel and Shirley Wurst, Sheffield Academic Press, 2000, pp. 60–72.

O'Connor, Kathleen M. *Genesis 1-25A*. Smyth and Helwys, 2018.

Rogerson, John W. "The Creation Stories: Their Ecological Potential and Problems," *Ecological Hermeneutics: Biblical, Historical, and Theological Perspectives*, edited by David. G. Horrell et al., T&T Clark, 2010, pp. 21–31.

Sarna, Nahum M. *The JPS Torah Commentary: Genesis*. Jewish Publication Society, 1989.

Schmid, Konrad. "The So-Called Yahwist and the Literary Gap Between Genesis and Exodus." *A Farewell to the Yahwist? The Composition of the Pentateuch in Recent European Interpretation*, edited by Thomas B. Dozeman and Konrad Schmid, Society of Biblical Literature, 2006, pp. 29–50.

Van Seters, John. *The Pentateuch: A Social-Science Commentary*, 2nd ed., Bloomsbury, 2015.

Wellhausen, Julius. *Prolegomena to the History of Ancient Israel*, translated by. J. Sutherland Black and Allan Menzies, Meridian, 1957.

White, Lynn Jr. "The Historical Roots of Our Ecologic Crisis," *Ecocriticism: The Essential Reader*, edited by Ken Hiltner, Routledge, 2014, pp. 39–46.

2 The Pentateuch, Part II: Exodus-Deuteronomy

Exodus

The Book of Exodus narrates the liberation of the people of Israel under Moses from slavery in Egypt, their receiving the Law from Yahweh on Mount Sinai, and their building the tabernacle to worship Yahweh in the wilderness. The Hebrew verb *avad*, to "work" or "serve," along with its cognate nouns *eved*, "servant," and *avodah*, "service," have a wide semantic range, covering all kinds of work and service, from enforced slavery to worship of God. The Book of Exodus describes a journey from one kind of *avodah* to another – from *avodah* ("slavery") to the Egyptians, to *avodah* ("service," or "worship") of God.

The Divine Name

Early in the first part of this narrative comes the episode of the burning bush, in which "the angel of the LORD appeared to [Moses] in a flame of fire out of a bush" on Mount Horeb (Exod. 3:2), and Yahweh tells Moses that he is going to deliver the people of Israel from their slavery in Egypt. In response Moses asks God his name. God replies, *ehyeh asher ehyeh*, "I AM WHO I AM." He adds, "Thus you shall say to the Israelites, '*ehyeh* [I am] has sent me to you'" (Exod. 3:14). The phrase *ehyeh asher ehyeh* has a range of possible meanings in English. The relative pronoun *asher* (which is not gendered in Hebrew) can mean either "who" or "what." *ehyeh* means "I will be" or "I am." There are only two tenses in biblical Hebrew, the imperfect and the perfect, and *ehyeh* is the imperfect of the verb "to be." Both the grammatical and the narrative contexts lead many commentators to prefer "I will be" here in Exodus 3:14, as I do myself. As William Johnstone puts it, "God's affirmation of the divine name is more likely to be a soteriological statement about the certainty of immediately impending future action [...] than an abstract ontological statement about God's intrinsic eternal being" (*Exodus 1-19* 81). Two verses earlier, as Moses protests that he is unable to confront Pharaoh or lead the Israelites out of slavery in Egypt, God replies, "I will be [*ehyeh*] with you" (Exod. 3:12). I agree with Fretheim that the use of the verb *ehyeh* here in Exodus 3:12, when Moses asks "Who am I?", suggests the basis of the primary sense of the verb in Exodus 3:14, when Moses asks "Who are you?." In both cases, the sense is "I will be with you," in the liberation

DOI: 10.4324/9781315751566-3

from slavery in Egypt and the journey into the good land which I have promised you. "The formula suggests a divine faithfulness to self [...] God can be counted on to be who God is; God will be faithful" (Fretheim 63).

A second sense of the name, in my view, is that it represents a partial refusal to reveal or indicate the divine nature. William Propp calls this passage a "type-scene," with parallels in Genesis 32:22–32 (in which Jacob wrestles with the divine "man") and Judges 13 (in which the angel of Yahweh comes to Samson's parents), where a divine figure refuses to reveal his name (*Exodus 1-18* 223). Johnstone argues that these parallels suggest that "'I WILL BE WHO I WILL BE' is not God's name but an avoidance of explanation and a reproof that Moses is making a demand impossible to grant" (*Exodus 1-19* 81). The second time the divine name is used, it is a verb (the verb "I am") used as a noun – "I AM [*ehyeh*] has sent me to you" (Exod. 3:14b). This means that the name is in one sense not a name. It is not a noun but a verb. As Johnstone rightly observes, "The breaking of the usual rules of grammar [...] matches the inscrutability of the name that defies definition in human speech" (*Exodus 1-19* 82). The meaning that can be discerned in the formula exists alongside the refusal of meaning that it also expresses. God reveals some of his name, some of his nature, to Moses, but no more than Moses in his situation needs to know. As Fretheim puts it, the formula signifies that "the more one understands God, the more mysterious God becomes" (63).

The Passover

The Exodus itself, Yahweh's deliverance of the people from slavery in Egypt, occurs on the night of the Passover. The death of every firstborn, person and animal, in Egypt is the last of the ten plagues by which Yahweh forces Pharaoh to allow the people of Israel to leave Egypt. The most striking aspect of the account of this event is the way in which, at the very climax of the story of the ten plagues, the narrative suddenly turns from narrating the dramatic events into a detailed prescription of how they should be ritually commemorated, both at the time in Egypt and once the people of Israel have settled in the land that Yahweh has promised them. The story of the death of the firstborn in Egypt, and of God's passing over the houses of the Israelites who have sacrificed the Passover lamb and sprinkled its blood on their doors, is interrupted at Exodus 12:1 with a long and detailed account of how to commemorate these events. The ritual for commemorating the events precedes the account of the events themselves. In the narrative of Exodus 11–12, God's deliverance of the people from slavery in Egypt is an event whose ritual commemoration is so important that the event itself has become altogether subsumed into its commemoration. As Brueggemann puts it, "the historical event fades off into or has been primarily cast in, through, and for liturgical reenactment" (773).

The final plague is announced in Exodus 11:1–10, in which at midnight, every firstborn male person and animal in Egypt will die. Then, before this happens (at Exod. 12:29), there is a detailed account of how to commemorate the events of this plague. Here the commemoration and the event merge. In Egypt, in the very month in which Yahweh gives Moses these instructions, the Israelites are to

28 *The Bible as Literature*

sacrifice a lamb (on the fourteenth day of the month, at twilight), and "take some of the blood and put it on the two doorposts and the lintel of the houses in which they eat it" (Exod. 12:7). When God passes through the land of Egypt that night, striking down all the firstborn, he tells Moses, "When I see the blood I will pass over [*pasach*] you, and no plague shall destroy you" (Exod. 12:13). Having given these instructions for the event of the Passover in Egypt, the text goes on, "This day [*ha-yom ha-zeh*] shall be a day of remembrance for you" (Exod. 12:14). The day is to be a festival (*hag*), a "perpetual ordinance [*chuqqat olam*]" to be observed "throughout your generations." Presumably this seven-day festival did not occur in Egypt after the event of the death of the firstborn and God's passing over the Israelite houses, since the Israelites could hardly have delayed in Egypt for a week under those conditions. So the term "this day" of Exodus 12:14 is constitutively ambiguous. On the one hand, it means the day in Egypt in which Yahweh destroys all the Egyptian firstborn but passes over the houses of the Israelites who have sacrificed the Passover lamb and sprinkled its blood on their doorposts and lintels. On the other, it also means the festival of Passover that annually commemorates this day in Egypt throughout the generations of the people of Israel (up to and including the time in which the text is written). It is the same with the account of the Exodus that follows the night of the first Passover in Egypt. The author writes, "That was for the LORD a night of vigil, to bring them out of the land of Egypt. That same night [*hu ha-lailah ha-zeh*] is a vigil to be kept for the LORD by all the Israelites throughout their generations" (Exod. 12:42). The referent, "that night," refers constitutively to both the first Passover in Egypt and to the annual commemoration of that Passover throughout the generations. The events of the first Passover night and the commemoration of these events in the Passover of the generations are so intertwined with one another in the narrative that they cannot be thought apart from one another. The event and the commemoration, the act and the reenactment, although logically distinct, are deliberately and carefully narrated in the book of Exodus as indistinguishable.

The meaning of this intertwining is clear. The event and the commemoration of the event are indistinguishable because Yahweh continues to act in the present, according to the writers of the text, as he acted in the past in delivering the people of Israel from slavery in Egypt and leading them into a good and broad land, flowing with milk and honey. What Yahweh did in the past in Egypt he continues to do in the present in Israel. The Priestly writer is emphatic about this. As Fretheim observes, the Passover Haggadah, the Jewish liturgy for Passover, "stresses that worshippers in every celebration are actual participants in God's saving deed: God brought *us* out of Egypt" (139, emphasis in original). This stress perfectly mirrors that of the text of Exodus. The event in Egypt is an event that continues throughout all the generations of Israel, including this one, in the present time of writing or reading the text, as it is ritually reenacted. Yahweh did not only liberate us from slavery and bring us into a flourishing place of our own in Egypt, hundreds of years ago, the text insists, but he continues to do so to this day. The text means that, in whatever situation the people of Israel find themselves in, year by year, in that very situation Yahweh is still present to deliver them and lead them to a good and broad place, flowing with milk and honey, as he was in Egypt.

TEXT FOR DISCUSSION

St. Augustine, *On Christian Teaching*

In On Christian Teaching *(396), St. Augustine, bishop of Hippo in North Africa, sets out a series of rules for understanding the difficult parts of the Bible. There are many kinds of knowledge outside the church, he writes, that can help the reader in understanding these texts, one of which is philosophy. In the passage below (II, 60–61), he compares pagan philosophy to the gold, silver, and clothing that the Israelites asked from their Egyptian neighbors before the Exodus (Exod. 3:22; 11:2; 12:35):*

Any statements by those who are called philosophers, especially the Platonists, which happen to be true and consistent with our faith should not cause alarm, but be claimed for our own use, as it were from owners who have no right to them. Like the treasures of the ancient Egyptians, who possessed not only idols and heavy burdens which the people of Israel hated and shunned but also vessels and ornaments of silver and gold, and clothes, which on leaving Egypt the people of Israel, in order to make better use of them, surreptitiously claimed for themselves [...] similarly all the branches of pagan learning contain not only false and superstitious fantasies and burdensome studies that involve unnecessary effort, which each one of us must loathe and avoid as under Christ's guidance we abandon the company of pagans, but also studies for liberated minds which are more appropriate to the service of the truth, and some very useful moral instruction, as well as the various truths about monotheism to be found in their writers. These treasures – like the silver and gold, which they did not create but dug, as it were, from the mines of providence, which is everywhere – which were used wickedly and harmfully in the service of demons must be removed by Christians, as they separate themselves in spirit from the wretched company of pagans, and applied to their true function, that of preaching the gospel [...] The event narrated in Exodus was certainly a figure, and this is what it foreshadowed.

Saint Augustine, *On Christian Teaching*, translated by R. P. H. Green © 1997 by Oxford University Press. Reproduced with permission of the Licensor through PLSclear.

QUESTIONS

1. Augustine begins by saying that pagan, that is, pre-Christian, philosophy contains many principles that are both true and useful for Christian thought and practice. What do you think of this view?
2. Augustine thinks of philosophy outside the church as containing principles useful for determining the truth (such as logic, rhetoric, or mathematics); useful moral principles; and even truths concerning belief in God. What would some of these be?

3. These true metaphysical and moral principles Augustine describes as precious metals that have been as it were "dug" from the "mines of providence" by philosophers outside the church, and which can be found in all times and places. He means that God has created the universe in such a way that much of the truth about its nature (as revealed in the Bible and taught by the church) is evident to those who try to understand it with their reason alone. What do you think of this view?
4. What do you think of Augustine's hermeneutic principle by which he is able to argue that the biblical text about the Israelites taking gold, silver, and clothing from their Egyptian neighbors before the exodus means that Christians should do the same with pagan philosophy? The New Testament writers interpret Old Testament texts in similarly allegorical ways (e.g., Gal. 4:21–5:1), and such modes of interpretation were widely used until the Reformation. On the other hand, it is difficult to see what a text could not be made to mean in this way. Is Augustine right or wrong to say that this is the meaning of the text of Exodus?

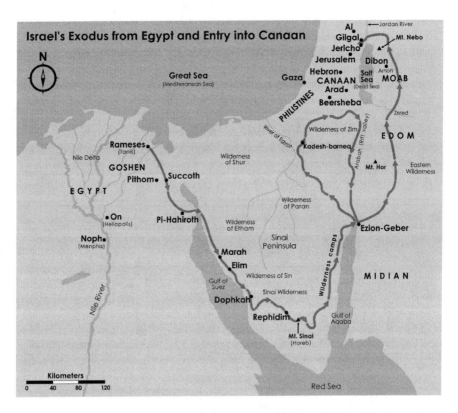

Figure 2.1 One of the possible routes of the Exodus. Credit: Leandro Perin Pissolato / Alamy Stock Vector.

The Pentateuch, Part II   31

The Ten Commandments

After the liberation of the people of Israel from Egypt, Moses leads them through the wilderness, until three months later they arrive in the wilderness of Sinai, camping there in front of the mountain. From Mount Sinai, God delivers the law to Moses. The law begins, in both Exodus and Deuteronomy, with the Ten Commandments, as they are traditionally known in English. In the Hebrew Bible, however, they are not called "the ten commandments," but rather "the ten words." The Hebrew noun ordinarily translated as "commandment" is *mitzvah* (plural *mitzvot*). But when the Bible speaks of the Ten Commandments, it calls them *aseret ha-devarim*, the ten words (Exod. 34:28, Deut. 4:13; 10:4). *Devarim*, the noun used in this phrase, is the plural of *davar*, "word," "matter," or "thing." The Septuagint translates the phrase as *deka logoi* ("ten words") at Exodus 34:28 and Deuteronomy 10:4, from which we get the word "Decalogue," which is perhaps the best English translation of the Hebrew.

The Decalogue is special. In both Exodus and Deuteronomy, the Ten Commandments are separated from all the other statutes of the law, and they are the first thing given in the law. They are given twice in the Pentateuch, emphasizing their importance, and while the two lists are somewhat different, they are recognizably the same list, unlike the rest of the laws that follow them, which are very different in Exodus 21–23 and Deuteronomy 12–26. They are spoken directly by God to all the people of Israel; the rest of the law God speaks only to Moses, and Moses relays his words to the people (Deut. 5:22–27). They are written with God's finger on two stone tablets, a material that seems to signify the everlasting nature of their content (Sarna 202; Johnstone, *Exodus 20-40* 228), and they are placed inside the Ark of the Covenant in the Tabernacle (Exod. 25:16; Deut. 10:5), whereas the rest of the law is written on a scroll and placed next to (*mi-tsad*) the ark (Deut. 31:24–26). Commentators ancient and modern have argued that all of the laws which follow the Decalogue, both in Exodus and Deuteronomy, can be understood as expositions of the Decalogue in given practical and developing circumstances. Johnstone describes the Book of the Covenant (the laws that follow the Decalogue in Exod. 21–23) as the "authorized exposition" of the Decalogue (*Exodus 20-40* 43); for Propp, it is a "commentary" on the Decalogue (*Exodus 19-40* 305). Ronald Clements perhaps puts it most succinctly: "The remainder of the Torah is, in effect, simply an elaboration of these basic commands" ("Deuteronomy" 893).

Despite (or rather, precisely because of) its position as the very heart of the covenant, from the perspective of literary criticism one of the first things that strikes the reader of the Pentateuch is how changeable and changing the Decalogue also seems to be. On the one hand, it is quite literally set in stone; but on the other its text and the meaning of this text seem to be constantly moving before our eyes. There are two main ways in which this is the case. First, as the history of the understanding of the Decalogue in the church makes clear, it is not clear how to divide its words into ten. In both Exodus and Deuteronomy, the commandments are called *aseret ha-devarim*, "the ten words" (Exod. 34:28, Deut. 4:13; 10:4). But as Propp puts it, "counting the commandments proves surprisingly difficult"

32 *The Bible as Literature*

(*Exodus 19-40* 302). There is no agreement as to what exactly the ten words are. In mainstream Jewish tradition, the first word is "I am the LORD your God who brought you out of the land of Egypt, out of the house of slavery" (Exod. 20:2); and the second is "You shall have no other gods before me. You shall not make for yourself an idol," all the way to the end of the prohibition on idols (Exod. 20:3–6). In the Roman Catholic and Lutheran Churches, by contrast, the first word is what Jewish tradition considers to be the second, namely the whole of Exodus 20:3–6, "You shall have no other gods before me. You shall not make for yourself an idol," and so on. There are then two commandments against coveting at the end of the list (which in Jewish tradition is just one commandment), which furthermore the Roman Catholic and Lutheran Churches divide up differently. The Lutheran Church follows Exodus 20:17 in counting "You shall not covet your neighbor's house" as the ninth commandment, and "You shall not covet your neighbor's wife [...] or anything that belongs to your neighbor" as the tenth; whereas the Roman Catholic Church follows Deuteronomy 5:21 in counting "Neither shall you covet your neighbor's wife" as the ninth, and "Neither shall you desire your neighbor's house [...] or anything that belongs to your neighbor" as the tenth. In Deuteronomy there are two separate verbs used for these two kinds of desire – *chamad* ("covet," NRSV) with respect to one's neighbor's wife; and *avah* ("desire," NRSV) with respect to one's neighbor's goods – whereas in Exodus, the verb *chamad* is used for both. In the Reformed churches, a third view is taken, in which the first word is "You shall have no other gods before me" (Exod. 20:3); the second "You shall not make for yourself an idol," all the way to the end of the prohibition on idols (Exod. 20:4–6); and there is only one commandment, the tenth, against coveting (Exod. 20:17; Deut. 5:21). The way the Masoretic text is divided into words, verses, and sections could support any of these views.

The second way in which the content of the Ten Commandments seems to change as we read them is in the differences between the two lists in Exodus 20:2–17 and Deuteronomy 5:6–21. The greatest difference between them is in the commandment about keeping the Sabbath, and especially in the rationale for this commandment. See Table 2.1.

Up to this point in the two lists of the Ten Commandments, the texts of Exodus and Deuteronomy have been exactly the same. Then the Sabbath commandment, the fourth in the Reformed numbering, is very different in Exodus and in Deuteronomy. The verb used for the Israelite's approach to the Sabbath is different – it is *zachar*, "remember," in Exodus; and *shamar*, "observe," in Deuteronomy – and there are several additions to the text of the commandment in Deuteronomy, which we have not seen so far in the previous three. The major difference in the two forms of the commandment is the reason for which Israel is commanded to remember or observe the Sabbath. In Exodus, it is related to God's creation of the heavens and the earth, as recorded in the Priestly creation account in Genesis 1:1–2:4a. Just as God created the world in six days and rested on the seventh, so shall the people of Israel do each week. In Deuteronomy, by contrast, a completely different reason is given. Here it is that the people of Israel used to be slaves in Egypt, where they had

The Pentateuch, Part II 33

Table 2.1 The commandment on the Sabbath in Exod. 20:8–11 and Deut. 5:12–15

Exodus 20:8–11	Deut. 5:12–15
Remember *the Sabbath day and keep it holy. Six days you shall labor and do all your work. But the seventh day is a Sabbath to the* LORD *your God; you shall not do any work—you, your son or your daughter, your male or female slave, your livestock, or the alien resident in your towns.* **For in six days the** LORD **made heaven and earth, the sea, and all that is in them, but rested the seventh day; therefore the** LORD **blessed the Sabbath day and consecrated it.**	**Observe** *the Sabbath day and keep it holy,* **as the** LORD **your God commanded you.** *Six days you shall labor and do all your work. But the seventh day is a Sabbath to the* LORD *your God; you shall not do any work—you, or your son or your daughter,* **or** *your male or female slave,* **or your ox or your donkey,** *or any of your livestock, or the resident alien in your towns,* **so that your male and female slave may rest as well as you. Remember that you were a slave in the land of Egypt, and the** LORD **your God brought you out from there with a mighty hand and an outstretched arm; therefore the** LORD **your God commanded you to keep the Sabbath day.**

Note: The text in bold is not contained in the companion passage in Deuteronomy or Exodus.

no rest. The Sabbath is a weekly sign that Yahweh has delivered them from slavery in Egypt, into a good and broad land flowing with milk and honey, where they are no longer slaves to another people but free to serve Yahweh as his covenant people. The Sabbath rest signifies that they are, because of Yahweh's faithfulness to them, free to rest.

What we see in these diverging forms of the fourth commandment is that the process of reflecting upon the Ten Commandments, of interpreting and applying their meaning to the community's lives in the changing circumstances of the present, is written into the texts of the commandments themselves. As Fretheim puts it, "the various canonical expressions of some commandments […] witness to an ongoing effort by Israel to address changing life situations" (222). Some scholars hypothesize an originally short form of all Ten Commandments (Weinfeld 242–243, 247–248; Biddle 105), in which all ten were of similar brevity to the sixth through ninth (in the Reformed numbering) in their final form in the Pentateuch. Whether or not such a form existed, the two forms of the Sabbath commandment seem clearly to bear witness to a long and continuous process of reflecting on its significance. Indeed, the Pentateuch emphasizes this process precisely insofar as it does not contain a short or repeated form of the commandment, but only the two different expanded forms. The process of reflecting on the meaning of the commandments, that is, is written into the commandments themselves. As Patrick Miller puts it, they "open up a moral and theological arc or movement that began long ago and is still going on. They are dynamic, open in meaning and effect" (*Ten Commandments* 6). In Johnstone's words, "A degree of indeterminacy is […] one might say necessarily, written into the very structure of the foundation document of Israel's relationship with its God, the Decalogue" (*Exodus 20-40* 46). What these scholars are pointing to is that text and interpretation are a single complex process

34   *The Bible as Literature*

written into the Ten Commandments themselves. The differences in form between the two lists of the Ten Commandments in Exodus and Deuteronomy make clear that they are on the one hand foundational for the Israelite community with respect to their relationships with Yahweh and with one another as his covenant community, and on the other hand mobile, demanding a constant process of reflection, interpretation, and application to the constantly changing circumstances in which that community lives.

Leviticus

Purity and Horror

The purity laws (Lev. 11–15) are often regarded in Christian tradition (but not in Jewish tradition) as the most difficult or unappealing parts of the Bible. Samuel Balentine writes, "On first encounter many will find its concerns with uncleanness not only extreme but perhaps also bizarre" (91–92). As we read the Bible as a literary text, by contrast, the purity laws of Leviticus 11–15 are extremely striking. Indeed to my mind, along with the powerful symbolism of the *aza'zel*, or "scapegoat" (KJV), in Leviticus 16:1–28, they have the most powerful emotional effect of any passage in the book. As literary critics, we are used to dealing with the effects on readers' emotions of literary texts, and the purity laws have a very strong emotional effect. The emotion expressed (or rather, felt by the modern reader) is primarily horror. This was surely not the intention of the Priestly tradents, authors, and editors of the text, but it is one very striking aspect of what it is now like to read it. What a modern reader of the purity laws as a literary text first finds there is horror at the porousness of the human body, at the fragility of its boundaries, constantly and in numerous ways threatened by the disgusting and dangerous things that can breach its apparent integrity both from within and without.

The purity laws deal with clean and unclean foods, childbirth, skin diseases, and emissions, both normal and pathological, from the male and female sexual organs. The effect of disgust conveyed in them is built up in several ways. In Leviticus 13, it accrues from the sheer repetition of the many ways in which the skin can become diseased so as to make a person unclean. The first section deals with a "swelling," an "eruption," or a "spot" on the skin (13:2); the second with a "leprous disease" (13:9), which includes a "white swelling in the skin that has turned the hair white," and "quick raw flesh" in the swelling (13:10); the third with a "boil" that has healed and formed a "scar," but "in its place there appears a white swelling or a reddish-white spot" (13:19); the fourth with a "burn," whose "raw flesh" becomes a "spot, reddish-white or white" (13:24); the fifth with a "disease" on the head or the beard, also called an "itch" and a "leprous disease," in which "the hair is yellow and thin" (13:30); the sixth with "spots," "white" or "dull white" (13:39); and the seventh with a "reddish-white diseased spot" on a bald head or a bald forehead, which "resembles a leprous disease" (13:43).

The Pentateuch, Part II   35

Reading about each of these skin flaws or diseases would individually produce a sense of disgust in most readers, but the constant repetition with difference of flaw after flaw, disease after disease that afflicts the skin over 46 verses strongly magnifies this sense. The effect is further magnified by the fact that, in all seven cases, the text portrays the priest carefully examining each kind of disease. To take the first section, on the "swelling," "eruption," or "spot":

> The priest shall examine the disease on the skin of [the person's] body, and if the hair in the diseased area has turned white and the disease appears to be deeper than the skin of his body, it is a leprous disease; after the priest has examined him, he shall pronounce him ceremonially unclean. But if the spot is white in the skin of his body, and appears no deeper than the skin, and the hair in it has not turned white, the priest shall confine the diseased person for seven days.
>
> (Lev. 13:3–4)

The text describes the priest looking as closely as possible at the diseased skin, to gauge whether the disease is visible beneath the surface of the skin as well as on its surface, and to assess the color of the spot. He also has to look closely at the body hair in the diseased part of the skin, to assess its color. In the second section (13:9–17), on the "leprous disease," he has to see if there is a white swelling in the skin, if the skin hair has turned white in the affected area, and if the skin has become raw there (13:10). The sense of disgust already created by the long list of diseases with which Chapter 13 deals is considerably increased in this way, as the reader cannot but imagine herself looking closely with the priest into these diseased areas of a person's skin.

There are several other features of the text of the purity laws that contribute to the sense of horror it produces in a modern literary reader. These include, first, the unclear rationale for the uncleanness of certain creatures or physical events. Scholars have spent a great deal of effort trying to identify this rationale, but it is certainly not immediately clear to a modern reader. So, at the very beginning of the laws we read, "Any animal that has divided hoofs and is cleft-footed and chews the cud – such you may eat" (Lev. 11:3). The mysterious nature of uncleanness here – why does an animal that does not have divided hoofs and chew the cud cause uncleanness? – gives it a kind of power over one's rational ability to judge how or whether to avoid it, contributing to the sense of horror it instills. Second, as the specific concepts of "unclean" (*tame*), "detestable" (*sheqets*), and "abomination" (*to'evah*) are used in conjunction with this unclear rationale, this sense of horror is magnified, as in phrases like, "Anything in the seas or streams that does not have fins or scales [...] they are detestable to you", or "These you shall regard as detestable among the birds. They shall not be eaten; they are an abomination" (Lev. 11:10, 13). Third, the texts frequently define as unclean, things of which many people have an irrational horror anyway: "Whatever moves on its belly [...] or whatever has many feet, all the creatures that swarm upon the earth, you shall not eat; for they are detestable" (11:42). Although it is difficult to explain why, it is

36   *The Bible as Literature*

common enough for people to find snakes, bugs, and other "creepy-crawlies" horrible or disgusting, and that irrational sense of horror is doubly evoked when the purity laws say that they cause uncleanness. This is also true of the many ways in which uncleanness can be contagious.

The Logic of Purity

From the most ancient Jewish exegetical and philosophical texts to the present, scholars have asked about the rationale behind the purity laws. In recent decades, there have been two particularly noteworthy attempts to discover this rationale. The first was by the anthropologist Mary Douglas, in *Purity and Danger*. She argues that the pure in the dietary laws is the whole or the complete. This begins with the "wholeness of the body seen as a perfect container" (65), and is extended to "species and categories," such that "hybrids and other confusions are abominated" (66). Purity "means keeping distinct the categories of creation. It therefore involves correct definition, discrimination, and order" (67). Hence, the fundamental principle dividing clean from unclean animals in the dietary laws is that clean animals "shall conform fully to their class. Those species are unclean which are imperfect members of their class, or whose class itself confounds the general scheme of the world" (69).

Much as it explains, this theory does not explain everything about the dietary laws, as it claims to do, and it is ultimately not persuasive. While wholeness certainly seems to be one consideration in the Priestly writers' concept of the pure, in practice Douglas has to extend the idea of wholeness so widely that it loses its meaning as an explanatory category. First, as she examines perhaps her most persuasive concept of the whole body as the pure one, she includes (as she must) the case in which "women must be purified after childbirth" (64). But why should this be the case? It is at the very least questionable that a woman who has given birth is not whole. Again, why is it the case, if the pure body is a whole one, that only "lepers should be separated"? What about sufferers from other diseases? – surely they would contradict the idea of wholeness just as lepers do. Furthermore, it is not true that "all bodily discharges are defiling" (64); only some are. Why do urine, feces, sweat, spit, mucus, or milk not defile? Wholeness certainly seems to be part of the Priestly idea of the pure, but it is not the complete explanation of the underlying rationale. We see something similar in Douglas's claim that swarming creatures (*sherets*) "[cut] across the basic classification" of the Priestly writers into land, sea, and air animals. This appears to be the case in English, in which it is difficult to translate the verb *sharats*, "to swarm," and its cognate noun *sherets*, "swarming creatures," precisely because there is no category in English that corresponds to that of "swarming creatures." But in Hebrew this is not the case. In Hebrew, there is a single and whole category denoted by the words *sherets*. It is a category in itself, not a cross-categorical term as Douglas claims, and so to say that "swarming creatures" are impure because animals that contravene categories in general are impure is false.

The second most influential account of the rationale behind the purity laws has been that of the Bible scholar Jacob Milgrom. He argues that the underlying rationale behind all of the purity laws is "reverence for life" (*Leviticus 1-16* 733). The system of dietary laws works like this, he argues:

> Its purpose is to teach the Israelite reverence for life by (1) reducing his choice of flesh to a few animals; (2) limiting the slaughter of even these [...] animals to the most humane way; and (3) prohibiting the ingestion of blood.
>
> (735)

Discharges of blood in childbirth and menstruation are "associated with the loss of life," and so are impure (767). Skin disease too is "an aspect of death," since (among other reasons) "the common denominator of all the skin ailments described in Lev 13 is that the body is wasting away." The entire system of the purity laws, Milgrom concludes, is "a symbolic system reminding Israel of its imperative to cleave to life and reject death" (1003).

As with Douglas's, Milgrom's theory seems to explain some of the thinking behind the purity laws, but it does not succeed as a complete explanation. The most obvious criticism is that, if the principle behind the dietary laws is reverence for life, why is any animal at all considered edible and therefore pure? Surely it would be most reverent to life not to kill and eat any animal. Second, Milgrom's theory, like Douglas's, is difficult to falsify. Menstruation and the blood lost in childbirth are unclean, he argues, because blood is the sign of life and its loss the sign of death. But it would be equally plausible (perhaps even more so) to think of childbirth as a sign of life. Similarly, menstruation could be considered a sign of fertility and therefore of life. The theory is too flexible; whatever the facts of the purity laws, the theory can explain them by associating whatever is considered clean with life and whatever is considered unclean with death. A third problem is that there are places where the theory explains too little. For example, if the range of skin diseases specified in the purity laws are unclean because they are associated with death, why only these diseases? There are many other kinds of disease whose symptoms could be considered "reminders of [...] the onset of death" (819), but none of them are specified as unclean. Reverence for life is surely part of the thinking behind some of the purity laws, but it cannot be said to be the unifying principle underlying all of them.

In fact there is no single principle that underlies the purity laws and that they could all be said to signify to the people of Israel as they practiced them. As Lloyd Bailey puts it,

> Not only has there been a failure to propose a single widely compelling theory, but also there is no reason to reject the idea that the list of "unclean" animals is composite, i.e. that a variety of factors has been at work.
>
> (139)

38 *The Bible as Literature*

I agree. In my view, the best explanation of the significance of the purity laws is the one that emerges most clearly from the Book of Leviticus as a whole, that holiness involves the people of Israel separating themselves for God:

> I am the LORD your God; I have separated [*hivdil*] you from the peoples. You shall therefore make a distinction [*hivdil*] between the clean animal and the unclean.
>
> (Lev. 20:24–25)

As we can see from the Hebrew here, the same verb (*hivdil*, to "divide" or "separate") is used to describe the distinction between Israel and the other nations, and between clean and unclean animals. Just as Yahweh has made a distinction between Israel and all the other nations, so Israel must distinguish between the clean and the unclean. The very difference reminds the community at every level of daily life of the difference between Israel, God's covenant people, and all the other nations of the earth. As Baruch Levine writes, "Pure creatures are [...] to impure creatures as the Israelites are to the other nations" (*Leviticus* 248).

This leaves us with the question of how we are to judge the nature of these distinctions as modern literary readers. We have already discussed the emotional effect of disgust, at the frailty of the boundaries of the human body, which the purity laws convey. The purity laws consider people with skin diseases, menstruating women, and women who have given birth to be unclean, as well as men and women who have emitted any kind of fluid, normal or pathological, from their sexual organs. How are we to judge this portrayal of the human body? As in all literary criticism, a reader's judgments are going to be determined by the interpretive frameworks she brings in advance to the text. From a post-Enlightenment perspective, a perspective that privileges human rights, human dignity, and equality before the law, the purity laws are often unjust, in particular toward women and toward sick people. No one chooses either menstruation or the way in which children are born, and it is irrational to suggest that either fact of bodily human life makes a person unfit for the presence of God or the community. The same is true of people suffering from skin diseases. No one chooses to do so, and it is similarly irrational to say that sick people are unfit for the presence of God or (except in the case of contagious diseases) the community. As David Wright writes:

> There are many parallels between the Bible's view of those suffering from *ṣāra'at* [skin disease] and unscientific popular views about those suffering from the serious diseases of modern concern [such as cancer or AIDS]. These popular views grow out of society's fears and attempts to explain evil [...] These explanations, while turning chaos to order for some, are sometime injurious, psychologically if not physically, to the sick [...] Knowledge about the ancients' symbolic understanding of biblical *ṣāra'at* and the effects it had upon sufferers in antiquity can serve as an avenue for critiquing our own thinking (or misthinking) about modern disease.
>
> (Milgrom, *Leviticus 1-16*, 824)

Wright observes that the injustices of the purity laws are by no means confined to one ancient time and place, but continue to be all too present in modern thought and practice toward sick people and, let us add, toward women. He is surely right about the reason for this, that what we see in the purity laws is the human desire to "[turn] chaos to order" inadequately checked by a liberal and rational sense of the full and equal humanity of every other person as such.

Numbers

Murmuring in the Wilderness

After the long section of Priestly cultic, legal, and ethical material from Exodus 25 through to Numbers 10 (with the exception of Exod. 32–24), the narrative of the Pentateuch begins again in Numbers 11. It begins with a remarkable series of stories, which are striking for two reasons. First, they (or rather, versions of them) have already been told, in Exodus 15:22–17:7; and second, they are all variations on the same theme. These are the stories of "murmuring in the wilderness" (Bailey 457), which occur from Num. 11:1–21:7. "Murmur" is the KJV's translation of the Hebrew verb *lun*, which is used almost exclusively in the Bible in these stories in Exodus and Numbers, as the people of Israel complain about the hardships they are enduring as Yahweh leads them from slavery in Egypt through the wilderness to the promised land of Canaan. Table 2.2 shows the parallels between the stories in Exodus and Numbers.

There are other parallels between the stories too. Furthermore, as Dennis Olson points out, there is a kind of antithetical parallelism between the stories marked as No. 1 in Table 2.2, in which the first complaint story in Exodus is about God's grace shown through the pleasure of water, and in Numbers about God's anger shown through the pain of fire (62). The murmuring stories seem to have been edited carefully and deliberately in the Pentateuchal narrative in order to emphasize their significance in that narrative. In Exodus, there are three stories, back-to-back, about the Israelites' complaining that Yahweh, and the leader he has chosen for them in Moses, is going to let them die in the wilderness. These stories are told of the people of Israel on their way to Mount Sinai, where they receive the covenant, the Ten Commandments, and the Torah. Seven stories on the same theme (two of them the very same stories – those of manna and quail, and of water from the rock) – are

Table 2.2 The parallel murmuring stories in Exodus and Numbers

Murmuring Stories in Exodus: On the Way to Sinai	*Murmuring Stories in Numbers: On the Way from Sinai*
Three days from the Red Sea (Exod. 15:22)	Three days from Mount Sinai (Num. 10:33)
1. Bitter Water Made Sweet (Exod. 15:22–26)	1. Fire from the LORD (Num. 11:1–3)
2. Manna and Quail (Exod. 16:1–36)	2. Manna and Quail (Num. 11:4–35)
3. Water from the Rock (Exod. 17:1–7)	3. Water from the Rock (Num. 20:1–13)

40   *The Bible as Literature*

then told in Numbers of the Israelites on their way *from* Mount Sinai to the borders of Canaan.

The stories emphasize the faithlessness of the people of Israel. This emphasis is so strong that the series of stories expresses a view of human nature. As Bailey argues, the complaint narratives express a "deep realization of the egocentric nature of human beings," often emphasized in biblical literature, such that "the portrait of Israel's spiritual nature [...] becomes mixed and complicated" (502, 462). This is surely true. The pattern of choosing material goods like food, water, or physical security in themselves, over against the covenant life with Yahweh of which these would be a part, is so constantly repeated in the complaint stories that it adds up to the portrayal of a kind of perversity in the human heart. The people of Israel, and a fortiori all the peoples to whom the covenant will extend, seem to tend toward choosing against what they at their best also recognize to be the highest good of fullness of life as Yahweh's covenant people.

The complaint stories begin in Exodus. The Israelites have just witnessed the plagues of Egypt, the Passover, and the miraculous parting of the Red Sea. They have seen that Yahweh can be trusted to lead them out of slavery. Three days into their journey from the Red Sea, however, they complain that there is no drinkable water. Yahweh provides water for them with a miracle. In the next story (Exod. 16:1–36), they complain again, this time that there is no food. They have just seen Yahweh's will to provide for them, but they still do not have faith in him, complaining that they are now going to die of hunger. Indeed, they even wish that Yahweh had not freed them from slavery in Egypt: "If only we had died by the hand of the LORD in the land of Egypt, when we sat by the flesh-pots and ate our fill of bread" (Exod. 16:3). They prefer slavery, if their bodily needs are met, to freedom to serve Yahweh. This kind of thinking, frequently repeated in the complaint stories, will eventually climax in Num. 14:4, "Let us choose a captain, and go back to Egypt." But, in Exodus 16, Yahweh graciously provides the Israelites with manna and quail. The very same pattern occurs in the next story (Exod. 17:1–7). Despite having seen Yahweh provide them with water and with food, the people again complain that he will not provide water. A third time he does.

Thomas Dozeman calls the journey from the Red Sea to Sinai, in which the first series of complaint stories occur, "a period of courtship between God and Israel" in which "complaint does not lead to divine judgement but to rescue" (100). In the second, and longer, series of complaint stories in Numbers, this is no longer the case. Now, the people of Israel have received the covenant at Mount Sinai, and "know their responsibilities in the law and the commandments" (Olson 63). In the second series of complaint stories, therefore, Yahweh's response changes from mercy to anger. Olson shrewdly observes that Israel is now accountable for the law, "beginning with the first and most important of the Ten Commandments: 'You shall have no other gods before me'" (63). Israel's continued pattern of complaint in the wilderness beyond Sinai, he means, is a pattern of thinking of material things and situations as gods, as rivals to God. In Numbers, the "rabble" have a "strong craving" (*hit'avvu*), which spreads to the people of Israel, and the second (non-Priestly) manna and quail story begins. In this story, Yahweh "struck the people with a very great plague," "while the meat was still between their teeth," so that "the place was called Kibroth-Hattaavah [Graves of Craving], because there they buried the people who had the craving [*ha-mita'vvim*]" (Num. 11:33–34). Dozeman comments, "The craving for meat is a rejection of manna," which is a rejection of the God who provides manna. Indeed the story, he argues, is about "anyone who craves meat more than the nourishment of God" ("Numbers" 105, 111). There are seven complaint stories in Numbers 11–21, each with the familiar pattern in which the people of Israel "crave" for other things, good in themselves, instead of God, or in the language of the first commandment, other gods before Yahweh. This is the perversity of the human psyche, according to the Pentateuch. Over and over again, apparently time without end, the people of Israel, despite knowing better and better with each story, have a kind of tendency, a "craving," a disorder in the sum of their desires, for subordinate goods, or other gods, rather than Yahweh, whom they have seen time and again to be their highest good.

What Did Moses Do?

One of the last complaint stories in Numbers is the second water from the rock story, in Numbers 20:1–13. It contains "one of the great puzzles of Biblical inter-pretation" (Olson 128), which has "troubled interpreters for centuries" (Bailey 498), namely, what is the sin for which Moses and Aaron are so heavily punished? At the end of the story, Yahweh tells Moses and Aaron, "You shall not bring this assembly into the land that I have given them" (Num. 20:12). Both will die before entering the promised land. Aaron dies a few verses later (Num. 20:22–29), at Mount Hor; Moses dies at the end of the Book of Deuteronomy (Deut. 32:48–52; 34:1–8), at Mount Pisgah. In the complaint story in Numbers, this is because "You did not trust in me, to show my holiness before the eyes of the Israelites" (Num. 20:12). But the way in which this is the case, the way in which Moses and Aaron have committed these sins, is very unclear.

When the people complain that there is no water, Yahweh tells Moses, "Take the staff, assemble the congregation [...] and command the rock before their eyes to yield its water" (Num. 20:8). What Moses does is this: "He said to them, 'Listen, you rebels, shall we bring water for you out of this rock?'" He then "lifted up his hand and struck the rock twice with his staff" (Num. 20:10–11). Where is the sin so serious, the lack of faith, the failure to show Yahweh's holiness, in this difference? First, we must be clear that the answer to this question is not at all clear in the text. As Levine rightly puts it, "The reader has the sense that he is missing something" (*Numbers* 483). Olson writes that the reason is "not entirely evident" (128); Bailey that it is "not plainly explained" (498). This is true. Many explanations have been offered. Milgrom lists 11 (*Numbers* 448), including the following: (1) Moses strikes the rock instead of speaking to it; (2) he strikes it twice instead of once; (3) he doubts God; (4) he calls Israel "rebels"; (5) he says "Shall we" bring water out of the rock instead of "Shall God." Milgrom argues at considerable length for a version of (5), which he says that the text shows with

42　*The Bible as Literature*

"startling clarity" (*Numbers* 451). Dozeman argues for a version of (4), in which he says that one aspect at least of Moses's sin is "clear" (160). But both are wrong to say that the story is clear. Both explanations are relatively plausible, but neither (nor any other explanation) is clearly stated nor implied by the text. Olson argues that the text is "intentionally ambiguous" (128). I find it difficult to judge intention here, especially since the text may reflect the result of more than one person's intention, but the text as we have it is (as the reader's experience will surely show) constitutively ambiguous.

I would suggest that the best clue the text gives us concerning Moses and Aaron's sin is the context of the complaint stories in which this sin is narrated. The stories are all about what we have called the perversity of the human heart, about the persistent tendency of the people of Israel to cease to trust in Yahweh, their highest good, and to place their ultimate concern in second-order material goods, such as food, water, and security. The place in which the story is set, and with which it concludes, is "the waters of Meribah," *merivah* meaning "quarrel," because "the people of Israel quarreled [*ravu*] with the LORD" there (Num. 20:13). The noun *merivah* and the verb *ravu* both derive from the root *riv*, to "quarrel" or "contend." This story, like all the complaint stories, is a story about the tendency of the people of Israel to quarrel or contend with Yahweh. Since Moses and Aaron's sin is both very grave and also not clear, the best assumption in the context of the complaint stories is that their sin too is of this kind. Olson, who argues that the people's need for water in this story is a legitimate one which Yahweh intends to satisfy, writes that Moses "calls the people 'rebels' when in fact it is he and Aaron who are the true rebels and are punished," since they are not "sensitive to the genuine needs" of the people (129). Dozeman takes the same view, arguing that by wrongly judging the situation as an act of rebellion by the people against God, Moses "becomes the rebel" instead (161). I am not sure that the story allows us to judge the nature of Moses's sin so clearly, but Olson and Dozeman are surely right to infer from the context of the complaint stories that Moses's sin is, like that of the people he calls "rebels," the very same tendency to rebellion. The nature of Moses's rebellion is largely hidden from the reader, in my view, among a series of possibilities, stated and unstated. This indicates two things about the perversity of the human heart that the authors and editors of the complaint stories portray. First, even the most apparently virtuous individuals, like Moses and Aaron, Yahweh's chosen servants, are subject to this tendency. Second, they are subject to this tendency even as they lead the congregation of Israel. Despite the stories in Numbers authorizing Moses's leadership against criticism from Aaron, Miriam, Korah, Dathan and Abiram, and the people, this story also indicates that not even God's most authorized leader is free from the tendency to deviate from what he also knows to be his, and the people's, highest good. As Olson puts it, this story expresses a "healthy realism about the frailty of human leadership" (130). This is what the complaint stories emphasize, that no one among the people of Israel, not even the leaders of the congregation, can be trusted to pursue the good, to trust in Yahweh, at every moment, with every choice in life. This is the view of human nature of the authors and editors of the complaint stories, and it is with human beings so conceived that they portray Yahweh making his covenant.

Deuteronomy

The Deuteronomists

Thus far we have dealt with the work of Priestly and non-Priestly writers in the Pentateuch. With the Book of Deuteronomy we come to the work of a recognizably distinct third group of writers, whom biblical scholars have called Deuteronomistic, because their thought and style appear first in and throughout the Book of Deuteronomy. Wilhelm de Wette first argued in 1805 that the Book of Deuteronomy was by a different author than those whose work is discernible in the first four books of the Pentateuch. He also observed that it is reasonable to conjecture that Deuteronomy was "the book of the law" discovered in the Jerusalem temple in the eighteenth year of the reign of King Josiah (622 BCE), as narrated in 2 Kings:

> The high priest Hilkiah said to Shaphan the secretary, "I have found the book of the law in the house of the LORD. When the king heard the words of the book of the law, he tore his clothes, [saying] [...] "Great is the wrath of the LORD that is kindled against us because our ancestors did not obey the words of this book."
>
> (2 Kings 22:8, 11, 13)

Both these claims have remained almost universally accepted, albeit in modified forms, by biblical scholars ever since. One of the reasons for the latter claim, that Deuteronomy is the "book of the law" found in the temple in King Josiah's reign, is that the account of Josiah's reformation of worship once he has read this book closely reflects the prescriptions for right worship in the Book of Deuteronomy. These prescriptions are not found, or at least are emphasized less, in Genesis through Numbers. Furthermore, Deuteronomy has a distinct rhetorical style, with numerous characteristic phrases and expressions repeated many times in the book, but never (or less frequently) used in Genesis through Numbers, such as "the land the LORD your God is giving you"; "with all your heart and with all your soul"; "observe diligently"; and "commandments, statutes, and ordinances." As Clements puts it, "There is a high level of consistency and homogeneity of style in Deuteronomy that makes it in general the most easily recognized of the entire Old Testament" (272).

In a 1943 text, the German biblical scholar Martin Noth argued that the Book of Deuteronomy only became the fifth book of the Pentateuch late in its history. It was initially written, he claimed, as an introduction to a much longer work, which scholars have called the Deuteronomistic History, consisting of the current books of Deuteronomy, Joshua, Judges, 1 and 2 Samuel, and 1 and 2 Kings. Noth's

44   *The Bible as Literature*

theory of the Deuteronomistic History has been highly influential in biblical criticism, and in outline remains accepted by many biblical scholars. There have been numerous modifications and developments of the theory, most of which involve positing more than one author of the history. Most scholars since Noth prefer to think not of a single Deuteronomistic author, but rather of a group or school of Deuteronomistic writers spanning several generations, before, during, and after the Babylonian exile. However, as Walther Dietrich says, scholars "cannot agree as to how many authors, when, and with what means and intentions [they] have been at work on the material" (478). The Book of Deuteronomy itself, with its multiple introductions and multiple additions to the central law code of Chapters 12–26, also seems to be the product of multiple authors or editors.

So this is the third group of authors, editors, and collectors whose work is discernible in the Pentateuch (and beyond), the Deuteronomists. They are a reform movement, associated with the reforms of Josiah's reign (640-609 BCE), and characterized above all by the "high premium they set on the commitment to an exclusive worship of the LORD God alone" (Clements 280). I find the hypothesis plausible that their momentum grew during the reign of Josiah's grandfather Manasseh (698/687–642 BCE), who ruled for 55 years and "misled [Israel] to do more evil than the nations had done that the LORD destroyed before the people of Israel" (2 Kings 21:9). As Richard Nelson puts it, "The existence of a reform movement like that mirrored in Deuteronomy would be understandable as resistance to the religious and international policies of Manasseh" (7). There are many theories as to who the Deuteronomists were, but no consensus.

The End of the Torah

The Book of Deuteronomy completes the narrative of the Torah. It is made up of speeches given by Moses to the people of Israel, the next generation after the Exodus generation has died in the wilderness, on the plains of Moab, east of the Jordan river, from which the people will enter the promised land. After he gives these speeches, he writes down the law (*torah*), which they constitute in a book or scroll (*sepher*). Then, as Yahweh tells him to do, Moses climbs Pisgah, the northwestern flank of Mount Nebo in the Abarim range east of the Dead Sea, from which he is able to see "the whole land" (34:1) to which he has led the Israelites, but which he himself will not be permitted to enter. On that mountain he dies.

The Book of Deuteronomy concludes the narrative of the Pentateuch in an altogether liminal way. The story ends on the border, with the audience of Moses's speeches, along with all subsequent readers of the text, poised between the wilderness on the one hand and the promised land on the other. This is the point, the message, of the story of Moses's death at the edge of the promised land to which he has been leading the people of Israel for 40 years. The narrative of the Pentateuch concludes on the borderline, with two possibilities, blessing and curse, ahead of the people of Israel. It is a story that does not have a traditional ending (although

The Pentateuch, Part II   45

it has become one of the most traditional stories of Western culture). There is no finality to it, but rather an open-ended choice, of motion, above all moral motion, in one or another of two directions. There are two accounts of Moses's death in Deuteronomy, one Priestly (32:48–52), the other Deuteronomistic (34:1–6). They differ on the reason for which Moses is not allowed to enter the promised land, but they both agree that he does not enter the land but only sees it from Mount Nebo. In both traditions, the climax of the story of the Exodus, of the 40 years in the wilderness, and of the journey to the promised land is the position of the people of Israel at the border of that promise. The narrative of the Pentateuch ends in a position of choice, of one direction or another, of blessing or curse, ultimately of life or of death, the fullness of life in covenant with Yahweh or a failure to live up to that covenant.

Nowhere is this borderline position more emphatically or dramatically portrayed than in the account of Moses's death on Mount Nebo. Moses climbs a mountain – indeed the phrase "Moses went up [...] to Mount Nebo, to the top of Pisgah" (34:1) may mean that Pisgah is the very highest point of Mount Nebo – and so occupies a position as it were between heaven and earth. His view allows him to survey the whole of the promised land, from Dan in the north to Zoar in the south, all the way to the Mediterranean Sea in the west (34:1–3), with the plains of Moab at his back. He occupies a position between the promised land west of the Jordan and the "wilderness," as Deuteronomy calls the plains of Moab, linking them with the wilderness of the Sinai peninsula in which Israel wandered for 40 years, to the east. Finally, since Moses dies on Mount Nebo, his vision of the promised land also takes place in a third and ultimate boundary position, that between life and death. All three boundaries that Moses occupies at the climax of the story of the Pentateuch – between heaven and earth, between wilderness and promised land, and between life and death – are experienced, both by the character of Moses and by the reader of the text at once, as a unity of experiences whose meanings bleed into and inform one another. This is the point to which the Pentateuch leads its reader, as it had led Moses, a forking path, a situation between heaven and earth, between God's promise and God's punishment, and ultimately – as the Torah itself will say so emphatically in Deuteronomy – between life and death. As Miller writes, "Torah does not guarantee land and security and blessing. It offers it and describes the way to it" (*Deuteronomy* 245). The end of the story of the Pentateuch is not an ending, not a conclusion, but rather a space between heaven and earth, between west and east of the Jordan, and between life and death. This is the space in which the reader of the text is herself left, along with the characters about whom she has been reading, with choice in front of her.

An Endless Call

Deuteronomy completes the Pentateuch as Genesis began it, with repetition. Just as Genesis begins with two creation accounts, so the Book of Deuteronomy as

46   *The Bible as Literature*

a whole consists of a second account of the law revealed to Moses at Sinai. As with the two creation accounts, this second account differs in significant respects from the first. Most strikingly with respect to the plot of the Pentateuch, in Deuteronomy all the people of Israel hear Yahweh giving the Ten Commandments at Horeb (Deut. 4:10–12; 5:4–24), as is the case in Exodus (Exod. 20:18–22). The rest of the law, however, Yahweh reveals only to Moses, who does not pass it on to the people of Israel until 40 years later on the plains of Moab, as they are about to enter the promised land, on the "today" (*ha-yom*) that the Book of Deuteronomy frequently invokes. In both Exodus and Deuteronomy, the people of Israel are afraid at the overwhelming event of hearing God speak, and after he has given the Ten Commandments, they tell Moses to approach him and to relay the rest of God's words to them (Exod. 20:19, 21; Deut. 5:25–27). Deuteronomy adds to Exodus that Yahweh approves of this idea. He tells Moses, "Say to them, 'Return to your tents.' But you, stand here by me and I will tell you all the commandments, the statutes and the ordinances, that you shall teach them" (Deut. 5:30–31). Three verses and 40 years later, on the plains of Moab, Moses tells the people of Israel, "Now this is the commandment – the statutes and the ordinances – that the LORD your God charged me to teach you" (Deut. 6:1). In Exodus, Moses relays God's words to Israel at Mount Sinai; in Deuteronomy he hears them on Mount Horeb (that is, Sinai) but does not pass them on until 40 years later on the plains of Moab.

What is the meaning of this difference in the time at which Moses passes on the law to the people of Israel in the two accounts in the Pentateuch – at Sinai according to Exodus; 40 years later in Moab according to Deuteronomy? The answer to this question is found in the fact that in Deuteronomy, the text is clear and emphatic on the following two facts. First, the people of Israel were punished for their failure to trust in Yahweh at Kadesh with 40 years of wandering in the wilderness, during which every adult male of the Exodus generation died. Second, Moses frequently refers to the people of Israel at Moab as the generation whom Yahweh liberated from Egypt and led through the wilderness for 40 years. These two things are true only of Joshua and Caleb. In every other case, the adult males at Moab were not adult males at Sinai or on the wilderness journey to Kadesh, from which Moses sent spies into Canaan. Nevertheless, the Book of Deuteronomy repeatedly says that this is case. Moses says at Moab:

> The LORD our God made a covenant with us at Horeb. Not with our ancestors [*avotenu*] did the LORD make this covenant, but with us, who are all of us [*kullanu*] here [*poh*] alive [*chayyim*] today [*ha-yom*].
>
> (Deut. 5:2–3)

The last clause is even more emphatic in Hebrew than in English because its syntax is broken into a series of loosely connected words whose principle of connection is simply an accretion of different ways of emphasizing the here-and-now quality of the people whom it denotes. In Hebrew the text says, "but with-us we these here today all-of-us ones-alive" (the hyphenated English words here each indicating a single word in Hebrew). Of the seven Hebrew words that follow the word "but," three have the first person plural ending *-nu*, phonetically emphasizing that it is "we," "us," those of us here today, who heard Yahweh at Horeb.

The Book of Deuteronomy says clearly that the Horeb generation all (but two) died in the wilderness and equally clearly, indeed thoroughly emphatically, that Moses's younger listeners in Moab were present at Horeb. Nelson's description of the conflicting storylines as "rhetorical sleight-of-hand" (66) is not right, in my view. Miller's assertion that the two times are "telescoped" (*Deuteronomy* 67) is better. Moshe Weinfeld expounds the sense rightly in speaking of "the eternal validity of the covenant" (238). The Deuteronomists have a theological concern that is of greater concern than any logical (or a fortiori chronological) one. There is something like a more important logic than logic at work in the final text. Here we should add that, in addition to conflating the generation that heard the Ten Commandments at Horeb with the generation that hears the rest of the law at Moab, Moses also emphatically states to his audience in Deuteronomy, "I am making this covenant [...] not only with you who stand here with us today before the LORD our God, but also with those who are not here today" (Deut. 29:14–15). The covenant is with all the people of Israel, past, present, and future. As Weinfeld writes, "The cyclic concept of all generations being present at the Exodus and at the Sinai revelation has been perpetuated in Jewish tradition to the present" (239). Deuteronomy says that God made a covenant with the people of Israel at Horeb, with the people of Israel (although entirely different individuals) at Moab, and in fact with all the people of Israel of all time, both those who were and those who were not present either at Horeb or at Moab. This is the theological concern of the Deuteronomists that matters more to them than logical or chronological consistency. God calls the people of Israel to enter into covenant relationship with him, whenever and wherever they are. He called them at Horeb; he calls them at Moab; and he calls the reader or hearer of the text, wherever and whenever that reading or hearing takes place. The truth of this constant call outweighs the principles of logic, for the Deuteronomists; it is a greater truth than those which can be articulated logically, and it is this greater truth, this theology beyond logic, that is at the heart of the book's concern.

TEXT FOR DISCUSSION

Michelangelo, *Moses*

This statue was commissioned by Pope Julius II for his tomb. Michelangelo initially designed a much larger monument than the one completed in 1545, and this statue (c. 1513–1515) was designed for the second story, to be seen from below. It stands in the church of San Pietro in Vincoli in Rome.

48 *The Bible as Literature*

Figure 2.2 Michelangelo Buonarroti, *Moses*, c. 1513–1515, marble, San Pietro in Vincoli, Rome. Credit: Classic Image / Alamy Stock Photo.

QUESTIONS

1. Michelangelo's Moses has horns on his head, reflecting a medieval iconographic tradition that derives from the Vulgate's translation of Exodus 34:29, "The skin of his face shone because he had been talking with

God." The Hebrew word translated "shone" is *qaran*, a rare verb cognate with the noun *qeren*, "horn," and so translated in the Vulgate as *cornuta*, "horned." But the Hebrew verb means something like to "send out rays," just as horns are "sent out" from a head. So, the horns on Michelangelo's statue signify that Moses has been glorified (that is, his face is shining) after having been in the presence of God. How and why does the statue portray Moses's glory?

2. Michelangelo's Moses is physically well formed. He has large, muscular arms and legs; a strong, athletic torso; and even large, imposing hands. The biblical Moses is 80 years old when he receives the Ten Commandments, which Michelangelo's statue is holding, and has been fasting for 40 days. Giorgio Vasari wrote of the statue in 1568, "Today more than ever Moses can be called the friend of God. For, through the skill of Michelangelo, God has wanted to restore and prepare the body of Moses for the Resurrection before that of anyone else" (345). What do you think is the significance of Michelangelo's Moses's physical strength and beauty?

3. Sigmund Freud interpreted the statue in psychoanalytic terms. He sees the position of the left leg and foot to indicate Moses's desire to get up and act, to smash the tablets of the Ten Commandments in anger when he sees the Israelites worshipping the Golden Calf. But the relative stillness in the statue's torso indicates that he has overcome this anger, and will not break the tablets. So Michelangelo's Moses is (a) "struggling against an inward passion for the sake of a cause to which he has devoted himself," and (b) morally superior to the biblical Moses, who gives in to his destructive anger (Freud 277). What do you make of these claims? If you disagree with Freud, what do you make of the apparently rising position of Michelangelo's Moses's legs?

4. What is Michelangelo's Moses doing with his beard? (Freud thinks this gesture expresses the emotional tension he sees in the character). What do you see in the biblical accounts of Moses that may be represented here?

Works Cited

Bailey, Lloyd R. *Leviticus-Numbers*. Smyth and Helwys, 2005.

Balentine, Samuel E. *Leviticus*. John Knox Press, 2002.

Biddle, Mark E. *Deuteronomy*. Smyth and Helwys, 2003.

Brueggemann, Walter. "Exodus." *The New Interpreter's Bible*, vol. 1, edited by Leander Keck et al., Abingdon Press, 1994, pp. 677–981.

Clements, Ronald E. "Deuteronomy," *The New Interpreter's Bible*, vol. 2, edited by Leander Keck et al., Abingdon Press, 1998, pp. 271–552.

Dietrich, Walther. "Historiography in the Old Testament." *Hebrew Bible / Old Testament: The History of Its Interpretation, Vol. III, Part 2: The Twentieth Century – From Modernism to Postmodernism*, edited by Magne Sæbø, Vandenhoeck and Ruprecht, 2015, pp. 467–99.

50   *The Bible as Literature*

Douglas, Mary. *Purity and Danger: An Analysis of Concepts of Pollution and Taboo.* Routledge, 2002.

Dozeman, Thomas B. "Numbers." *The New Interpreter's Bible*, vol. 2, edited by Leander Keck et al., Abingdon Press, 1998, pp. 1–268.

Fretheim, Terence E. *Exodus.* John Knox Press, 1991.

Freud, Sigmund. "The Moses of Michelangelo." *The Penguin Freud Library, Vol 14: Art and Literature*, translated by James Strachey et al., edited by Albert Dickson, Penguin, 1990, pp. 253–82.

Johnstone, William. *Exodus 1-19.* Smyth and Helwys, 2014.

———. *Exodus 20-40.* Smyth and Helwys, 2014.

Levine, Baruch A. *The JPS Torah Commentary: Leviticus.* Jewish Publication Society, 1989.

———. *Numbers 1-20: A New Translation with Introduction and Commentary.* Doubleday, 1993.

Milgrom, Jacob. *The JPS Torah Commentary: Numbers.* Jewish Publication Society, 1990.

———. *Leviticus 1-16: A New Translation with Introduction and Commentary.* Doubleday, 1991.

Miller, Patrick D. *Deuteronomy.* John Knox Press, 1990.

———. *The Ten Commandments.* Westminster John Knox Press, 2009.

Nelson, Richard D. *Deuteronomy: A Commentary.* Westminster John Knox Press, 2002.

Noth, Martin. *The Deuteronomistic History.* Translated by Jane Doull et al., 2nd ed., JSOT Press, 1991.

Olson, Dennis T. *Numbers.* John Knox Press, 1996.

Propp, William H. C. *Exodus 1-18*: A New Translation with Introduction and Commentary. Doubleday, 1998.

———. *Exodus 19-40: A New Translation with Introduction and Commentary.* Doubleday, 2006.

Sarna, Nahum M. *The JPS Torah Commentary: Exodus.* Jewish Publication Society, 1991.

Vasari, Giorgio, *Lives of the Artists*, Vol. 1, translated by George Bull, Penguin, 1987.

Weinfeld, Moshe. *Deuteronomy 1-11: A New Translation with Introduction and Commentary.* Doubleday, 1991.

3 The Histories

The Deuteronomistic History

As we saw in our section on the Deuteronomists in the last chapter, Martin Noth's theory of a Deuteronomistic historian, collecting traditional stories about the history of Israel and carefully incorporating them into a unified work of his own theological conception, has been very influential in biblical studies. There has been considerable consensus among biblical scholars that the books of Joshua, Judges, 1 and 2 Samuel, and 1 and 2 Kings, with Deuteronomy as a kind of theological introduction, were produced as a single historical work. As Noth's work was developed by subsequent scholars, the view that there are multiple writers at work in the Deuteronomistic history, a group of authors, collectors, and editors who share a similar worldview, rather than a single creator of the history, became especially popular. There are very different accounts, though, of who these writers were and where in the Deuteronomistic history their work can be found.

Frank Moore Cross argued in a 1973 book that there is evidence for a first edition of the Deuteronomistic history (Dtr[1]) dating from the reign of King Josiah (640-609 BCE), and a second edition (Dtr[2]) dating from the Babylonian exile (c. 550 BCE), whose author "retouched or overwrote" the first edition into a "document relevant to exiles" (285). In Germany, Rudolf Smend maintained Noth's view that the history was written during the exile. He sees the first version (DtrH), however, to have been interpreted by a second editor (or editors) whose concern is noticeably "nomistic" or legal in nature, whom Smend therefore designates as DtrN (98). Smend's student Walther Dietrich discerns the work of a third editor in the books of Samuel and Kings, at work before DtrN, whom he designates DtrP, because of his concern with prophecy and its fulfillment (Dietrich 482; cf. Römer, *So-Called* 30).

We should also note that some scholars continue to argue for Noth's single Deuteronomistic historian. More recently, others have begun to deny the existence of a coherently Deuteronomistic history at all, arguing that "the deuteronomistic texts in the books of the Former Prophets are extremely different one from one to another," or that "the importance of the Davidic monarchy in the book of Kings is incompatible with the book of Deuteronomy, which is not interested in kingship at all" (Römer, "So-Called" 311–312). As Thomas Römer points out, this would

DOI: 10.4324/9781315751566-4

52   *The Bible as Literature*

return thought on the books of Joshua, Judges, Samuel, and Kings to that of scholars before Noth who saw "an important number of deuteronomistic additions and revision in the Former Prophets but did not recognize any coherence or comprehensive theology in those additions" ("So-Called" 312).

So, as with the Pentateuch, we have almost no extra-textual facts about the history books from Joshua to Kings, but only an ongoing history of hypotheses as to their composition. In our literary criticism of these books, we will assume only that we are dealing with a series of traditional stories that have been edited into their final form in a long and complex process. We will notice that the recognizably Deuteronomistic passages in these books sit together with stories whose concerns are often remarkably opposed to those expressed in the Book of Deuteronomy as well as to those expressed in other stories. The rather conflicting and sometimes positively contradictory nature of these stories and concerns (such as the question of whether the monarchy is or is not a desirable institution in 1 Sam. 8–12) we will assume only to derive from the traces of multiple writers expressing multiple ideas during the complex process of the stories being passed on, written down, collected, and edited. Some of these writers seem to have been Deuteronomists, and some do not.

Joshua

TEXT FOR DISCUSSION

The Ethics of the Conquest Narratives

In the text and questions below, we think about perhaps the single most difficult question in biblical interpretation, that of the divine command to kill the native peoples of Canaan, down to the last man, woman, and child, so that the covenant people of Israel can possess the land. The first text below is from the first conquest story, the sack of Jericho. For similar stories, see Joshua 8:1–2, 18–29; 10:8–11, 28–43; 11:6–15. Joshua 10:40 sums up, "Joshua defeated the whole land [...]; he left no-one remaining, but utterly destroyed all that breathed, as the LORD God of Israel commanded."

6 [16] [...] When the priests had blown the trumpets, Joshua said to the people, "Shout! For the LORD has given you the city. [17]The city and all that is in it shall be devoted to the LORD for destruction [*cherem la-YHWH*] [...]" [20]So the people shouted, and the trumpets were blown [...] and the wall fell down flat; so the people charged straight ahead into the city and captured it. [21]Then they devoted to destruction by the edge of the sword all in the city, both men and women, young and old, oxen, sheep, and donkeys. (Josh. 6:16–21)

---

5 [13]Once when Joshua was near Jericho, he looked up and saw a man standing before him with a drawn sword in his hand. Joshua went to him and said to him, "Are you one of us, or one of our adversaries?" [14]He replied, "Neither [*lo*, lit. "No"]; but as commander of the army of the LORD [*sar tseva YHWH*] I have now come." And Joshua fell on his face to the earth and worshipped, and he said to him, "What do you command your servant, my lord?" [15]The commander of the army of the LORD said to Joshua, "Remove the sandals from your feet, for the place where you stand is holy." (Josh. 5:13–15)

QUESTIONS

1. There are several historical hypotheses adduced by biblical scholars that give some context to the practice of *cherem*, or "devoting to destruction" people and things to God described in Joshua:
   (a) The archeological record does not clearly give evidence for the wholesale destruction of Canaanite towns in the late Bronze Age described in the Book of Joshua. It may be, therefore, that the Israelites did not historically practice such destruction.
   (b) Devoting people and things to the nation's god for destruction was practiced elsewhere in ancient Near East. The closest parallel is the Moabite Stone, an inscription from the ninth century BCE, discovered in 1868, on which the king of Moab says, "Chemosh said to me, 'Go, take Nebo from Israel!' So I went [...] taking it and slaying all, seven thousand men, boys, women, girls, and maid-servants, for I had devoted them to destruction for the god Ashtar-Chemosh" (Pritchard 320).
   (c) If the Book of Joshua is written or edited after the experience of exile, the brutal destruction by the imperial Babylonians of the people, culture, and homeland of Judah, it may be in part a "reactionary fantasy about the destruction of a superior people" (Dozeman 92).
   Do any of these hypotheses affect your reading of the conquest stories in Joshua, such as our first text above (Josh. 6:16–21)?
2. The early Christian exegete Origen argued in his *Homilies on Joshua* that the conquest stories should be understood according to the spiritual rather than the literal sense that God had given them. The native tribes of Canaan signify the vices of the soul that the Christian must completely annihilate in order to live in peace in the kingdom of heaven. "If in this manner we understand what is written," he says, "perhaps the reading will seem worthy of the pen of the Holy Spirit" (8.6), rather than cruel and inhuman. What do you think of this interpretation?

54   *The Bible as Literature*

3. The Protestant reformer John Calvin, in his *Commentary on Joshua*, uses a version of divine command theory in interpreting the conquest stories. He argues that what God commands is good, whether our moral intuitions agree with it or not. Where the divine command is morally incomprehensible, he says, "let us remember that the judgement seat of heaven is not subject to our laws" (10.40). What do you think of this argument?

4. Jerome Creach argues that "there is a self-critical feature of the text itself that must guide our interpretation" of the conquest stories (18). I agree with this, and I have included the second text in our "Texts for Discussion" above because, in my opinion, it is one of several such examples in the Book of Joshua. When Joshua asks the commander of the army of the LORD whether he is "one of us" (*lanu*, lit. "for us") or "one of our adversaries" (*le-tsarenu*, lit. "for our enemies"), the latter replies, "Neither." Since Joshua "worships" him, we can assume that the commander of the army of the LORD is an appearance of Yahweh, who says that he is neither on Israel's side nor the Canaanites'. Despite all the texts in the book that say that Yahweh is on Israel's side, to the point of wanting all the peoples of Canaan killed, here is one text that says that this is not the case. How does this point affect your understanding of the conquest stories such as our first text above?

Samson

There are many fascinating stories in the Book of Judges, each of which is rich material for literary critics. We will focus here on the longest series of these stories, those about Samson. There is little consensus as to the history of the composition of the Samson stories. Noth argued that the Deuteronomistic historian (Dtr) used two basic traditions in writing the history of the judges – a "series of stories about various tribal heroes and their victories" (42); and a list of "judges," which gave basic details about them. On the whole, Dtr allowed the stories to "speak for themselves" (46) and added his theological interpretations of them in introductions and conclusions. In our literary criticism of the Samson stories, we will follow the broad scholarly consensus that two major layers can be discerned in them – a series of traditional stories about an Israelite hero; and the work of an editor or editors of these stories.

Israel's Worst Nazirite

Whoever the editors of the Samson stories were, if the hypothesis is correct that they were editing traditional stories, they had a difficult task, particularly if they were Deuteronomists with a definite theological agenda. The stories themselves seem to conflict with each other, even before any question of an editorial voice conflicting with the stories arises. The story of Samson's divinely announced birth

The Histories 55

and consecration in Judges 13 seems to conflict with the rest of the stories in Judges 14–16, in which he proves himself thoroughly unworthy of such an introduction. In Judges 13, Samson's conception and birth is announced by the angel of Yahweh to his mother, who has previously been barren (13:3). This scene strongly suggests that Samson, whose conception, birth, and consecrated life the angel of Yahweh announces, will be a significant heroic figure in the history of Yahweh's covenant relationship with his people. Furthermore, Samson's divinely mandated rule of life will be that of a "nazirite to God [*nezir elohim*]" (13:5). The Hebrew term *nazir* means someone "consecrated" or "devoted" to God. The rules for making a vow to dedicate oneself to Yahweh in this way are set out in Numbers 6. The nazirite must (a) not drink wine, or eat or drink any product of the vine, (b) not cut their hair, and (c) not go near a corpse (Num. 6:1–8). Samson's birth story seems to emphasize that he will be an especially holy person, someone set apart by and for Yahweh for great deeds as a judge of Israel in the time of Philistine oppression.

Once Samson has grown, however, and the next story about him begins, it quickly becomes apparent that the opposite seems to be true. The very first event in this story is that "Samson went down to Timnah, and at Timnah he saw a Philistine woman," whom he wants for his wife (14:1). Timnah is about four miles west of where Samson grows up, and in the time of the story's setting "had become a Philistine town" (Webb 364). In the introductory sections of the Book of Judges, the Israelites are warned not to associate closely with the native peoples of Canaan (2:2). A Deuteronomistic narrator includes the Philistines among the nations that "the LORD left to test all those in Israel" (3:1), to see whether the people of Israel would remain faithful to the covenant, which test they fail: "they took their daughters as wives for themselves [...] and they worshipped their gods" (3:6). Samson is one such failure: he takes a daughter of the Philistines as a wife, and this is the very first thing he does after the impressive annunciation story about the coming of a man especially consecrated to Yahweh.

The story of Samson's marriage to the woman of Timnah continues to be one failure after another. As we have seen, there are three rules specified for nazirites in Numbers, and in the next two events in this story Samson breaks two of them. The most important rule is not to go near a corpse. Every Israelite is made unclean by the presence of a corpse, and there is a ritual for cleansing this impurity (Num. 19:10–22). But a nazirite may not go near a corpse under any circumstances, not even if a close relative has died (Num. 6:7). This is a stricter rule even than that for priests (Lev. 21:1–3). The second event in the story of Samson's marriage is that he kills a lion (Judg. 14:5–6), thereby coming into the presence of the corpse of an unclean animal and defiling himself. Worse, after some time has passed (*mi-yomim*, lit. after some days), Samson goes back to see the corpse again, puts his hands inside it to eat the honey made by the bees who have made a hive in it, and then eats the "ritually contaminated" honey (Olson 850). This is an extremely unholy act, taboo even for an ordinary Israelite. For a nazirite, it seems to be a blatant irreverence toward his vow. Worse follows, as Samson gives this unclean food to his parents without telling them that it is unclean (14:9). In the next event of the story, he goes down to Timnah and "made a feast there as the young men

56   *The Bible as Literature*

were accustomed to do" before a wedding (14:10), which would surely involve drinking wine, especially since the story specifically mentions Timnah's vineyards as the setting for the killing of the lion (14:5), thereby breaking the second of his three nazirite vows. The fact that the feast lasts for seven days suggests a similarly blatant disregard for his consecrated status.

As if this were not strange enough in the story of the judge whose annunciation seemed to promise so much, the text of the story repeatedly specifies that these actions, apparently clearly against God's will, are in fact willed by God. When Samson violates the covenant prohibition on marrying a Philistine woman, the narrator glosses, "His father and mother and mother did not know that this was from the LORD; for he was seeking a pretext [*to'anah* – "opportunity"] to act against the Philistines" (14:4). When Samson breaks the nazirite vow not to go near a corpse, it is because "the spirit of the LORD rushed on him" so that he kills the lion (14:6). Samson also seems to break the sixth commandment when he murders 30 men in Ashkelon in an act of mere revenge. This too is because "the spirit of the LORD rushed on him" (14:19). The text is a very conflicted one. It is as if the narrative voice itself is confused and does not make clear moral or religious sense. Since we have only hypotheses as to the extent to which this effect may be the result of a history of writers editing and reediting older stories, we are left as literary critics to understand the effect of the text as we now have it. It seems to me that the effect is fairly clear. The text of the stories of Samson seems to portray the judgeship of Samson as a period of such moral and religious confusion – as a result of Samson's failure to live up to the covenant – that the narrative voice of the text itself that portrays this is just as confused as the rest of Israel. As with certain modern novels, the narrator himself is a part of the confusion, chaos, and lack of values that he is narrating. In an aesthetically compelling way (whether or not this was the result of any one writer's intention), the text portrays the degeneration of Israel's life under Samson by degenerating itself into the theological and moral chaos unleashed by his failure to rule in a manner faithful to the covenant.

Sex and Violence

Samson never shows any interest in living according to the covenant, far less in delivering Israel from its oppressors, which is the primary function of the judges. He is driven primarily by his sexual and aggressive instincts. The stories of his adult life are linked as stories in which he pursues one woman after another – the woman of Timnah, the prostitute in Gaza, and Delilah. In the first story, Samson goes down to Timnah and "saw [*ra'ah*]" a Philistine woman (14:1). He repeats this to his parents – "I saw [*ra'ah*] a [...] woman [...]; now get [*qanah*] her for me as my wife" (14:2). Although Samson is forbidden to marry a Philistine woman, he is so attracted to her physical appearance that he ignores the precepts of the covenant. When his parents protest that he wants to marry among "the uncircumcised Philistines," Samson is clear as to the reason – *yasherah be-einai*, "she is right in my eyes" (14:3). The Hebrew idiom makes Samson's motivation clear – it is with his eyes that Samson has been attracted to the woman, regardless of the prohibitions of the covenant and

The Histories 57

his nazirite status. Although he later talks to her and still finds that she is right in his eyes (14:7), the text never even gives her the personal intimacy nor the personal respect of a name. Samson's overriding motivation has been his sex drive.

In the final story of Samson's adult life, that of his relationship with Delilah, there initially seems to be an improvement in the quality of his relationship with her. He is said to "love" (*ahev*) Delilah (16:4). Furthermore, she has the dignity of a name in the text, which the women in the two previous stories do not. Nevertheless, the cycle of pursuing one woman after another remains as the fundamental plot of the stories about Samson's adulthood. No sooner has the story of Samson and the prostitute in Gaza finished than the text continues, "After this [*acharei chen*], he fell in love with a woman in the valley of Sorek" (16:4). Delilah seems not to return whatever kind of love Samson feels for her, since the very first thing we hear about her is that she agrees to betray him for money (16:5–6). The story of Samson and Delilah is the third story about the women Samson pursues in which his sex drive leads him into a situation that culminates in acts of violence against his Philistine enemies. In all three stories, his divinely given strength is used not to deliver Israel from their Philistine oppressors, but only to get revenge on the Philistines in situations to which his sex drive has led him. In the final story, this revenge includes his death. He has never effectively "judged Israel" (15:20; cf. 16:31), but has been no more than a highly "flawed hero" (McCann 95), governed by his libido rather than the covenant, whose divinely given strength has therefore been almost entirely wasted.

Samson represents something like a biblical version of the state of nature. He is a portrait in the final text of what human beings would degenerate into without the covenant to guide them. The judges Gideon and Jephthah, despite their increasing sins, still deliver Israel from its enemies. But Samson does not, because the covenant is never the guiding principle of his actions. After Samson's failure to judge Israel faithfully, the degeneration into sex and violence we see in him occurs throughout Israelite society in the final chapters of the Book of Judges (17–21), the moral nadir of the entire Hebrew Bible. The editorial voice in Judges 17–21 four times repeats the phrase "In those days there was no king in Israel," twice adding, "All the people did what was right in their own eyes" (17:6; cf. 18:1; 19:1; 21:25). This voice seems to imply that the monarchy will solve the moral and religious anarchy into which Israel has degenerated throughout the Book of Judges, but the Deuteronomistic historians go on in the books of Samuel and Kings to be highly ambivalent about the monarchy. This is the message of the stories of Samson – only faithfulness to Yahweh's covenant leads to the good life, whether individually or for the whole community of Israel. Samson shows us what this is not; it is primarily up to the reader to work out in practice what it is.

Ruth

Introduction

With the Book of Ruth, we transition into a book that is not part of the Deuteronomistic history, nor is it a book of history at all in the sense that the Deuteronomistic historians

58   *The Bible as Literature*

and the writers of the books of Chronicles, Ezra, and Nehemiah think of themselves as writing the history of Israel. In Christian Bibles, as in the Septuagint, the Book of Ruth follows the Book of Judges. No doubt this is in part because the book begins, "In the days when the judges ruled" (Ruth 1:1). Since the book ends with King David, of whom Ruth becomes the great-grandmother, then whatever the intention of those who developed the canon of the Christian Bible, it reads in that Bible as a transitional story about life between the period of the judges and the period of the Davidic monarchy (cf. Farmer 893–894). Furthermore, the sexual violence with which the Book of Judges ends cannot but contrast with the good, mutually supportive relationship between Ruth and Boaz in the following book.

There is little agreement on the authorship or date of the Book of Ruth. Most scholars believe that it is mostly the product of a single author, although "significant debate remains about whether 4:7,18–22 are later redactions" (Schipper 19). The possibility that a woman or women were involved either in the oral tradition on which the book draws or in the composition of the book itself is increasingly suggested. Edward Campbell points to the biblical tradition of "wise women" who are storytellers or singers, suggesting that they may be responsible for the story of Ruth (22–23). Fokkelien van Dijk-Hemmes argues that the book stems from a "women's culture," in which women speak but are also marginalized by the male-dominated culture in which they do so (134–139). Irmtraud Fischer believes that it is "quite realistic" that Ruth was written by a woman, arguing primarily for the "authentic female voice" expressed throughout the book, "perhaps even by a male author" (33–34). There is no agreement on the dating of the book, and dates from the Davidic monarchy to the early Persian period have been proposed.

A Moral Story

Ruth and Boaz are both said to possess *chayil*, strength or power. This word has a wide semantic range, including moral strength, the wealth that leads to power, and, as in the English phrase a "fighting force," an army. Boaz is called an *ish gibbor chayil*, a man great in power (2:1), and Ruth an *eshet chayil*, a woman of strong character. Tamara Eskenazi points out that the Targum translates the term *chayil* to mean "strong in Torah" (28), which is an excellent interpretation of its meaning in the Book of Ruth as a whole. The *chayil* or strength that unites Ruth and Boaz derives precisely from their love of and obedience to the Torah. Eskenazi cites the rabbinic saying "There are no mighty men other than mighty in Torah" (28). Once we add mighty women to the saying, this is the meaning of the Book of Ruth.

Boaz obeys the Torah. As many commentators point out, the fact that Ruth has to ask the servant in charge of Boaz's reapers to exercise her right to glean behind them (2:7) suggests that the rule prescribed in the Torah (Lev. 19:9–10; Deut. 24:19–22) may not always have been carried out in practice (Eskenazi 29; Nielsen 54–55; Sakenfeld 45). In Boaz's case, however, not only does he allow the foreigner to glean, but he goes above and beyond the rule of the law, obeying the spirit, the purpose of the law. He orders his young men not to bother Ruth, inviting her to drink from his vessels when she is thirsty, sharing food with her, allowing her to glean among the standing sheaves, and even instructing his young men to pull handfuls of grain from the sheaves and scatter them on the ground so that she can glean them (2:8–9, 14–16). He has understood the divine purpose, the divine will to bless, behind the gleaning laws, and he has followed that purpose in exceeding what the law demands. He knows that the laws that say "You shall love your neighbor as yourself" (Lev. 19:18) and "You shall love the alien as yourself; for you were aliens in the land Egypt" (Lev. 19:34) are also to be obeyed as he encounters Ruth, and he has understood what it means to obey them. It means this bountiful excess of generosity toward her, a despised foreigner (Deut. 23:3–6), since that is what Yahweh has done for him, as a son of Israel, from the Exodus to the present.

This is the principle that drives the plot of the story of Ruth. The central event of the plot is Boaz's agreement to Ruth's request to act as a redeemer in marrying her. As many commentators point out, what Ruth is asking for is not something prescribed by the Torah. It is not exactly for Boaz to act as a redeeming kinsman, since the duties of this role concern buying back a relative's property (Lev. 25:25–34), buying back a relative after he has sold himself into slavery (Lev. 25:47–55), and avenging a relative's killing (Num. 35:9–29). Nor is it exactly levirate marriage that Ruth is asking for, since it is only a man's brother's wife with which levirate marriage is concerned (Deut. 25:5–10), and Ruth is a more distant relative of Boaz. Boaz is not obliged, according to the letter of the Torah, to redeem Ruth with marriage. He does so, if we take his actions throughout the story as the guide to this central one, because he knows that the *chesed*, the loyal love, which he mentions in Ruth in agreeing to her request (3:10), is the fundamental principle of the Torah, both underlying and exceeding any given specific prescription within it. The story of Ruth and Boaz is a story of lives lived according to the Torah, not only according to the details of each individual statute but above all according to its heart, the *chesed* or loyal love shown by Yahweh to the people of Israel and that the Torah therefore asks them to show back to him and to each other.

A Love Story

As this story about relationships lived according to the Torah develops, the story that attracts most modern readers, the love story, with its positively erotic undertones, develops along with it. The greatest aesthetic achievement of the Book of Ruth is the way in which its author has told the moral story and the love story in such a way that they are irreducibly part of one whole story, greater than the sum of its parts. Neither love nor sexual attraction is explicitly mentioned in the Book of Ruth, but the story of the relationship between Ruth and Boaz is told in such a way that erotic love is constantly suggested beneath the surface of the narrated events, and by the time this story climaxes in the threshing floor scene, it is scarcely beneath the surface at all. The first two verses of Chapter 2, in which Boaz is introduced as a character, juxtapose the introduction of Boaz into

60   *The Bible as Literature*

the world of Naomi and Ruth, with Ruth deciding to "find favor in the eyes [*be-einai*]" of a man:

> Now Naomi had a kinsman […] a prominent rich man, of the family of Elimelech, whose name was Boaz. And Ruth the Moabite said to Naomi, "Let me go to the field and glean among the ears of grain, behind someone in whose sight I may find favor".
>
> (Ruth 2:1–2)

The relationship between these two sentences is reminiscent of Jane Austen's understated humor. It is not directly said that Ruth is planning to find favor in the eyes of the "prominent rich man," her kinsman who could redeem her in marriage, but what else could the connection between the two sentences be? It could be just a coincidence that, no sooner do we hear of the marriageable Boaz, than we also hear of Ruth's plan to find favor in the eyes of some man, but it is very likely that it is not a coincidence, since marriage to Boaz would give Ruth all that she wants. The strong suggestion underneath what the text directly states is that the narrator of the Book of Ruth, like Austen's narrators, knows that a timely encounter may lead to love and then to marriage, with all its advantages.

The love story beneath the surface of the text becomes positively sexual, flirting with the limits of socially acceptable behavior, in the threshing floor scene. No sexual act takes place, nor is any sexual attraction between Ruth and Boaz mentioned, but the story is made up of events that, although not described as such, are the components of a story of a sexual encounter. Ruth bathes, anoints herself with fragrant oil so that she smells good (Eskenazi 51; Nielsen 68), and "[puts] on her best clothes" (3:3). She looks for Boaz asleep during the night, "[uncovers] his feet," and lies down next to him (3:4). Commentators argue over what exactly is meant by the phrase "uncover his feet [*gillit margelotayv*]." Katherine Sakenfeld describes the meanings well:

> The term translated "feet" by the NRSV is not the usual word, but a less common synonym (appearing only in Ruth […] [and] Dan.10:6) better taken as "legs." Nonetheless, the possible connotation of genitalia, for which the ordinary word for feet is sometimes a euphemism, hovers near at hand.
>
> (54)

"Lower body" perhaps best conveys the sense of the word here. Although it is not clear exactly what Ruth does, it certainly has sexual connotations. Kirsten Nielsen argues that Ruth uncovers herself at his feet (68–71), which is possible, but the most likely sense is that she uncovers Boaz's lower body in an intimate, erotic way as if they are or are about to be sexual partners. Boaz too, although speaking and acting chastely throughout, nevertheless concludes the encounter by telling Ruth, "Lie down until the morning" (3:13). The Hebrew verb *shachav*, "to lie down," especially when used concerning a woman, has sexual connotations, as does the sentence in general in this context. The story is constantly told as if it is the story of a sexual encounter, although no such encounter is in fact narrated as having occurred.

In fact, the narrator has brilliantly managed to tell two stories at once, an erotically charged love story, and a moral story about right relationships between people. The effect of this intertwining of two stories into one, greater than the sum of its individual parts, is to make clear that, for the Book of Ruth, love – erotic, sexual love – is an integral part of the good life. Love and the Torah are as closely intertwined as the love story and the moral story in the narrative, the Book of Ruth says. The Torah itself goes into some detail concerning negative sexual relationships, especially in Leviticus 18, a text linked to the story of Ruth by its use of the verb *galah*, "to uncover," in speaking of sexual relationships. The Book of Ruth tells the story of a positive sexual relationship, of a sexual relationship carried out according to the Torah. It is an account of what love looks like in the light of the Torah.

One of the qualities of love in the Book of Ruth is the considerable equality in agency of the two protagonists of the love story. Ruth takes the initiative to determine and shape her life for the good, albeit within the limited opportunities of a patriarchal society. She chooses to look for a husband by gleaning; she risks being socially ostracized by her nighttime advance to Boaz; she risks Boaz taking advantage of her, for which only she would be censured by the community. She makes her marriage happen. The story of Ruth, the love story entwined within the moral story, both acknowledges and rewards agency in the female character just as much as in the male character, although the latter has all the social power and influence. If the Book of Ruth shows what love looks like according to the Torah, one of the things that it looks like is a relationship between two equals, equals in agency, intelligence, dignity, and responsibility. Indeed, it is precisely because of this equality, this common humanity, this equal sharing in the image of God, that the love between the couple occurs and grows in the first place.

David

Introduction

With the stories of David in 1 Samuel 16 through to 1 Kings 2, we are back with the Deuteronomistic history. The two books now called 1 Samuel and 2 Samuel in the Hebrew and Christian Bibles were originally a single volume. The division into two books was introduced by the Septuagint, "perhaps to create scrolls of a more manageable size" (Birch 950). Noth argued that "for the story of Saul and David Dtr. had access to an extensive collection of Saul-David traditions compiled long before Dtr. from different elements" (54). He describes these as "diverse, disparate and hitherto scattered traditional material" (57). There is considerable agreement among scholars that at least three sets of stories seem already to have been compiled before they were edited into the books of Samuel. These are the "Ark Narrative" (1 Sam. 4–6); the "History of David's Rise" (1 Sam. 16:1–2 Sam. 5:10); and the "Succession Narrative" or "Court History" (2 Sam. 9–20; 1 Kings

62   *The Bible as Literature*

1–2), although there is disagreement about exactly where each set of stories begins and ends.

The Hebrew Bible preserves many more stories about David than about anyone else. Other characters in the Deuteronomistic history, although interesting and complex, are dwarfed by the sheer amount of space devoted to David and by the sheer number of stories collected about him. Graeme Auld describes 1 and 2 Samuel as "the book of David," since they are "about David: all the other personalities are there so that we may see and know David better" (1–2). Walter Brueggemann writes:

> The text is deeply and endlessly fascinated with David [...] David is portrayed as man of many parts, with all those parts subjected to close scrutiny [...] What finally preoccupies this literature, however, is the conviction that, in this passionate man, Israel discerned something more than David [...] Israel can scarcely find words for this David, to whom it does not wish to concede everything but before whom it pauses with a sense of awe.
>
> (2)

Tony Cartledge adds,

> David was a such a powerful character in history that many stories grew up around him and were remembered with great reverence. Sometimes these accounts seem to contradict each other, but the editors were so respectful of David's heritage that they included several divergent traditions with little attempt to harmonize them.
>
> (199)

Israel loves David, just as so many characters in its stories about him do, because he is a complex man of many parts who seems to live out human experience to its fullest extent, and because as he does so they see their God expressed in him.

David as an Artist

As we think about the Bible as literature, perhaps the most significant fact about the many traditional stories about David is that, according to one of the traditions about him, he is an artist. He is the "sweet psalmist of Israel [*ne'im zemirot yisra'el*, lit. the lovely one of the songs of Israel]" (2 Sam. 23:1, KJV). Seventy-three of the Psalms are attributed to him in the Masoretic Text, 85 in the Septuagint, and a rabbinic tradition ascribes all 150 to him. The New Testament also attributes psalms to him that the MT does not. In the books of Chronicles, David establishes the songs and music for worship in the Temple (1 Chron. 6:31–48; 16:4–42), and leads the song, music, and dance as he brings the Ark of the Covenant there (1 Chron. 15:16–28; cf. 2 Sam. 6:5,14–15). He is invoked as a legendary composer by the prophet Amos (Amos 6:5). In the books of Samuel, he is said to be the author of a lament (*qinah*) on the death of Saul and Jonathan (2 Sam. 1:17–27), a psalm (*shirah*, lit. song) of thanksgiving (2 Sam. 22:1–51), almost exactly identical to

Psalm 18, and a final poem described as a *ne'um*, a prophetic "declaration," in praise of the Davidic king (2 Sam. 23:1–7).

David is introduced in three separate stories at the beginning of the story of his rise from shepherd boy to king. In the second of these (1 Sam. 16:14–23), he becomes King Saul's court musician. David plays the lyre well, and his playing, as Saul's courtiers had thought would happen, makes the king better (16:16, 23). At the beginning of the story, Saul is troubled by "an evil spirit from the LORD [*ruach ra'ah me'et YHWH*]" (16:14). It is difficult to know what this means exactly, since as Bruce Birch observes, "the notion of an evil spirit from the LORD is disturbing" (1102). But as Cartledge points out, "In ancient Israel, there were no secondary causes: all things were traced back to God" (206; cf. Birch 1102; Brueggemann 125). Brueggemann is right to say that the affliction of this evil spirit in the story is both theological and psychological in nature, and that "we shall misunderstand [...] if we appropriate the sickness as mere theology or only psychology" (124). Birch points out that, throughout the story of Saul, the king "evidences brooding and melancholy states, fits of anger and rage that issue in violence, and irrational actions that divert from the needs of his kingdom and finally lead to his own suicide" (1102), while adding that "Saul's condition has a spiritual dimension." He is right to speak of the simultaneously "troubled mind and spirit" of Saul.

It is this holistic affliction of mind, spirit, and perhaps even body that David's playing of music heals. David is "skillful in playing the lyre [*yodea menaggen be-kinnor*]" (16:16), and the result is that, as Saul's courtiers had predicted, Saul is made to "feel better" (16:23: cf. 16:16). Here the Hebrew phrase is *tov lo*, which means "good [is done] to him." David's playing causes Saul to "be better." The modern English translation "feel better" is too weak – the Hebrew says that Saul "is well," that "good" is done to him by David's music. Indeed the writer uses the unusual verb *ravach*, "to be spacious," or figuratively "to experience relief," at the end of the story: "Saul would be relieved [*ravach*, רוח] and feel better [*tov lo*], and the evil spirit [*ruach*, רוח] would depart from him" (16:23). The writer uses this word deliberately because *ravach* is cognate with *ruach*, "spirit" – indeed, as the reader can see from my transcription of the Hebrew here, the two words are written identically in the Hebrew text. David's music heals Saul at the level of the spirit, throughout his whole person. The text has a very high view of the power of music to do good to the whole of a person. Indeed, with its structuring of the story around the concept of *ruach*, "spirit" (16:14, 15, 16, 23), it suggests that it is the spirit of Yahweh that heals the spirit of Saul, that brings good to him – to his mind, spirit, and perhaps body too – through David's music.

David, Bathsheba, and Uriah

The stories about David in Samuel and Kings are arranged as the story of a rise and fall. Interestingly, along with this story a second story runs, like a second line of a different shape on a graph, in which Yahweh remains constantly faithful to David and to his descendants whether David is faithful to him or not. In diagrammatic form, the shape of David's story looks something like Figure 3.1.

64 The Bible as Literature

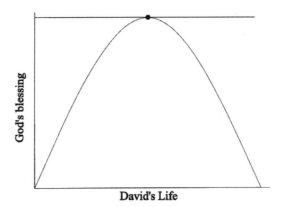

Figure 3.1 The two stories of David's life.

The watershed point of the story (marked with a black dot in Figure 3.1), where David's rise peaks and becomes a fall, is the episode of Bathsheba and Uriah (2 Sam. 11–12). Birch calls this episode a "major shift in David's story" (1283); Brueggemann the "pivotal turning point in the narrative plot of the books of Samuel" (271). Cartledge describes it best, to my mind, calling the episode "the beginning of the end for David, for he finally meets an enemy he cannot defeat," namely himself (495).

The story begins with David uncharacteristically remaining behind in Jerusalem as the Israelite army goes out to war with the neighboring Ammonites. Ever since Saul's death in battle, David has been fighting war after war to establish, protect, and extend his kingdom. In the previous chapter (2 Sam. 10), David has been at the head of the army fighting the Arameans in Transjordan. After the story of Bathsheba and Uriah ends, David goes back to his usual position at the head of the army and is victorious against the Ammonites just as he was victorious against the Arameans (2 Sam. 12:29). David is continually fighting for Israel before the episode of Bathsheba and Uriah, and continues to do so afterward. The episode occurs in the first place, however, precisely because he does not go out with the army to fight, but stays behind in Jerusalem:

> In the spring [*teshuvah*, lit. return] of the year, the time when kings go out to battle, David sent Joab with his officers and all Israel with him; they ravaged the Ammonites, and besieged Rabbah. But David remained at Jerusalem.
>
> (2 Sam. 11:1)

David is uncharacteristically idle. As many commentators point out, when Israel insisted upon Samuel appointing a king, it was "so that our king may govern us and go out before us and fight our battles" (1 Sam. 8:20). David has ceased to be this king. Next, we read that "late one afternoon," David "rose from his couch" and saw Bathsheba (2 Sam. 11:2). The first phrase *le 'et ha-erev* means "at the time of

The Histories   65

the evening." David has been asleep for most of the day, which cannot but seem morally questionable in comparison to fighting at the head of Israel's army. As Cartledge puts it, "The narrator's careful location of David 'on his couch' in the late afternoon implies that David is giving less attention to his work and showing more regard for his personal pleasure" (496).

No reason is given for David's idleness. Furthermore, no reasons are given for any of his actions after he catches sight of Bathsheba while walking on the palace roof. The lack of anything but the briefest description of the characters' actions in the account of David's seeing and taking Bathsheba is very marked: "David sent messengers to get her, and she came to him, and he lay with her [...] Then she returned to her house. The woman conceived; and she sent and told David, 'I am pregnant'" (2 Sam. 11:4–5). This extreme terseness of style continues throughout the story. Biblical narrative is typically opaque with respect to characterization, but even by the standards of biblical stories, the style of the episode of Bathsheba and Uriah is exceptionally terse. As P. Kyle McCarter points out, "The narrator gives us no clue to David's motives in his conduct towards Bathsheba [...] This is in striking contrast to the situation elsewhere in the stories about David" (289).

In his classic study of biblical characterization, Robert Alter relates the opacity of the characters of biblical narrative to "the biblical view of man" as "a bundle of paradoxes," "created by an all-seeing God but abandoned to his own unfathomable freedom" (115). He argues that the reticence of biblical writers with respect to the inner life of the characters whose stories they tell expresses their sense of "the fluctuating or multiple nature of motives," the "unsoundable capacities for good and evil in human nature," and their "underlying [...] conception of character as often unpredictable, in some ways impenetrable, constantly emerging from and slipping back into a penumbra of ambiguity" (119, 126, 129). This impenetrability, this irreducible opacity of the human person to reason and to the conscious self, has a marked moral dimension in the story of David and Bathsheba. This is a story about the moral darkness of the human person. David slides with breathtaking speed from one moral crime to another. He forces himself sexually upon the married Bathsheba, who may be worrying about her husband at the front, and who gives no consent in the text to sex with the king. He commits adultery, a crime to be punished in the Torah with both parties being stoned to death (Deut. 22:22–24). He tries to cover up these crimes by persuading Uriah to sleep with his own wife, but Uriah is so virtuous a man that he refuses, out of loyalty to his fellow soldiers (2 Sam. 11:11). The Deuteronomic law demands sexual abstinence in a military camp (Deut. 23:8), and David himself had once been in the habit of keeping this law (1 Sam. 21:5). Uriah's loyalty to the covenant is a mirror of David's previous faithfulness, from which he is now slipping further and further. Furthermore, the text repeatedly emphasizes that Uriah is a Hittite, a non-Israelite, and that he behaves with precisely the faithfulness to the covenant that David has lost. Uriah is one of David's elite soldiers (2 Sam. 23:39), and he has a Hebrew name (meaning "Yahweh is my light"). As Cartledge puts it, "Uriah had a name and a faith that belonged to Yahweh alone" (508). The text emphasizes that this man of foreign ancestry, "not even a child of the torah" as Brueggemann says (275), is the model

66   *The Bible as Literature*

of loyalty to Yahweh and his covenant with Israel that David ought to be, once was, but is no longer. In response to Uriah's virtue, David sinks further and further into vice. The story concludes with David arranging to murder Uriah to mitigate the scandal that he has fathered a child with Uriah's wife, and he does it in such a way that many other soldiers are killed with him (2 Sam. 11:17).

This story, at the peak of the larger collection of stories about David's rise and fall, is a story about the human heart and its tendency, as the Deuteronomists put it, to turn aside to the right or the left (*sur yamin u-semol*) (Deut. 5:32; 17:20; 28:14; Josh. 1:7; 23:6), to turn away from what a person also knows to be the good. David's uncharacteristic idleness at the beginning of the story puts him into contact with himself, and what he sees and experiences there is horrifying (and at the same time entirely predictable). It is the perversity of the human heart. The story functions on three levels, since David represents three things at once in the story. He is Israel's greatest king; he is a king; and he is a person. At all three levels, in all three social roles, the moral of the story is that he is not to be trusted. No king is to be trusted, not even the very greatest in the nation's history. Samuel warned the people as much when they wanted a king, to be "like other nations" (1 Sam. 8:5). He warned them that a king will above all "take" (*laqach*) from his people:

These will be the ways of the king who will reign over you; he will take [*laqach*] your sons [...] He will take [*laqach*] your daughters [...] He will take [*laqach*] the best of your fields and vineyards and olive orchards [...] He will take [*laqach*] one tenth of your flocks, and you shall be his slaves.

(1 Sam. 8:11, 13, 14, 17)

The Deuteronomists are clear. This is what happens in a monarchy. A king takes, even David, the greatest of them. When he sees and wants Bathsheba, although she is married, he "takes" her (2 Sam. 11:4). The NRSV softens the translation here, obscuring the relationship between Samuel's prophecy and its fulfillment. The KJV more accurately reads, "David sent messengers, and took [*laqach*] her." Why is a king not to be trusted? The story of Bathsheba and Uriah, like many other passages in the Hebrew Bible, is clear: because he is a person, and what is inside David is inside every human being, the tendency to turn aside from what he also knows to be good, good for him and good for society.

TEXT FOR DISCUSSION

Rembrandt, *David and Uriah*

Rembrandt van Rijn (1606–1669), the great Dutch painter and printmaker, painted this enigmatic picture toward the end of his life, circa 1665. Rembrandt painted and sketched numerous biblical scenes, including many episodes from the stories of David.

The Histories 67

Figure 3.2 Rembrandt van Rijn, *Haman Recognizes His Fate (David and Uriah)*, 1665, oil on canvas. The State Hermitage Museum, St. Petersburg, Russia. Credit: Heritage Image Partnership / Alamy Stock Photo.

QUESTIONS

1. The picture emphasizes Uriah, whereas the story of David, Bathsheba, and Uriah emphasizes David's experience and point of view. It is as if Rembrandt is filling in one of the gaps in the terse biblical narrative with his representation in painting of Uriah's experience. What do you think of this technique of adding details to the biblical story that are not given in it? Is it a valid or productive way of interpreting the biblical story?
2. Uriah's downward gaze, bowed head, and right hand on his heart all suggest that (a) he knows his fate and (b) unable to change the will of the king, he accepts it with philosophical and religious resignation. What do you think

68   *The Bible as Literature*

of this interpretation of Uriah's experience in the biblical story? To what extent is it faithful to the biblical text, or to the Bible more generally?

3. David in the painting (on the right) is smaller than Uriah, because seated in the background; is less well lit; and is as it were, peering around the back of Uriah rather than sitting erect or on a throne. Even his crown is small compared to Uriah's headdress. The biblical stories about David emphasize that he is physically attractive and personally charismatic, but he does not have these qualities in Rembrandt's painting. What do you think of Rembrandt's depiction of David? To what extent is it faithful to the biblical story?

4. Until the early twentieth century, this painting was thought to represent a scene from the Book of Esther, and was catalogued as *Haman Recognizes His Fate*. To my mind, the painting is of David and Uriah, since Haman never achieves the kind of philosophical resignation depicted in the central figure. First, which do you think it is? Second, what do you think of the fact that the discussion can arise at all? That is, Rembrandt has not clearly represented a definite biblical scene, but rather interpreted the biblical story (whether of Uriah or Haman) in his own way. The painting does not clearly depict Uriah's parting from David, since then he would have a letter in his hand (2 Sam. 11:14). Rather, Rembrandt has imagined a scene for himself based on multiple elements of the biblical story. What do you think of this way of engaging with the biblical text?

Esther

Introduction

The Book of Esther, the final book in the historical section of the Protestant Old Testament, is neither part of the Deuteronomistic history nor part of the history that comprises the books of Chronicles, Ezra, and Nehemiah. Most scholars date the book from about 400 to 200 BCE. The story is set in the time of the Persian emperor Xerxes I, who reigned from 486 to 465 BCE. In the Hebrew text his name is written as *achashverosh*, and transliterated in the KJV and NRSV as "Ahasuerus," which as Jon Levenson writes, "seems to be how Hebrew speakers heard the Persian name that the Greeks rendered as Xerxes" (23).

Different Bibles contain different versions of the Book of Esther, because multiple versions of the text exist. First, there is the Masoretic Text (MT), which is used in the Hebrew and Protestant Bibles. The Septuagint (LXX) is a translation of the MT or of a "lost Hebrew original quite close to the MT" (Levenson 27), which notably includes 107 extra verses not in the MT, in six major additions to the text. These additions dramatically change the nature of the story. In the MT, there is no mention of God, the Torah, nor of any concern in Esther or Mordecai to maintain their Jewish identity by living according to the Torah. This all changes with the

LXX additions. Since St. Jerome could find no Hebrew version of the six additions to the LXX, he doubted their authenticity and placed them at the end of the Book of Esther in the Vulgate. As Levenson puts it, "in that location they lost much of their meaning, since they are there deprived of their natural and original placement in the narrative" (27). The Protestant Reformers argued that only the biblical books written in Hebrew were authoritative, and so did not consider the LXX additions canonical. Protestant Bibles therefore translate the MT, and relegate the additions to the Apocrypha. Modern Roman Catholic Bibles, such as the New Jerusalem Bible, put the additions in their logical place in the narrative. Eastern Orthodox Bibles translate the LXX version.

The genre of the Book of Esther seems to be something like historical fiction (Queen-Sutherland, 200–201; Bechtel 3–4; Levenson 23–25; Crawford 856, 859). On the one hand, the author provides some authentic details about the Persian empire: "the author knows [...] about its size, its postal system, and a considerable number of details about its court life [...] and employs a number of words and a few names of indisputable Persian origin" (Levenson 24). On the other hand, the main events of the book's plot do not correspond with any extra-biblical sources. The Greek historian Herodotus says that the Persian king could only marry from within seven noble families, none of whom would have been Jewish (3:84). Xerxes's queen was named Amestris, whom Herodotus recounts as behaving cruelly (7:61, 114; 9:109–112). In the seventh year of his reign, when Esther is taken into Ahasuerus's harem, that is, 480 BCE, Xerxes is in Greece, fighting the battle of Salamis. There is no record of a Haman or a Mordecai (or any non-Persian) as Xerxes's top official, nor is there any record of a massacre of tens of thousands of people during Xerxes's reign (Crawford 859). Nor would a banquet that lasts six months seem likely; nor an edict calling for the genocide of an entire people almost a year from the time of its publication; nor a slaughter by this people of over 75,000 without suffering any losses of their own (Levenson 25; Bechtel 3–4). As Levenson puts it, "The enormous amount of exaggeration and inaccuracy in Esther suggests a motive other than that of precise reporting in the modern, Western sense" (26).

Vashti's Refusal

The first of the interlocking stories in the Book of Esther is that of Esther's rise to power. King Ahasuerus gives a banquet of excess. There are two banquets, one lasting 180 days, the next seven, with gigantic guest lists; gorgeous decorations, furnishings, and drinking vessels; and unlimited food and drink for all. At the conclusion of this banquet, a gender struggle takes place, in which both sides lose. Ahasuerus commands his eunuchs to "bring Queen Vashti before the king, wearing the royal crown, in order to show the peoples and the officials her beauty [*yophyah*]" (1:11). In rabbinic tradition, this means that she is to be wearing nothing except the crown (Berlin 14–15). This tradition makes more emphatic what the text already says, that the king is sexually humiliating Vashti, drunkenly forcing her against the ethical codes of their society into being the object of his own and his male guests' sexual gaze. As Berlin puts it, "a gathering of rich drunken men want to get a look"

70   *The Bible as Literature*

at her (12). Herodotus tells similar stories of such improper behavior, even by their own culture's standards of proper relationships between men and women, among the Persians (5.18–20; 1.8–12). Vashti refuses, maintaining her dignity and her humanity. Her punishment for doing so is a grim one. She simply disappears, from the throne and from the story. Ahasuerus's courtiers tell him, "Let the king give her royal position [*malchutah*] to another who is better than she" (1:19). This is what happens; Esther will be the person who takes her place and so becomes the heroine of the story, and this is the last we hear of Vashti.

The word *malchut* used here, which means essentially "royalness," is a very noticeable one in the Book of Esther. In this part of the story, the fact that Vashti's *malchut*, or royalty, can be so easily removed from her quietly points out how precarious a thing royalty is, and so how precarious that of even the king of the vast Persian empire is. Ahasuerus's unjust exercise of power over the queen shows in fact how fragile his own position of royal power is. It shows that royal power is not at all intrinsic to the individual person of the king or queen. This point is emphasized by the comic plot device of the decree sent throughout the empire declaring that "every man should be master [*sorer*, lit. "be a prince"] in his own house" (1:22). The king's wise men and advisers massively exaggerate the threat to male authority constituted by Vashti's refusal to obey the king's improper command: "This deed of the queen will be made known to all women, causing them to look with contempt [*havzot*] on their husbands [*ba'alim*, "lords"] (1:17). One act of disobedience by his wife, even in a case where disobedience was proper by their society's own standards, and the entire Persian empire seems to the king's advisers to be about to crumble. Ahasuerus's situation goes from bad to worse as the comedy progresses. His advisers have him send the decree throughout the empire, written "to every province in its own script and to every people its own language," which of course has the effect of publishing Ahasuerus's humiliation by his wife to every citizen of the vast Persian empire. Most importantly, it has the effect of publishing the fragility of his power throughout the entire empire. The fact of a comically unenforceable law, that "all women [...] give honor to their husbands" (1:20), increases this fragility all the more.

There is no doubt, however, that this comedy has a dark side. Levenson is too sanguine when he writes that "we may rightfully suspect that Vashti greeted the edict [that she never again come into the king's presence] with something other than grief" (52). Her life as she has known it is over. She is a threat to the king's power, a possible figurehead for a coup, and execution or imprisonment are the most likely results. She would be forbidden her old associates, and probably her children too, if she has any. Carol Bechtel is right to speak of the "oppressive" nature of the comic plot of the story of Esther's rise (26). Not only is Vashti's life diminished, if not actually ended, but the law requiring every wife in the Persian empire to submit to her husband, to give him "honor" (*yeqar*) and to have him "rule" (*sarar*) over her (1:20, 22), is also sure to lead to widespread cruelty, both physical and mental, to women throughout the empire.

The Sex Contest

The next part of the story of Esther's rise to power is the bawdy story of the imperial sex contest. Levenson calls this part of the book "The Search for Miss Persia and Media" (53), but even this phrase, explaining the subject matter of the story as a beauty contest, is too dignified. While beauty is involved, what Esther wins, in the lowest – that is, most bodily – comedy in the book, is a sex contest. Once again, the comedy is a dark one. On his servants' advice, seeming to miss his former queen, Ahasuerus appoints commissioners "in all [*kol*] the provinces of his kingdom to gather all [*kol*] the beautiful young virgins to the harem in the citadel of Susa" (2:3). The tone of the story is of gigantic excess. As Berlin puts it, "The excess of wine in Chapter 1 is matched by the excess of women in Chapter 2" (21). The king is supplied with a gigantic number of beautiful young women, all of whom have submitted to a year-long beauty regimen to increase their already attractive appearance. Each of this excessively high number of excessively beautiful women has one night with the king. Furthermore, each young woman "was given whatever she asked for to take from the harem to the king's palace" (2:13), which is presumably something designed for a particularly arousing sexual encounter for the king. Bechtel writes, "Perhaps the details are best left to the imagination" (33), which seems to be what the author of the Book of Esther thinks. His Greek contemporary Aristophanes, by contrast, enjoys specifying just such details (cf. *Lysistrata*, ll. 47–48, 109–110, 149–151, 219–232). Whatever Esther takes to the king's bed, however, she wins the sex contest. After her one night with the king, "he loved [*ahev*] Esther more than all the other women," and so "he set the royal crown on her head and made her queen instead of Vashti" (2:17).

This is how Esther rises to the position of power, of *malchut*, in and because of which she is able to save the Jewish people from Haman's genocide. She needs intelligence, justice, bravery, political skill, rhetorical skill, and personal charm to thwart Haman's plan, but she is only able to use these qualities to save her people by having become queen through winning the imperial sex contest. Once again, as throughout the Book of Esther, the comedy takes place in the dark. The Jewish people are subjects of the Persian empire, vulnerable to genocide. The women of the Persian empire are subjects of men, vulnerable to physical, mental, and sexual violence. Bechtel rightly points out that the harem to which every beautiful young woman in the empire is uprooted, and in which she then has to stay, is "a poor substitute for freedom, home, and family" (31). The Book of Esther is the story of a victory, but it is a victory, the book emphasizes, that takes place against the larger trend of the history of the Jewish people of oppression, violation, and injustice. The Jewish people were almost exterminated. To use Bechtel's words again, Esther has to be "doubly violated, both as a woman and a Jew" (31), in order to prevent this. And while she saves the Jewish people as a result, she does not save the women of the empire, who remain altogether the sexual subjects of men. The young women do not get to go home; Vashti does not get to remain queen; and the edict requiring all wives to be ruled over by their husbands is not revoked. If the Book of Esther

72 *The Bible as Literature*

wants to make us laugh, and it does, it wants us to be equally clear that we are laughing so as not to cry, and that opportunities for such laughter are all too rare.

The Slaughter of the Enemies

The climax of the story of Esther's salvation of the Jews turns the screw of this message one more time. When Esther defeats Haman's plan to have all the Jews in the empire killed, she does not have his genocidal edict reversed, as a reader familiar with Western comic tradition might expect. Rather, the king allows Mordecai to send another edict throughout the empire in which he allows all his Jewish subjects to gather together and kill any group of people who might be threatening them, along with all their wives and children, and to take their property (8:11–12). Nine months later, this is what happens. The Jews in the citadel of Susa kill 500 people on the thirteenth of Adar, and when Esther asks for the edict to be extended for a second day, a further 300 on the fourteenth. In the provinces of the empire, the Jews kill 75,000 of their enemies (*oyvehem*) (9:16).

Jewish and Christian readers have often been troubled by the Jews' mass slaughter of their enemies in the story of Esther. The Greek translators made a rather feeble attempt to mitigate the damage by lowering the number to 15,000 (9:16, LXX). Most of the explanations that attempt to justify the slaughter are unconvincing. Perhaps the best is that of André LaCocque, who writes, "The Jewish victory in Susa is equivalent to a successful insurrection in the World War II-era Warsaw ghetto with the result of 75 000 S.S. troops being slaughtered" (80). The Book of Esther does indeed emphasize that the Jews are defending themselves against the anti-Semitic citizens of the empire who were preparing to massacre them, man, woman, and child. But when it becomes a state law that a group of citizens have the right to define, without any checks and balances, any other citizen as an enemy of that group, and kill him as such, abuse of such a right is certain. Even if every one of the 75,810 people killed by the Jews were certainly planning to kill or harm them, there is a morally greater response to this fact than revenge in the form of mass slaughter. The text itself hints as much, when it says that the Jews "did as they pleased" [*vayya'asu...ki-retsonam*]" to those that hated them (9:5). This phrase picks up the one used of the banquet of excess given by Ahasuerus at the beginning of the story, where the king instructs his officials "to do as each [guest] pleased" [*la'asot ki-retson*] (1:8). The verb *asah*, "to do," followed by the phrase *ki-retson*, "according to the desire of," is used in both cases. In their slaughter of their enemies at the end of the story, the Book of Esther suggests, the Jews are behaving in the same way as the guests at the king's banquet at the beginning – that is, indulging their desires to excess, because they have the power to do so for a while.

Adele Berlin is wrong to argue that the mass slaughter of the enemies of the Jews is part of the comic genre of the book. She writes, "The killing is no more real than anything else in the plot, and is completely in character with the story's carnivalesque nature" (xii); "scenes of tumultuous riots and violent mock-destruction are completely at home in farcical and carnivalesque works" (81). The slaughter of the enemies of the Jews in the Book of Esther cannot be understood in this way, however. It is in no way "mock" destruction, but real destruction, on a large scale. Western comedy, including farce and burlesque, does not include mass killing. The deaths of the Jews' enemies are not part of the comic genre of the book; they are the place where the book shows its difference from comedy. In Aristophanes's *Lysistrata*, the Western comedy most comparable to the Book of Esther, the half-chorus of old men attempts to burn the women occupying the Acropolis alive. But this does not happen. They are foiled in their plan by the half-chorus of women. While there is plenty of talk and gestures of violence between them, in fact they end up forming a whole chorus and dancing together. "Let us join our ranks together, then embark upon a song" (l. 1042). The killing at the climax of the Book of Esther is not part of its comic genre, not part of farce, burlesque, or any other "low" form of comedy. It is not the case that "it is all in fun; nothing here is real" (Berlin 81). It is real, it is deeply disturbing, and it is deliberately so.

The Book of Esther ends with a festival. Mordecai and Esther send letters to all the Jews in the Persian empire instructing them to keep the fourteenth and fifteenth days of the month of Adar as "the days on which the Jews gained relief from their enemies, and as the month that had been turned for them from sorrow into gladness and from mourning into a holiday [*yom tov*]" (9:22). The festival of Purim is instituted at the end of the story. It is a celebration of victory over hatred, injustice, and death, a celebration of life, of the joy of being alive in a world that has all too often threatened the lives of the people of Israel. But the Book of Esther is clear, and deliberately so, that there is a dark underside even to this festival of life. The forces of evil, of injustice, and of death by which the people of Israel are threatened exist in them too, and in all peoples to whom the covenant with Israel will be extended. There is a sober reflection enjoined by the Book of Esther for the joyful celebration of Purim with which it ends. Evil is not only in others, in whom we have defeated it; it is in us too, in whom we have not.

TEXT FOR DISCUSSION

The Greek Additions to Esther

The LXX translation of Esther, which dates from the second century BCE, contains six major additions to the Hebrew MT added either at the time of translation or later (Crawford 860). Their likely date of composition is the second century BCE. Below are extracts from additions C and F:

14 ¹Then Queen Esther, seized with deadly anxiety, fled to the Lord. ²She took off her splendid apparel and put on the garments of distress and mourning, and instead of costly perfumes she covered her head with ashes and dung, and she utterly humbled her body [...] ³She prayed to the Lord God of Israel, and said: "O my Lord [...] ¹⁵you know that I hate the splendor of the wicked and abhor the bed of the uncircumcised and of any alien. ¹⁶You know my necessity – that

74 *The Bible as Literature*

I abhor the sign of my proud position, which is upon my head on days when I appear in public. I abhor it like a filthy rag, and I do not wear it on the days when I am at leisure. [17]And your servant has not eaten at Haman's table, and I have not honored the king's feast or drunk the wine of libations" [...]

* * * *

10 [4]Mordecai said [...] [9]"The Lord has saved his people; the Lord has rescued us from all these evils [...] [10]For this purpose he made two lots, one for the people of God and one for all the nations, [11]and these two lots came to the hour and moment and day of decision before God and among all the nations. [12]And God remembered his people and vindicated his inheritance. [13]So they will observe these days in the month of Adar, on the fourteenth and fifteenth of that month, with an assembly and joy and gladness before God, from generation to generation for ever among his people Israel."

QUESTIONS

1. The first extract is from Addition C, which follows 4:17 in the Hebrew text. Esther has agreed to Mordecai's request to intercede for the Jewish people with the king, although she may die for it. In the Hebrew text, God is never mentioned; here in the Greek text, however, Esther fervently prays to "the Lord God of Israel." In the Hebrew text, Esther saves the Jewish people through her ingenuity; here she prays to God for help, and that prayer is answered. What do you think of this difference between the texts? Is the Greek text more religious, or should readers of the Hebrew text assume that her ingenuity is a God-given gift?
2. In Esther's prayer we learn that she has lived a pious Jewish life in secret in the king's court, keeping the dietary laws when she can, and hating her forced marriage to a Gentile and the wealth of his court. Her joy has only been in God. Do you think this interpolation makes explicit something that was already implicit in the Hebrew text, or does it change the nature of the story?
3. The third extract is from Addition F, which is the end of the Greek book, following 10:3 in the Hebrew. Here Mordecai refers to the fulfillment of a dream he had in Addition A, which begins the Greek book, in which Esther's saving the Jews appeared in symbolic images. The Greek book begins with a dream and ends with its fulfilment, both of which come from God (11:12; 10:4). From beginning to end, God has been directing events. God is not mentioned once in the Hebrew book. What do you think of this difference?
4. The Greek text retains the Hebrew text's account of the name of the Jewish festival of Purim, that it derives from the word *pur*, for the "lot"

> that Haman cast to determine when the Jews of the empire should be killed (3:7; 9:24–26). In our second extract above it adds another account, that God made two "lots," one for the Jewish people, one for the nations, and cast the lot for the Jewish people (15:10–12). The broad sense of this is that God, rather than luck, is in charge of all the events narrated in the Book of Esther. What do you think of this addition to the Hebrew text?

Works Cited

Alter, Robert. *The Art of Biblical Narrative*. Basic Books, 1981.

Aristophanes. "Lysistrata." *Birds and Other Plays*, translated by Stephen Halliwell, Oxford UP, 1998, pp. 79–141.

Auld, A. Graeme. *I and II Samuel: A Commentary*. Westminster John Knox, 2011.

Bechtel, Carol M. *Esther*. Westminster John Knox, 2002.

Berlin, Adele. *Esther*. Jewish Publication Society, 2001.

Birch, Bruce C. "The First and Second Books of Samuel." *The New Interpreter's Bible*, Vol. 2, edited by Leander Keck et al., Abingdon Press, 1998, pp. 949–1383.

Brueggemann, Walter. *First and Second Samuel*. Westminster John Knox, 1990.

Calvin, John. *Commentaries on the Book of Joshua*, translated by Henry Beveridge, Baker Books, 2009.

Campbell, Edward F., Jr. *Ruth*. Doubleday, 1975.

Cartledge, Tony. *1 and 2 Samuel*. Smyth and Helwys, 2001.

Crawford, Sidnie White, "Esther." *The New Interpreter's Bible*, vol. 3, edited by Leander Keck et al., Abingdon Press, 1999, pp. 855–972.

Creach, Jerome F. D. *Joshua*. John Knox Press, 2003.

Cross, Frank Moore. *Canaanite Myth and Hebrew Epic: Essays in the Religion of Israel*. Harvard UP, 1973.

Dietrich, Walther. "Historiography in the Old Testament." *Hebrew Bible / Old Testament: The History of Its Interpretation, Vol. III, Part 2: The Twentieth Century – From Modernism to Postmodernism*, edited by Magne Sæbø, Vandenhoeck and Ruprecht, 2015, pp. 467–499.

Dozeman, Thomas B. *Joshua 1-12: A New Translation with Introduction and Commentary*. Yale UP, 2015.

Eskenazi, Tamara and Tivka Frymer-Kensky. *Ruth*. Jewish Publication Society, 2011.

Farmer, Kathleen A. Robertson. "Ruth." *The New Interpreter's Bible*, vol. 2, edited by Leander Keck et al., Abingdon Press, 1998, pp. 891–946.

Fischer, Irmtraud. "The Book of Ruth: A 'Feminist' Companion to the Torah?" *Ruth and Esther: A Feminist Companion to the Bible (Second Series)*, edited by Athalya Brenner, Sheffield Academic Press, 1999, pp. 24–49.

Herodotus. *Histories*, translated by Robin Waterfield, Oxford UP, 1998.

LaCoque, André. *The Feminine Unconventional: Four Subversive Figures in Israel's Tradition*. Fortress Press, 1990.

Levenson, Jon. *Esther: A Commentary*. Westminster John Knox, 1997.

McCann, J. Clinton. *Judges*. John Knox Press, 2002.

McCarter, P. Kyle, Jr. *II Samuel*. Doubleday, 1984.

Nielsen, Kristen. *Ruth*. Westminster John Knox Press, 1997.

76 *The Bible as Literature*

Noth, Martin. *The Deuteronomistic History*, translated by Jane Doull et al., 2nd ed., JSOT Press, 1991.

Olson, Dennis T. "Judges." *The New Interpreter's Bible*, vol. 2, edited by Leander Keck et al., Abingdon Press, 1998, pp. 721–888.

Origen. *Homilies on Joshua*, translated by Barbara J. Bruce, edited by Cynthia White, Catholic University of America Press, 2002.

Pritchard, James B. *Ancient Near Eastern Texts Relating to the Old Testament*. 3rd ed., Princeton UP, 1969.

Queen-Sutherland, Kandy, *Ruth and Esther*. Smyth and Helwys, 2016.

Römer, Thomas. "The So-Called Deuteronomistic History and Its Theories of Composition." *The Oxford Handbook of the Historical Books of the Bible*, edited by Brad E. Kelle and Brent A. Strawn, Oxford UP, 2020, pp. 303–322.

———. *The So-Called Deuteronomistic History: A Sociological, Historical and Literary Introduction*. T&T Clark, 2007.

Sakenfeld, Katherine Doob. *Ruth*. John Knox Press, 1999.

Schipper, Jeremy. *Ruth*. Yale UP, 2016.

Smend, Rudolf. "The Law and the Nations: A Contribution to Deuteronomistic Tradition History." *Reconsidering Israel and Judah: Recent Studies on the Deuteronomistic History*, edited by Gary N. Knoppers and J. Gordon McConville, Eisenbrauns, 2000, pp. 95–110.

Van Dijke-Hemmes, Fokkelien. "Ruth: A Product of Women's Culture?" *A Feminist Companion to Ruth*, edited by Athalya Brenner, Sheffield Academic Press, 1993, pp. 134–139.

Webb, Barry G. *The Book of Judges*. William B. Eerdmans, 2012.

4　Biblical Poetry

The Psalms

Introduction

The authors of the psalms are anonymous, despite the tradition of superscriptions ascribing them to various characters from Israel's sacred history. There is very little possibility of precisely dating any individual psalm. As William Brown puts it, the Psalter is "the product of centuries upon centuries of compositional and editorial work, from its oral roots to its Masoretic arrangement" (1). Approximate dates can be suggested for some psalms, but as James Crenshaw points out, "every attempt to date psalms encounters enormous difficulty, for their content is altogether indifferent to historical events" (6). The Psalter suggests a division into five books or sections with the doxologies that conclude each one (41:13; 72:18–20; 89:52; 106:48). There are also several other noticeable collections within the Psalter, including the Davidic collections (3–41; 51–72; 138–145); the Korahite collections (42–49; 84–85; 87–88); the Elohistic collection (42–83); the Asaphite collection (73–83); and the Songs of Ascents (120–134). As Walter Brueggemann and William Bellinger put it, the Psalter is a "collection of collections" (2).

Most scholars think that the superscriptions to the psalms were added later than their time of composition, probably during these processes of collection. David, to whom 73 psalms are ascribed in the MT, "was remembered as the initiator of psalmody in worship" (McCann 283), and most scholars argue that this is more likely to be the reason for which psalms are ascribed to him than that David himself wrote them. As Crenshaw puts it,

> The tendency during the postexilic period to attribute sacred writings to revered leaders – the Pentateuch to Moses, the Wisdom literature to Solomon, prophetic texts like Isaiah 40–66 to Isaiah – led to an identification of David as the author of numerous psalms.
>
> (5)

The Septuagint carries the process further, increasing the number of psalms ascribed to David to 85. The midrash on the Psalms ultimately ascribes all the

DOI: 10.4324/9781315751566-5

78   *The Bible as Literature*

psalms to David, and a note in the Qumran manuscripts attributes 4,050 psalms and songs to him (Crenshaw 5; Brown 3).

There are several genre designations in the superscriptions of the psalms, such as *maskil*, *michtam*, and *shiggaion*. The meanings of these terms are mostly a matter of speculation, and they are typically left untranslated. The most frequent genre designation is *mizmor*, which appears 57 times. It is translated by the LXX as *psalmos*. The cognate verb *zamar* is often used in the psalms, and means to sing or make music in praise of God. The Greek word *psalmos* derives from a verb to "strike" or "twang" a string, and comes to mean song or music and then pious song or music. The LXX entitled the book *Psalmoi*, from which the English title "Psalms" comes. The traditional Hebrew name for the Psalter is *tehillim*, "praises."

For much of the twentieth century, scholarship of the Psalms was dominated by the method of "form-criticism" pioneered by Hermann Gunkel. In literary-critical terms, Gunkel's German term *Gattung* is perhaps best translated as "genre" rather than "form." Form-criticism (or "genre-criticism") means first, understanding a given psalm in relation to its genre, such as the thanksgiving song of an individual, the lament of the community, the hymn or song of praise, royal psalm, or Wisdom or Torah psalm. Second, form-criticism means identifying the *Sitz-im-Leben*, or "setting in life," of the genre – the social situation out of which each genre developed. Most of these were Israel's communal worship, for Gunkel (although he argues that most of the psalms in the Psalter are "spiritualized" imitations of older poems actually used in such worship). For example, in the case of individual laments, although these are spiritual compositions by later authors, the authors based them on earlier works that had originated out of the context of a sick person coming to the Temple to pray for God's help. While still respected, form-criticism has increasingly given way in the last few decades to literary criticism that pays attention to the qualities of the individual psalm. As Clinton McCann writes, "Regardless of the circumstances out of which the prayers arose, the language and imagery were eventually heard and appropriated metaphorically [...] This means that the language and imagery are symbolic enough to be applicable to a variety of situations" (277). It is clear from the texts of the psalms that they have a relationship to public worship, but since there are only hypotheses as to the nature of that relationship, I will focus on the meaning of the psalms in themselves, both as individual works and as a collection of such works.

Intimacy

One of the first things to strike the modern reader of the Psalms is the intimate relationship with Yahweh described in many of them. Psalm 4 concludes:

> I will both lie down and sleep in peace
>   for you alone, O LORD, make me lie down in safety.
>
>   (4:8)

The word translated "both" by the NRSV here, *yachdav*, in this case means "at once." The psalmist is saying, "I lie down in peace and at once fall asleep." So confident is his trust in Yahweh's promise to bless him that his peace is complete, permeating throughout his whole body. He falls asleep as soon as he lies down, because he has no fears or anxieties to keep him awake. "There are many who say 'O that we might see some good!'" (4:6), but the psalmist is not one of them. He prays neither for a good harvest (4:7), nor for the kind of peace and prosperity that follow a good harvest. His peace and prosperity come from Yahweh alone. The text strongly emphasizes that God alone is the source of his security. The last half-line of the psalm – "you alone, O LORD, make me lie down in safety" – includes the personal pronoun "you" (*attah*) (and the double "t" in the Hebrew word *attah* makes it especially emphatic, as one has to dwell on the doubled letter, almost spitting the word out), although it is not needed grammatically and Hebrew poetry typically elides such personal pronouns. Furthermore, the psalmist adds for even greater emphasis the word *levadad*, "alone," making an unusually long half-line of poetry, with five stresses (Hebrew half-lines usually have between two and four stresses). He wants strongly to emphasize that the complete peace, body and soul, that he feels, even in a time of trouble, comes from Yahweh and Yahweh alone.

He sleeps in peace because Yahweh causes him to "lie down in safety" (4:8). The word for "safety" here, *betach*, comes from the root "to trust." The verb *yashav*, translated as "lie down" here, has a broad range of meaning – to sit, remain, or dwell – and could be translated as "to dwell" in safety. *la-betach toshiveni* means, "You make me dwell in the safety that comes from trust in you." Yahweh's covenant presence with and promise to bless the people of Israel cause the psalmist to live in mental, physical, and emotional peace that extends throughout every aspect of his dwelling in the world, including his most intimate and vulnerable moments such as when he comes to bed at night in a time of trouble.

The psalmists often write from this most intimate position, reflecting on and rejoicing in Yahweh on their beds at night. In Psalm 63, the psalmist writes:

> My soul is satisfied as with a rich feast,
>   and my mouth praises you with joyful lips
> when I think of you on my bed,
>   and meditate on you in the watches of the night.
>   (63:5–6)

The psalmist is filled with joy and peace as he "thinks of" God on his bed at night. The verb here is *zachar*, which means to "remember" or "call to mind." In the next half-line, he "meditates" (*hagah*) on God through the watches of the night. In Psalm 4, we saw the psalmist lying down to sleep at night; here he is already in his bed, but stays awake out of sheer love of Yahweh in order to reflect on the divine source of his joy. This is a deeper joy to him than that of spending the night with a lover in that same bed. The psalmist's relationship with Yahweh brings him complete satisfaction: "My soul is satisfied as with a rich feast" (63:5). The word translated as "soul" here, *nephesh*, means the whole living person. The psalmist is

80 *The Bible as Literature*

satisfied in every aspect of his life as with a "rich feast," literally "fat and fatness" (*chelev va-deshen*). He concludes, "My soul [*nephesh*] clings to you; / your right hand upholds me" (63:8). With every part of himself, body and soul, the psalmist clings close to God and feels God clinging close to him.

Anguish

Perhaps the most striking aspect of the intimate relationship to Yahweh expressed in the Psalms, for the modern reader, is the detailed and explicit way in which the psalmists express their anguish as they call on Yahweh for help. The psalmists' emotional states are described with a sometimes shocking candor. In Psalm 6, the speaker says:

> I am weary with my moaning:
>   every night I flood my bed with tears;
>   I drench my couch with weeping.
> My eyes waste away because of my grief.
>   (6:6–7)

The psalmist speaks both of God's anger – "O LORD, do not rebuke me in your anger / or discipline me in your wrath" (6:1) – and prays that God will "heal [*rapha*]" him (6:2). He also speaks of ill health, terror, and his enemies. The theological relationship between sin and sickness is neither asked about nor answered in the psalm. God's anger, the psalmist's physical failing to the point to death, his mental anguish, and his torment by his enemies are all part of a continuum, a whole experience of life lived in covenant relationship to Yahweh. James Mays describes Psalm 6 as "one of the profoundest efforts to fulfil in the realities of life the first commandment" (60), and he is right to say so. The psalmist is describing his experience of the absence of Yahweh's blessing in a life in which he has no other god, no other highest good, than Yahweh. In the end, this is what the distress that the psalmist describes in such vivid detail is about. The lines quoted above are a series of images for the terrible experience, agonizing to the point of death, of Yahweh withdrawing his blessing. What exactly is the psalmist "moaning" or "flooding [his] bed with tears" about? Everything. Everything that Yahweh gives in covenant blessing – life, health, peace, good relationships with others – he has withdrawn, and it is this experience, this moment in the experience of a whole life lived according to the first commandment, that drives the profundity of the psalm's lament.

There is a clear caesura in Psalm 6 between verses 7 and 8. After the multifaceted lament of the first seven lines, the last lines express the psalmist's confident faith that Yahweh has heard and will answer his prayer. "The LORD has heard my supplication; / the LORD accepts my prayer" (6:9). Just as the many things that the psalmist laments in verses 1–7 are all part of the experience of Yahweh withdrawing his blessing, so the confident faith of verses 8–10 that those prayers have been heard are all part of a whole life's experience of covenant relationship with Yahweh. McCann calls this a "thoroughly theocentric understanding of reality" ("Psalms" 703). The psalm is about a whole lifetime's experience of relationship with Yahweh, from the anguish of the periods in which he withdraws his blessing to the peace and prosperity of the periods in which he gives it. With the striking exception of Psalm 88, all the lament psalms, in their different ways, work in this manner. They articulate the complex journey of covenant faith with an aesthetic power that is coextensive with their candor. Like the Psalter as a whole, they do so in such a way as to articulate their authors' belief, even in their darkest moments on this journey, that it is an upward one, a journey from lament to praise. Psalm 30 says that "weeping may linger for the night, / but joy comes in the morning" (30:5). Psalm 88 says that the night of God's absence may last a whole lifetime, that it may never leave. All the other lament psalms say that, in their experience at least, it will, some morning, however unimaginable.

Enemies

A third very striking feature of the psalms, especially to the modern reader, is the frequency with which the psalmists complain of attacks, of many kinds, by their enemies. So frequent is this kind of complaint that the psalms as a whole give the impression that their speakers are constantly surrounded by actual or potential enemies. Psalm 3 begins, "O LORD, how many are my foes! / Many are rising against me" (3:1). Psalm 56 begins, "Be gracious to me, O God, for people trample on me; / all day long foes oppress me" (56:1). Psalm 35 begins by pleading with Yahweh to "contend" (*riv*) and "fight" (*lacham*) with those who contend and fight against the psalmist (35:1). They also pursue him (35:3) – the verb here is *radaph*, "to chase, pursue, persecute," used of Pharaoh's pursuit of the Israelites in Exodus. The mention of weapons of war in verses 2–3 makes it clear that the situation the psalmist is speaking of, whether literally or metaphorically, is one of battle. The psalmist goes on to say that his enemies "seek after my life" and "devise evil [*ra'ah*] against me" (35:4), emphasizing that the battle is an especially personal one. For an unstated reason, the psalmist's enemies want to harm or kill him personally, as an individual. As the psalm goes on, the situation becomes more complex and multifaceted, almost with each new idea introduced. Next we hear, "For without cause they hid their nets for me; / without cause they dug a pit for my life. (35:7). This is a common complaint about the psalmists' enemies (cf. Psalms 38:19; 69:4; 109:3; 119:86, 161), that they persecute the psalmists *chinnam*, "without cause." The enemies become a particular kind of enemy here, a kind that attacks gratuitously and irrationally. They start to embody an idea of evil rather than the psalmist's fellow human beings who, even for a reason he regards as unjustified, are hostile to him.

The situation changes again in verse 11. The psalmist says, "Malicious witnesses rise up; / they ask me about things I do not know" (35:11). Perhaps these malicious witnesses are harming the psalmist's reputation in public or, since the phrase "malicious witness [*ed hamas*]" seems to be a technical legal term (cf. Exod. 23:1; Deut. 19:6), perhaps they are doing so in a legal proceeding. Either way, we see

82   *The Bible as Literature*

the context changing as the psalm progresses. The nature of the enemies of which it complains is Protean, assuming multiple and changing forms. The psalmist gets still more specific. We hear that the malicious witnesses "repay me evil for good" (35:12). These are people to whom the psalmist himself actively did good (*tovah*). He mourned and fasted when they were seriously ill, grieving for them as if he were grieving for his own mother (35:13–14). The malicious witnesses are now people close enough to him for him to have cared deeply for them while they were sick, as deeply as for his brother or his mother. This is why he is "forlorn" (*shechol*, lit. "bereaved") when they do him evil in return (35:12). It is not clear in the psalm whether these people are the same enemies as the armed attackers of the first verses or a different group. This effect of unclarity is achieved deliberately by the psalmist, as one can tell from the fact that the same aesthetic strategy is used in the other psalms that complain of the psalmists' enemies, such as Psalm 55. The psalmist creates an impression of accretion, of being surrounded by one kind of enemy after another, who loosely merge into one another as a kind of crowd of enemies all persecuting him at once.

Brueggemann and Bellinger call scholarly speculation about the precise circumstances of the psalmist "futile" (174). They are right to say so, not only because, as they put it, "the rhetoric of the psalm is open enough to relate […] to many circumstances," but because it has deliberately been written to be so open. Rather than complaining, or even wanting to complain, of specific enemies or specific acts of hostility by them, the author of Psalm 35 has created a general, existential sense of being surrounded by people who are ready and willing, at a moment's notice, to do him harm. The portrayal of enemies in the psalms is a portrayal of what it is like, according to the Psalter, to be human, to live in society. Gunkel makes the following perceptive observation about individual lament psalms:

> Commonly, the images of the complaint contradict one another and do not allow themselves to be coordinated into one self-contained situation […] Whatever unites these images has to be sought outside the images themselves. This unity may lie in the spiritual condition of the poet.
>
> (134)

Gunkel goes on to claim that the impression of being surrounded by enemies derives from the spiritual condition of "extreme illness and terrifying mortal danger" (148), but this is not the reader's experience of the psalmists' accounts of their enemies. The portrayal of enemies in the psalms is not so much about the approach of death as it is about life. It is a portrayal of what human life in society is like, in the psalmists' view. Life, in their view, involves being surrounded by actual or potential enemies. The psalmists love peace and prosperity, or *shalom*. They look for peace, for quiet in the society in which they live. But they never get it; their enemies never stop their multiple hostilities. The portrayal of enemies in the psalms thus makes both an existential and a theological point. Valuable as social relationships are, the psalms say, they are always susceptible of failing, of

Biblical Poetry   83

falling apart into war or enmity. This is true even of one's closest friend. Peace and prosperity are what human beings are fulfilled by, and what Yahweh promises to the people of Israel in the covenant. But, the psalms say, they are not to be found in any lasting way here, even in the land promised in the covenant. Praising the justice of Yahweh's anointed king, the psalms quietly and indirectly say that the kingdom of righteousness, justice, and peace over which he will rule is still coming. Psalm 72 says of the king:

> In his days may righteousness [*tsedeq*] flourish
> and peace [*shalom*] abound, until the moon is no more.
> (72:7)

The constant presence of enmity in human life in the psalms makes clear that these days are not yet. The reader can only imagine, therefore, that they are still to come, that the rule of Yahweh's anointed is a future kingdom, one of a different kind than all the societies' human beings, even the people of Israel living under Yahweh's covenant, have ever known.

The Wicked

The enemies of the psalms are to some extent associated with another significant presence in the lives of the psalmists, the "wicked" (*resha'im*). Several psalms associate these concepts in parallelism, such as Psalm 3: "You strike all my enemies [*oyevai*] on the cheek; / You break the teeth of the wicked [*resha'im*]. (Psalm 3:7; cf. 17:9;55:3). Psalm 10 goes into detail about the behavior of the wicked. First, they "persecute the poor" (10:2). The word for "poor" here is *ani*, which means poor, afflicted, or humble. It is the most frequent of a group of related words used to describe the least powerful members of society in the psalms. The next most frequent of these words is *evyon*, which means "in want," "needy," or "poor." Used in parallel with both is *dal*, which means "low," "weak," or "poor" (and can also mean "thin"). Psalms 9 and 10 also use the less frequent words *dach*, literally "crushed"; and *chelchah*, "hapless" or "unfortunate." The wicked in the psalms are primarily those who take advantage of the poor, who use the powerlessness of the least powerful members of society for their own gain. In modern English usage, the term "wicked" connotes primarily licentiousness. The wicked in the psalms are not licentious people, however, given over to excessive self-gratification, but oppressors of the poor. The Nicaraguan poet Ernesto Cardenal represents this well in his series of poems entitled *Psalms*. In Psalm 1, the wicked are mentioned four times in the psalm's six verses, and the psalm contrasts the way of the righteous (*derech tsadiqim*) and the way of the wicked (*derech resha'im*). This is Cardenal's version:

> Happy the man who does not follow the party line
> attend its meetings
> does not sit at table with gangsters

84   *The Bible as Literature*

or with Generals in the War Council
Happy the man who does not spy on his brother
or denounce his fellow student
Happy the man who does not read advertisements
does not listen to their radios
does not believe their slogans

He will be like a tree planted near running water.
(11)

The poem accurately represents the fact that the wicked of the psalms are primarily oppressors, those with power in society who exploit the least powerful for their own ends.

The next trait of the wicked in psalms is that they either positively disbelieve in God or they do not believe that God will call them to account for their oppression of the poor. Peter Craigie calls this "functional atheism" (126).

In the pride of their countenance
the wicked say, "God will not seek it out";
all their thoughts are, "There is no God."
(10:4)

The wicked behave as if Yahweh did not exist. They do not have a clear or consistent position on the existence or nonexistence of God; the question is simply irrelevant to their concerns, which are for the material gains that come from power. They believe only in their own power (10:6). Psalm 12 attributes to them the phrase, "Our lips are our own – who is our master?" (12:4). This phrase is particularly striking in Hebrew. As several commentators point out, it is literally, "Our lips [are] with us," *sephatenu ittanu*, a kind of self-affirming parody of the covenant confession *YHWH ittanu*, "the LORD [is] with us" (Num. 14:9; cf. 2 Chron. 32:8). The wicked are their own gods, and so ignore the call for peace and prosperity for all, including and especially the weakest members of society, that Yahweh's covenant and Torah constitute.

The King

The Psalter's first solution to the problem of the wicked is Yahweh's anointed king. The second book of the Psalter ends with Psalm 72, which opens with a prayer that the king will rule in righteousness and justice (72:1–2). The psalm defines these qualities as follows: "He delivers the needy when they call, / the poor who have no helper" (72:13). The ideal king, according to the psalms, does what Yahweh requires of a king, and what the psalmist prays for in a king, namely to act in righteousness and justice toward the *aniyim*, the poor, who in Psalm 72:2 are called "your [God's]" *aniyim*. The king, Yahweh's anointed, will prevent the wicked from exploiting the poor, as Psalms 72 and 45 in particular make clear. Psalms 2 and 110

Biblical Poetry   85

have a similarly high view of the king as the embodiment of Yahweh's righteousness and justice.

However, these are only four psalms. The Psalter complains far more frequently about the oppression of the poor and needy by the wicked than it celebrates their defense by the righteous king. Indeed, the king most frequently referred to in psalms is David, and in the psalms ascribed in the Masoretic text to him, he is most frequently *ani*, or poor, himself, not protecting the needy from the ruthless greed of the wicked but himself needing such protection from them. Many lament psalms have superscriptions that attribute them to David during times of trouble or persecution. Psalm 54 is called "a maskil of David, when the Ziphites went and told Saul, 'David is hiding among us'"; Psalm 56 is said to be "Of David [...] when the Philistines seized him in Gath." In many psalms ascribed to David, the speaker describes himself as "poor" (*ani*) or "needy" (*evyon*), or with a related term that indicates his great need. Psalm 86 is ascribed to David, and the psalmist writes, "Incline your ear to me, O God, for I am poor (*ani*) and needy (*evyon*)" (86:1). Psalm 69 is ascribed to David, and the psalmist prays, "I am lowly (*ani*) and in pain (*cho'ev*); / let your salvation, O God, protect me" (69:29). Since David on the whole, in the psalms, has not presided over the kind of society envisaged in Psalm 72, the reader can only infer that this society is still to come. As the psalms deal with the problem of the wicked, their answer is prophetic. They imagine another kind of society, with another kind of king. They imagine Yahweh's covenant with David, about whom they cannot stop thinking, being fulfilled in a new way. It is in this sense that the wicked are, in the words of Psalm 73, "like a dream when one awakes; / on awaking you despise their phantoms" (73:20). The society to come, in which Yahweh's anointed king will rule over all people in righteousness, justice, and peace, will be like waking from this dream into reality itself.

Praise

The Psalms express a wide variety of religious emotions. They speak to God in a wide variety of ways, all of which are candid to the point of being shocking, at least initially to a modern reader. As we have seen, the most frequently expressed emotion is anguish. Suffering is the most frequent experience in human life, according to the Psalter. The next most frequently expressed emotion is love of God, expressed in the form of praise. The suffering by which human life is primarily characterized, according to the Psalter, tends in general, although not always, toward love of God who creates, provides for, and delivers from suffering the men and women whose lives are so characterized.

Gunkel speaks of the "overwhelming enthusiasm" of the psalmists for Yahweh (25). "His heart is so full everything God does," he writes of the Hebrew psalmist, "so full of all the grace that God pours out so bountifully, that the poet cannot do enough to tell of all this" (30). Gunkel is right. The psalmists cannot imagine enough people singing, dancing, and making music, or people and things making a loud or joyful enough noise, adequately to express the love they feel for Yahweh.

86   *The Bible as Literature*

The psalmists very frequently ask the hearers of their psalms to join them in singing to Yahweh. As Psalm 95 begins: "O come let us sing to the LORD; / let us make a joyful noise to the rock of our salvation!" (95:1). The verb translated as "sing" in line 1 here is *ranan*, "to give a ringing cry." It means to shout or cry out loudly, usually for joy. The verb translated as "make a joyful noise" in line 2 is *rua*, "to shout," which can also mean to give a blast on a horn. The psalms also use the verb *shir*, "to sing," as in Psalm 96, "O sing [*shiru*] to the LORD a new song; / sing [*shiru*] to the LORD all the earth" (96:1). The psalmists very frequently ask their hearers to make as loud and as joyful a noise as they can in singing to Yahweh.

They feel the same way about music. There cannot be enough instruments or enough noise on those instruments to express the blessings given by Yahweh to his covenant people. Psalm 98 exhorts its hearers:

Sing praises [*zammeru*] to the LORD with the lyre [*kinnor*],
  with the lyre and the sound of melody [*zimrah*].
With trumpets [*chatsotserot*] and the sound of the horn [*shophar*]
  make a joyful noise [*hari'u*] before the King, the LORD.
(98:5–6)

The verb *zimmer*, from which the verb translated as "sing praises" in line 1 and the noun translated as "melody" in line 2 here comes, means to make music in praise of God. It gives us the word *mizmor*, the Hebrew word translated as "psalm." It can mean music made with the voice or with musical instruments. In either sense, the Hebrew Bible has a term for music made specifically in response to God. It is similar in this sense to the English word "hymn," but it connotes something louder and more unreserved. Psalm 150 concludes the Psalter with images of a great noise being made on many musical instruments at once – the trumpet, the lyre, the harp, the tambourine, stringed instruments, the flute, and cymbals, all played loudly, and with the people of Israel dancing enthusiastically to them all.

Indeed, the psalmists imagine the whole creation turning into praise. "Make a joyful noise to God, all the earth," Psalm 66 begins. "Let the peoples praise you, O God; let all the peoples praise you," Psalm 67 repeats like a refrain. *Kol goyim* – all the peoples who are not Israel – the psalmists think of Yahweh as so delightful that, although they write as members of a people which believes that it has been chosen by God as his covenant people, they envisage that, if Yahweh were clearly revealed to or understood by all the other peoples of the earth, they too would see as much and praise him with as much enthusiasm as the psalmists of Israel.

TEXT FOR DISCUSSION

Psalm 1: Hebrew Poetry

Below is the Masoretic text of Psalm 1:

Biblical Poetry   87

$$
\begin{array}{r}
\text{1,א}^{\text{5}} \text{ אַשְׁרֵי־הָאִישׁ אֲשֶׁר} \mid \text{לֹא הָלַךְ בַּעֲצַת רְשָׁעִים} \\
\text{וּבְדֶרֶךְ}^{a} \text{ חַטָּאִים לֹא עָמָד וּבְמוֹשַׁב לֵצִים לֹא יָשָׁב:} \\
\text{² כִּי אִם בְּתוֹרַת יְהוָה חֶפְצוֹ וּבְתוֹרָתוֹ יֶהְגֶּה יוֹמָם וָלָיְלָה:} \\
\text{³ וְהָיָה כְּעֵץ שָׁתוּל עַל־פַּלְגֵי מָיִם} \\
\text{אֲשֶׁר פִּרְיוֹ} \mid \text{יִתֵּן בְּעִתּוֹ וְעָלֵהוּ לֹא־יִבּוֹל} \\
\text{וְכֹל אֲשֶׁר־יַעֲשֶׂה יַצְלִיחַ}^{b} \text{:} \\
\text{⁴ לֹא־כֵן הָרְשָׁעִים}^{a} \\
\text{כִּי אִם־כַּמֹּץ אֲשֶׁר־תִּדְּפֶנּוּ רוּחַ}^{b} \text{:} \\
\text{⁵ עַל־כֵּן} \mid \text{לֹא־יָקֻמוּ רְשָׁעִים בַּמִּשְׁפָּט וְחַטָּאִים בַּעֲדַת צַדִּיקִים:} \\
\text{⁶ כִּי־יוֹדֵעַ יְהוָה דֶּרֶךְ צַדִּיקִים וְדֶרֶךְ רְשָׁעִים תֹּאבֵד:}
\end{array}
$$

Figure 4.1 The Masoretic text of Psalm 1. *Biblia Hebraica Stuttgartensia*, edited by Karl Elliger and Wilhelm Rudolph, 5th revised edition, edited by Adrian Schenker, © 1977 and 1997 Deutsche Bibelgesellschaft, Stuttgart. Used by permission.

QUESTIONS

In order to understand the poetic craft of the author of this psalm, we will need to know some of the basic rules of Hebrew poetry.

(1) Each line in Hebrew poetry is composed of two (or sometimes three) half-lines. The divide between these half-lines is represented by a space in the MT above.

(2) Each half-line usually has between two and four stressed syllables. (This isn't meter, but rather a kind of heightening of the rhythm of ordinary speech.) In my transliterations below, acute accents will indicate the stressed syllables.

(3) The second half-line in each line is typically related to the first by parallelism, that is, a restatement with difference of the first-half line.

1. Read Psalm 1 in English translation. Now, let's look at v. 1 in the Hebrew, which is composed of two lines (i.e., four half-lines). The parallelism in the first half-line (v. 1a) is not perfect. In the third and fourth half-lines (v. 1c-d), it is perfect: "or stand in the way of sinners" (v. 1c) is restated with difference in, "or sit in the seat of mockers" (v. 1d). The second half-line of v.1, "does not walk in the counsel of the wicked," also parallels both these half-lines. But the first half-line of

88 *The Bible as Literature*

v. 1 jars against this neat pattern. The first two words, אשרי האיש (*ashréi ha-ísh*), "Happy the man," do not parallel the second half-line. Furthermore, the fourth and fifth words of v. 1, לא הלך (*ló halách*), "does not walk," logically belong to the second half-line (which would then neatly parallel "does not stand in the way of sinners" and "does not sit in the seat of mockers"). But in fact they are part of the first half-line, interrupting the otherwise neat parallelism of v. 1b-d. This has the effect of emphasizing the words that interrupt the parallelism, that is, אשרי האיש (*ashréi ha-ísh*), "Happy the man." That is, the poet has deliberately broken the rules of parallelism in order to emphasize these first two words of v. 1. Why do you think he has he done this? (I would suggest that he does so in order to emphasize his most fundamental point in the psalm, that it is righteousness rather than wickedness that makes a person happy. Would you agree, or not?)

2. Look at v. 4, which has three half-lines (or "hemistiches" or "cola" as scholars sometimes call them). The first one is set out in the MT on its own line because there is no other half-line with which it clearly stands in parallel. It is the half-line לא־כן הרשאים (*lo-chén ha-reshaím*), "Not so the wicked" (v. 4a). Standing alone without a parallel half-line strongly emphasizes the statement. Furthermore, its being a half-line without a parallel half-line has the effect of placing it in an unusual kind of parallel with the similarly unparalleled half-line we have just discussed in v. 1, אשרי האיש (*ashréi ha-ísh*), "Happy is the man." The poet has cleverly broken the ordinary rules of parallelism to have two half-lines parallel each other across different lines (which does not usually happen in Hebrew poetry). They both have two stresses (*ashréi ha-ísh; lo-chén ha-reshaím*); they are both emphatically unparalleled half-lines; and they are antithetical in meaning to one another – the first means that the righteous man is happy; the second that the wicked man is not. Why do you think the poet has done this? (I think he is cleverly emphasizing at the level of poetic form what he is also saying in the content of the poem, that the way of the righteous and the way of wicked are (a) the antithesis of one another and (b) the only two ways facing a person. Would you agree, or not?)

3. Let's look again at the two lines of v. 1. The second, third, and fourth half-lines are very neatly paralleled in terms of their form. All three half-lines have the form "does not [verb] in the [singular noun] of the [masculine plural noun]." Look closely at the Hebrew words of the third and fourth half-lines (i.e., vv. 1c and 1d, which make up the second line of the psalm). See that the first words of both half-lines begin with the letters ובּ (*u-ve*). These are both prefixes; the ו (*u*) means "nor"; the בּ (*ve*) means "in." Next, look at the second word of each half-line – see that it ends in both cases with the letters ים (*im*). This indicates a masculine plural noun (in v. 1c it is "sinners," חטאים

[*chatta'im*]; in v. 1d "mockers," לֵצִים *letsim*]). Then look at the third word in each half line – it both cases it is לֹא (*lo*), "not." Finally, look at the final word of each half line – see that it has just three letters (עָמַד [*amad*] in 1c; יָשַׁב [*yashav*] in 1d). In both cases, this is a very common verb ("stand" in 1c; "sit" in 1d). The three letters indicate in both cases that the verb is in its simplest form, the third-person perfect masculine singular. The last four words of the first line (v. 1a-b) also have exactly the same form, but with their order differently patterned. The poet has created a very detailed pattern of parallel forms between the three half-lines. Why do you think this is? (I would suggest that it indicates at the level of poetic form that there are numerous ways to be wicked, but they all have the same result, of which the psalmist speaks in v. 5. Would you agree, or not?)

The Song of Songs

Introduction

The superscription of the Song of Songs reads, "The Song of Songs [*shir ha-sherim*], which is Solomon's" (Song 1:1). The form of the phrase "song of songs" primarily indicates intensification, as in the similar phrases "holy of holies" (*qodesh qodeshim*), or "vanity of vanities" (*havel havalim*). Just as "holy of holies" means the most holy place in the Temple, so "song of songs" can mean the "best of songs." It can also mean the most songlike of songs, that is, the most beautiful song, or even the very essence of what song is or should be. It can also refer to the way in which the Song is a collection of lyrics, that is, a song made up of songs.

Most scholars believe that it is unlikely that King Solomon wrote the Song, since there is little support in the text itself for this view (Murphy 3; Weems 1024–1025; Fishbane xxi). Rather, the ascription to Solomon is more likely to be a late scribal addition, based on several factors. First, Solomon is referred to several times in the third person in the Song (3:7–11; 8:11–12; 1:5). Second, he is known in Israel's tradition as a prolific composer of songs – "he composed three thousand proverbs, and his songs [*shir*] numbered a thousand and five" (1 Kings 4:32). Third, Solomon is also known as a lover, with over a thousand wives and concubines (1 Kings 11:1–3). These issues probably suggested Solomon as an appropriate figure from Israel's history to whom to ascribe the Song. It may also be the case that the ascription is intended to confer the gravity of the Wisdom tradition upon the Song (Weems 1024–1025; Murphy 121–122), since Solomon is also known in biblical tradition for his wisdom (1 Kings 3–4).

The author or authors of the Song are unknown. The predominance of women's voices in the Song, as well as the book's "pronounced [...] female point of view" (Weems 1024), has led some scholars to suggest the possibility that a woman wrote the song, or alternatively that the author "drew on traditional materials, some of which were the products of women's culture" (Exum 65), but as Exum writes,

90   *The Bible as Literature*

"the sex of the author cannot be deduced from the poem" (65). A wide range of dates for the Song have also been suggested, from the time of Solomon in the tenth century BCE to the Hellenistic period (the fourth to second centuries BCE). Most commentators prefer a postexilic date, in part because the language appears to be late, including foreign loan words such as *pardes* ("orchard") (4:13), from Persian and *appiryon* ("palanquin," NRSV; "carriage," KJV) (3:9), perhaps from Greek (Murphy 149; Exum 139; Fishbane 96). Michael Fishbane suggests that the book is "a collection of lyrics composed over many centuries – beginning (perhaps) in mid-tenth century BCE and continuing to the fifth or fourth centuries BCE, when the Song achieved something like its present form" (xxi). The author's class context seems clearer – he (or possibly she) seems to be a member of the elite, or at least "acquainted with the accoutrements of the privileged class" (Weems 1025), as the references to the woman's vineyard, the royal wedding procession, and the references to fine spices, fruits, and perfumes suggest. As Exum adds, the Song is "a very sophisticated artistic composition, with a rich vocabulary, and versed in the poetic traditions of the ancient Near East – all of which suggests that the poet moved in educated elite circles in ancient Israel" (63).

Ancient Near Eastern Love Poetry

The Song is frequently compared to extant love poetry from the ancient Near East, especially to Egyptian love poetry, written between the thirteenth and eleventh centuries BCE, and to Mesopotamian love poetry, with dates ranging from the twenty-first to the seventh century BCE. The Egyptian poems share with the Song of Songs the language of brother and sister in which the lovers speak to each other; imagery of food, spices, flowers, liquor, oils, scents, and animals (including doves and gazelles); the rural setting of the lovers' meetings; the Springtime setting; the topos of the male lover knocking at his beloved's door, and the double entendres that can be used of this situation; and references to the mothers of the lovers (Fox 3–81). The Sumerian poems share with the Song of Songs imagery of food (most commonly honey), liquor, jewels, and architecture; the topos of the lover at the door; the topos of the night watchmen; and references to the lovers' mothers (Jacobsen 88–98, 3–84).

From this fragmentary evidence, little more than hints, of the conventions of the genre in which the Song of Songs is written, it is clear that the Song is a fine example of ancient Near Eastern love poetry. One might compare one of the "songs of description" in the Egyptian poems to those in the Song of the Songs:

> Behold her, like Sothis rising,
>   at the beginning of the year:
> shining, precious, white of skin [...]
> Long of neck, white of breast,
>   her hair true lapis lazuli.
> Her arms surpass gold,
>   her fingers are like lotuses.
>   (Fox 52)

Biblical Poetry 91

With the exception of the line "her fingers are like lotuses," and perhaps also "her hair true lapis lazuli," this song of description lacks some of the metaphoric energy of that of Song of Songs 4:1–5. The woman's body parts are described in terms of things more immediately comparable to them than in the Song, where a greater energy of the imagination is required to understand the ways in which the woman's hair is like a flock of goats, or her neck like "the tower of David" (Song 4:4). There are occasional lines in the Egyptian poems that articulate a similar metaphoric energy, including a fascinating description of the woman by a tree as if she were an especially beautiful tree (Fox 46). Nevertheless, a comparison of the Song with the fragments that remain make it clear that it both uses a series of conventional images, forms, and topoi, and that, whatever can be said about other examples of ancient Near Eastern love poetry, the Song is an especially beautiful and profound example of such poetry.

The Eros of the Senses

One of the many striking effects of the Song is its use of a dizzying wealth of sensual imagery to describe, without directly naming, the pleasures of sexual love that the two lovers sing about. One of the most widely used rhetorical strategies of the Song is its constant blurring of the boundaries between one thing and another. People and things, I and you, we and them, are always fusing in and out of being themselves and other than themselves, such that the very concept of self begins to dissolve in the song. This strategy is used in describing the lovemaking (*dodim*) of the lovers. A rich sensual panoply of imagery is used that overwhelms not only the senses but also the mind of the reader, such that all is confusion, merging, loss of self and of the boundaries of self, other and world. This gives the love so described a profounder, more deeply affecting quality than its more bawdy counterparts in Egyptian and Sumerian poetry. The Song is not bawdy at all, in fact, but a profound portrayal of the merging of self, other, and world that the most intimate forms of relationship between one person and another constitute.

The gorgeous assault on the senses begins right away:

> Let him *kiss* me with the *kisses* of his *mouth*!
>> For your *love* is better than *wine*,
> your *anointing oils* are *fragrant*,
>> your name is *perfume poured out*.
>>> (Song 1:2–3, italics added)

I have italicized all the words in these two couplets that pertain to the senses of touch, taste, and smell, which demand the closest proximity to the body of the other. The rhythms and sound patterns in the Hebrew lines are also very beautiful. The sense of touch is strongly invoked with the erotically charged repetition of "let him kiss me with kisses" (the Hebrew says "from kisses," as if her lover's mouth were a rich store of kisses from which she wants to draw) and then on top of that "the kisses of his mouth." The repetition of *sh* and *n* sounds in the Hebrew for "Let

92   *The Bible as Literature*

him kiss me with kisses" – *yish-shaqéni minneshiqót* – adds to the sensuality of the line, as does the rhythm of the first couplet (i.e., Song 1:2):

> *yish-shaqéni minneshiqót píhu | ki tovím dodécha mi-yáyin*

The sensuality of the woman's appeal to the "kisses" of her lover's "mouth" is heightened still further by her appeal in the next line to his "lovemaking" (*dodim*). The NRSV translates this as "love," but the plural noun in Hebrew has more definitely physical connotations. As Exum puts it, the word denotes "not love in the abstract but rather sexual activity, which can include kisses, caresses, and sexual intercourse" (93; cf. Murphy 125).

These four consecutive ideas pertaining to the sense of touch ("to kiss," "kisses," "mouth," "lovemaking") are followed by appeals to the senses of taste and smell. Your love is better than "wine" (*yayin*), the woman says in the second half-line of verse 2. In fact, the image of wine appeals not only to taste, but also to smell and touch, as wine is aromatic and as drinking it is a physical activity. Your "oils" (*shemanim*) are "fragrant" (*le-reach [...] tovim*), she goes on, and your name is "perfume" (*shemen*) poured out (1:3). The word *shemen*, repeated in this couplet, appeals both to the sense of touch, because it refers to oils rubbed into the body, and also to the sense of smell, because they are fragrant, and used deliberately to make the man smell attractive. The sense of smell is as overcharged as the sense of touch was in verse 2, as the woman says that the "fragrance" (*reach*) of her lover's fragrant anointing oils is "delightful" (*tovim*). Indeed the word *tovim* is repeated in the two half-lines 1:2b and 1:3a, in a way that it is difficult to render into English, but which adds to the sense of sensual delight in the Hebrew:

> *ki **tovím** dodécha mi-yáyin*
> *le-réach shemanécha **tovím***

("For your lovemaking is **better** than wine / the fragrance of your anointing oils **delightful**"). Finally, the man's name – the very thought of him – is like perfume "poured out" (*turaq*) to the woman. The verb here is feminine, although its subject (*shemen*, "perfume") is masculine, and so should take a masculine verb. The rules of gender agreement are broken several times like this throughout the Song. If the text and translation here reflect the intention of the author, then the overwhelming effect of all the sensual imagery is at work even in the grammar of the poetry, as the proper differences between masculine and feminine, between him and her, start to break down in the couple's overwhelming love for each other.

The Songs of Description

A second very striking feature of the Song of Songs to the modern or Western reader are its "songs of description," sometimes known by the Arabic name *wasf*, which means "description," and denotes a similar genre of Arabic poetry. The beauty of the songs of description in the Song of Songs consists not so much in the poet's use of the genre itself, which was a staple of contemporary poetry, but in the ways in which he (or she) uses it. First, the images suggest that the experience of love is a sensual, physically delightful one. "Your cheeks are like halves of a pomegranate / behind your veil" (4:3); "His cheeks are like beds of spices, / yielding fragrance. / His lips are lilies, / distilling liquid myrrh" (5:15). The effect of the first line is not to create an exact parallel between some aspect of pomegranate halves and some aspect of the woman's cheeks. Rather, the sensual connotations of the split pomegranate – the sweet taste, the bright color and soft texture of the fruit, the juice oozing from it, the curved shape of the half-fruit, and perhaps even the connotations of fertility in its many seeds – all these images and ideas arise from the image of the pomegranate halves and cluster around the referent, the poet's lover, along with all the other images in the song of description, as a whole. The erotic effect of concealing and revealing is at work in the next half-line, as the man looks at what is now a cluster of sensual delights through the woman's veil.

Many more of the images in the songs do not primarily have these sensual connotations. They do, however, have aesthetic, moral, and religious connotations, which constitute their main effect. "Your head crowns you like Carmel" (7:5), the man says to the woman (literally, "your head upon you is like Carmel"), and this line is perhaps the best introduction to this effect. It is very difficult to make this comparison of the woman's head to a mountain range refer primarily to the beauty of her head. Rather, the poet means that he loves the woman as much as he loves the natural beauty of Israel. His love for her, the image says, is like his love for the covenant land that Yahweh gave to his treasured people, flowing with milk and honey. This image, like many others in the songs of description, associates, in an almost sacramental way, the lovers' love for each other with their love of the land to which Yahweh brought their people, and so with their love of Yahweh. The images indirectly and poetically say that the lovers' love for each other is a covenant love, comparable to and a part of the covenant relationship between Yahweh and Israel.

In fact, the incongruity of some of the images is the most effective technique in the songs of description. It is because the comparison of the woman's head to Mount Carmel or her neck to the tower of David does not work easily in our immediate interpretive lexicon that the reader is forced to find the actual constellation of meanings the image sets up. And once we do so, we realize that the poet is speaking of and praising a very grand, a very ennobling love. His love for his beloved is like his love for the promised land in which he lives – it is a love for Yahweh's precious gift to him, and to all of his people from Abraham to his immediate family. Their love transforms every aspect of the couple's lives – the poet loves his beloved with a complete and completing love, for her beauty, for her body, for their interactions, for his country, for the traditions of the covenant, and for Yahweh himself who enters into that covenant with him and his people. The images of songs of description convey, with their combination of variety and incongruity, that the love of which the man and woman sing is truly sacramental. It is a love physical and spiritual, sexual and religious, private and public. It is a love that knows no bounds, the center of the world whose circumference is endless.

94   *The Bible as Literature*

Each image in the songs of description, in proportion to its incongruity, adds to the constellation of ideas, feelings, and experiences in whose terms the young man and the young woman describe their love. Particularly striking is the following, from the fourth song, in the man's voice:

> You are beautiful as Tirzah, my love,
>   comely as Jerusalem,
>   terrible as an army with banners.
>
> (6:4)

Tirzah was the capital city of the northern kingdom of Israel from just after Solomon's reign until the time of Omri, about 50 years later, who built Samaria as the new capital. The man compares the woman to the two capital cities of the kingdoms of Israel and Judah, to the two great centers of power in the divided countries. The main burden of this twin image is power. He emphasizes the woman's power, and he continues to do so with his next half-line, *ayummah ka-nidgalot*, which the NRSV translates as "terrible as an army with banners." *Ayom* (here in the feminine, *ayummah*) means terrible, dreadful, or awe-inspiring, and the only other time the adjective appears in the Hebrew Bible is at Habakkuk 1:7, where Yahweh tells the prophet how terrible the Chaldean army is that he will bring against the nations. The woman is as awesome, even terrifying in her power, as the mighty and merciless Babylonian army who will destroy Jerusalem and force the people of Judah into exile. As terrible as the Babylonians, she truly overpowers him in their mutual love.

There is no certainty on how to translate the word *nidgalot* – it may derive from the word for "banner," and so mean "an army with its banners," or more generally from the verb "to look," and so mean an "exalted" or "distinguished" sight or thing. What is clear is the overwhelming power of the woman as the man relates to her in love. This is not just her sexual power over him, although it is partly that in the context of the sensual love poem. It is also the power she has, both in herself and over him, in their mutual relationship of love. As much power as the young man has by virtue of being a man, which includes at the very least the freedom of the city, so much, if not more, does the woman have in their relationship, as he likens her to the very centers of power in which that relationship takes place. In their love, according to the songs of description, there is no subordination. In her song, he is like the golden, bejeweled statue of a god. In his, she is like Jerusalem itself, and its companion capital of the northern kingdom, and possibly their armies too. Both are free for each other; neither forced by the other. The songs of description imagine marriage as a relationship of mutual love between equals, equals in power, equals in rights, and equals in responsibility.

Searching in the Night

Exum emphasizes that, whereas the man in the Song tends more to filter his love through his sense of sight, the woman tends more to tell stories. These stories, she adds, "are the only parts of the Song that display narrative development or what one might call a plot" (14). We should emphasize here that it is in these stories primarily that the author (or authors or editors) of the Song carefully and deliberately choose to portray the agony as well as the ecstasy of erotic love. The two stories of the woman's nighttime searches for her mysteriously elusive lover emphasize this in particular. After the sense of consummation in 2:16, the woman narrates a scene in which she wakes up in her bed at night, wanting but not having her lover present with her:

Upon my bed at night
  I sought him whom my soul loves;
I sought him but found him not;
  I called him but he gave no answer.
(3:1)

Some scholars have thought these scenes were dream scenes, but there is no clarity as to whether the woman is awake or dreaming, and this unclarity is precisely the point. The stories are stories of absence, of desire, of a lack of fulfillment that the woman feels, even in her otherwise apparently perfect and thoroughly fulfilling relationship with the man. Whether she feels it as she dreams or while she is awake, she feels it, and feels it very strongly. She wants something – presence, touch love, fulfilment, consummation – from the man, but he is oddly not there for her to give her these things. This is part of the love the Song portrays – a love overwhelmingly delightful when it is present, but that is not always present.

The woman's unfulfilled desire takes the form of a nighttime search through the city for her lover, an act that would have been extremely dangerous for a young woman in the patriarchal society which produced the poem. She risks scandal, rape, and even murder. It is not a lightly made or inconsequential decision when she says to herself: "I will rise now and go about the city, / in the streets and in the squares" (3:2). This nighttime search throughout the public spaces of the city is an index, a symbol of the intensity of her sense of lack – she is in pain, the pain caused by the absence of her desired lover, to a very intense degree. If the sense of consummation in their love during the day is blissful, her sense of lack, longing, unfulfillment, and even pain during the night is equally agonizing to her. The poet is clear – love hurts as strongly as it satisfies.

The first time she sees the "sentinels" (*shomerim*) who "go about" (*savav*) in the city, they let her pass. In the second story, however, they physically attack and sexually abuse her. A grim and brutal episode is contained in the following single verse of the largely idyllic poem:

Making their rounds in the city
  the sentinels found me;
they beat me, they wounded me,
  they took away my mantle [*redid*].
(5:7)

96   *The Bible as Literature*

As Exum writes, "All is not well in the garden of erotic delights" (198). The woman knowingly risks the brutal, dehumanizing abuse of the sentinels, whose abuse of her is no doubt socially sanctioned, and she suffers it grievously in her own person. This was how intense her sense of lack was, whether asleep or awake. Delightful as it has been in the fields and the orchards, her love is agony to her at night, and she will put herself through the most terrible of humiliations and abuse to assuage this agony. Even after being beaten and sexually abused by the sentinels, she tells the daughters of Jerusalem (the women of Jerusalem, functioning as a kind of chorus), "If you find my beloved, tell him this: I am faint with [*cholat*] love" (5:8). She seems to have no regret or remorse or anger at her abuse by the watchmen – all she can think about, the idea that still dominates her mind and her emotions, is how much she wants, indeed needs, to be back in the presence of her absent and elusive beloved.

In the second nighttime search, this agony occurs at the very point of presence to her lover. He is knocking at her door, she opens, but just as she opens, he has gone. Almost at the very point of togetherness, consummation, coming together physically, emotionally, sexually, at that very point, the agony of his absence to her begins. Agony is at the very heart of the ecstasy of erotic love, according to the Song. Erotic love, in all its delights and joys, is also flawed to the core with the pain of absence, the pain of non-relationship and non-consummation. The man knocks at the woman's door at night, saying, "my head is wet with dew, / my locks with the drops of the night" (5:2) – a sensual, physical image of him, covered physically in moisture. She is naked and bathed in bed. The situation is very sexual, very much one that seems to be leading to sexual consummation. The next verses positively drip with sensual imagery (in a way that some commentators associate with sexual organs and fluids):

> My beloved thrust his hand into the opening,
>   and my inmost being yearned for him.
> I arose to open to my beloved,
>   and my hands dripped with myrrh,
> my fingers with liquid myrrh,
>   upon the handles of the bolt.
>
>   (Song 5:4–5)

The imagery very strongly suggests that the (or a) moment of sexual bliss and consummation is about to happen. But it is just here, just at this climactic moment that seems to be leading overwhelmingly and inevitably to sexual consummation, that he is gone from her. This dramatic caesura takes place within a single line of the Hebrew poetry:

> I opened [*patachti*] to my beloved,
>   but my beloved had turned and was gone.
>   (5:6)

Between these two half-lines, what takes place is that, at the very moment of consummation, hands dripping with myrrh, what happens is non-consummation. At

Biblical Poetry 97

the very moment of blissful presence to one another, the two are suddenly absent to one another. The poet is clear – absence, with all its pain, longing, agony, and anxiety, exists and torments at the very heart of the presence of their mutual love. Love hurts, essentially and centrally, according to the Song of Songs. The poet tells his readers that however blissful love is or seems for a time, it does not remain that way. However much it feels like consummation, it will not continue to do so. It is ultimately flawed, presumably because the people who love are flawed, and they live in and are affected by a society full of other flawed people. Blissful though it is in the day, love cannot be relied upon in the night.

David and Solomon

While the text of the Song itself does not go so far as to say this, there are hints in the relationships between the letters of the words, always significant to Hebrew thinkers, in the poem that point at a relationship between the erotic love of the poem and the covenant between Yahweh and his therefore similarly beloved people. The first of these is the comparison of the woman's neck, in her beauty to the man, to the "tower of David." Nothing is now known of a tower of David in Jerusalem or anywhere else in Israel. It may be that the tower is, even at the time the text of this song is being written, a fiction. Its name is significant in itself insofar as it picks up on the nickname *dodi*, "my beloved," that the woman uses frequently for her lover. In Hebrew *dodi* is written דודי. Now "David" is written with the same letters, דויד. Read from right to left, the first two letters in both words are exactly the same, and then the second two are also the same, but in reverse order:

דו | די‎   "my beloved"
דו | יד‎   "David"

This physical relationship at the level of the letters of the word is more than word-play; it is a relationship between words that indicates a relationship between things. It associates the love of the two lovers, in which the woman calls the man by the endearment "my beloved," with the covenant, with David, Yahweh's anointed king. If the tower of David, to which the man compares the beauty of the woman's neck, is fictional, then the comparison of the lovers' love to David's place in Yahweh's covenant is especially clear. The reader needs to find a reason for the poet's mention of a fictional structure, and the relationship between the very frequent word *dodi* and David's name is the easiest solution in a literary language that places a high value on the relationship between the letters in words. Even if the tower of David were a real place, known to the contemporary readers of the Song but lost now to biblical scholarship, the relationship between the two words remains significant, and could well seem to be reason for the otherwise rather incongruous comparison. As דודי is to דויד, so the love of the lovers is to the covenant, is to the relationship between David and Yahweh. Just beneath the surface of the text, at the level of its letters rather than its words, the grounding of the erotic love of couple in the covenant relationship of full blessing that Yahweh offers to his people, is strongly suggested.

98   *The Bible as Literature*

A similar set of relationships between words is set up by a second term whose historical meaning, if any, is also now lost to biblical scholars, the word "Shulammite," with which the woman is described in 6:13. The word most obviously means a person from Shulam, but such no town or place is known. There have been many explanations of the term by commentators, all of them ultimately speculative. Whatever the term meant to the poet and his expected readers, it exists in a pattern of related key terms that underlie the plot or setting of the love poem. These are:

Solomon – *shelomoh* (שלמה)
Shulammite – *shulammit* (שולמית)
Jerusalem – *yerushalam* (ירושלם)

The love poem is spoken between a man who is associated with King Solomon and a woman who is called the Shulammite, in Jerusalem. The two lovers and the place in which they sing of and conduct their love are identified with closely related names. Above all, all three of those names cluster around the three-letter root *sh-l-m*, the verb "to be complete," which gives the noun *shalom*, peace, prosperity, or well-being. See how the three Hebrew words are patterned:

ה | שלמ | *shelomoh*
ית | שולמ | *shulammit*
| שלם | ירו   *yerushalam*

The three key terms for the two lovers and the place in which they love are terms all patterned around each other, and specifically all three patterned around the word *shalom* – peace, prosperity, well-being, in the sense of the root verb *shalem*, to be complete. The Song draws the reader's attention explicitly to this pattern in its last verses, where the woman says:

> Then I was in his eyes
>   as one who brings peace [*shalom*, שלום]
> Solomon [*shelomoh*, שלמה] had a vineyard at Baal-Hamon;
>   he entrusted the vineyard to his keepers.
>
>   (8:10–11)

The text closely associates Solomon's name with *shalom*, with peace, the fullness of well-being that the lovers sing about. Indeed, this collocation here may well indicate to the reader that some of the purpose of partly identifying (and partly distinguishing) the man in the Song with Solomon is to indicate the *shalom* that the two lovers bring to each other in their love. The addition of the term Shulammite, otherwise difficult to explain, seems to do the same, as does the setting of the poem in Jerusalem, the woman often in dialogue with the *banot yerushalam*, the "daughters of Jerusalem." Two of the three terms in relationship are the names of Solomon, Yahweh's anointed king, and Jerusalem, the city of David, Yahweh's

Biblical Poetry 99

anointed king. The poem clearly suggests, at the level of these foregrounded key terms, that the love shared and experienced by the couple in the poem is comparable to, related or relatable in some way to, the relationship between Yahweh and the people of Israel in the covenant. There are many extra-textual reasons for which Jewish and Christian writers have related the erotic love sung about in the Song to a more intellectual or spiritual relationship between human beings and God. But the germ of this tradition is at work in the text itself. The Song carefully and deliberately patterns the relationship between Yahweh and his people, into the fabric of its text, into the very ways in which it sings of the joys and sorrows of erotic love. The text itself, at the level of these lexical patterns, invites, indeed almost demands, the reader to think that, delightful as erotic love is in itself, it is also the gift of Yahweh and a sign of what covenant relationship to him is and perhaps will be like.

TEXT FOR DISCUSSION

St. Bernard of Clairvaux, *On the Song of Songs*

> *St. Bernard (1098–1153), the influential abbot, mystic, and doctor of the church, wrote a series of 86 sermons on the Song of Songs, which expounded the text up to Song 3:1. The series was continued after his death by a fellow Cistercian. The excerpt below is from Sermon 45, on Song 1:15.*

"Behold, how beautiful you are, my dearest, O how beautiful, your eyes are like doves!" [Song 1:15] [...] He calls her his dearest one, proclaims her beauty, repeats that proclamation, only to win a like response from her. It is no idle repetition that gives firm assurance of love, and hints at something that demands investigation.

Let us see what is meant by the soul's twofold beauty, for that is what seems to be intimated here. Humility is the soul's loveliness. This is not my opinion merely, the Prophet has already said: "Sprinkle me with hyssop and I shall be cleansed," [Psalm 51:7] symbolizing in this lowly herb the humility that purifies the heart. He who was once both king and prophet trusts that this will clean him from his grave offence, and give him back the snowy brightness of his innocence [...] If, however, a man retains an innocence now graced with humility, do you not think that his soul is endowed with loveliness? Mary never lost her holiness, yet she did not lack humility, because she joined humility to innocence. As she said: "He looked graciously upon the lowliness of his handmaid." [Luke 1:48] [...]

When reproved, [the bride] repented and said, "My beloved is to me a little bag of myrrh that lies between my breasts" [Song 1:13]. As much as to say: It is enough for me; I desire to know nothing any longer except Jesus and him

100 *The Bible as Literature*

crucified [1 Cor. 2:2]. What great humility! [...] What [the bridegroom] actually says is "Behold, how beautiful you are." And he repeats this encomium to show that the grace of humility is joined to the glory of holiness [...]

"Your eyes are like doves" [Song 1:15]. You no longer occupy yourself with great affairs or marvels beyond your scope [Psalm 131:1], but like that guileless bird who builds her nest in the crevices of the rock [Song 2:14], you are content to be unpretentious, to linger near my wounds, happy to contemplate with dove-like eyes the mysteries of my Incarnation and Passion.

QUESTIONS

1. Bernard's presupposition, formed by centuries of church tradition on the Song of Songs, is that the poem uses the language of erotic love to describe the relationship between God and the soul. The Bible often speaks of God's relationship to Israel or to the church as a relationship between a bridegroom and bride (Isa. 62:5; Jer. 2:2; Hosea 2:16–20; Mark 3:19–20; John 3:29; 2 Cor. 11:2; Rev. 19:7–8; 21:9). What do you think of Bernard's view? Is it a valid or productive way to interpret the text?

2. In the excerpt above, Bernard expounds the meaning of Song 1:15, "Ah, you are beautiful my love; / ah, you are beautiful; your eyes are doves." He finds significance in the fact that the phrase "you are beautiful" is repeated. The fact that God says to the soul that she is beautiful twice means that the soul has a "twofold beauty," that of humility and of innocence. Bernard says, "this is not my opinion merely," quoting from Psalm 51:7 to prove the first point, and from Luke 1:48 to prove the second. By modern standards, this is a great deal to get from the repetition of the phrase "You are beautiful." What do you think of this interpretation? Does it make sense to see significance in the repetition of the phrase? Does it make sense to see this particular significance?

3. Bernard sees an example of the ideal humility of the soul two verses prior to Song 1:15, in the phrase "My beloved is to me a bag of myrrh / that lies between my breasts" (Song 1:13). He interprets this to means that the blessed soul is humbly content with the knowledge of Christ crucified rather than with the vision of the glory of God. Since myrrh was given to Christ on the cross and used to anoint him at his burial, in this line of the Song of Songs the soul is expressing love for Christ in his death by crucifixion. What do you think of this interpretation? The literal meaning of Song 1:13 is very physical, very erotic; do you think Bernard has interpreted it well or not in arguing that it is about the soul's relationship to Christ crucified?

4. In the final section of the extract above, Bernard interprets the next clause of Song 1:15, "Your eyes are doves," to mean that God loves the humility

Biblical Poetry 101

of the soul. He refers to Song 2:14, where a dove is mentioned again as an example of humility. Bernard argues that when the lover tells his beloved that her eyes are doves, God means that her beauty consists in her humility. What do you think of this interpretation? Note that the meaning of the comparison of the beloved's eyes to doves is not immediately clear, even to modern interpreters. Do you think Bernard has clarified it well or not?

Works Cited

Brown, William P. "The Psalms: An Overview." *The Oxford Handbook of the Psalms*, edited by William P. Brown, Oxford UP, 2014, pp. 1–23.

Brueggemann, Walter and William H. Bellinger, Jr. *Psalms*. Cambridge UP, 2014.

Cardenal, Ernesto. *The Psalms of Struggle and Liberation*. Translated by Emile G. McAnany, Herder, 1971.

Craigie, Peter C. *Psalms 1–50*, 2nd ed., Nelson Reference and Electronic, 2004.

Crenshaw, James L. *The Psalms: An Introduction*. William B. Eerdmans, 2001.

Exum, J. Cheryl. *Song of Songs*. Westminster John Knox Press, 2011.

Fishbane, Michael. *Song of Songs*. Jewish Publication Society, 2015.

Fox, Michael V. *The Song of Songs and the Ancient Egyptian Love Songs*. U Wisconsin P, 1985.

Gunkel, Hermann. *Introduction to Psalms: The Genres of the Religious Lyric of Israel*. Translated by James D. Nogalski, Mercer UP, 1998.

Mays, James Luther. *Psalms*. John Knox Press, 1994.

McCann, J. Clinton, Jr. "Psalms." *The New Interpreter's Bible Commentary*, edited by Leander Keck et al., vol. 3, Abingdon Press, 2015, pp. 271–729.

Murphy, Roland E. and O.Carm. *The Song of Songs*. Fortress Press, 1990.

Weems, Renita J. "Song of Songs." *The New Interpreter's Bible*, vol. 3, edited by Leander Keck et al., Abingdon Press, 2015, pp. 1021–1080.

5 Wisdom Literature

Job

Introduction

The Book of Job's genre, a complaint about the suffering of the righteous, is well attested in the ancient Near East. There are Egyptian, Sumerian, and Mesopotamian texts, all dating probably from the second millennium BCE, that deal with the problem of pain, some in ways very reminiscent of the Book of Job. As Samuel Balentine writes, "Textual evidence confirms that innocent suffering, random disorder, divine injustice, and the futility of life were issues of major concern throughout ancient Egypt, Mesopotamia, and Syria-Palestine" (5). The text closest in form and content to the Book of Job is the "Babylonian Theodicy," an acrostic poem of 27 stanzas, written around 1000 BCE. This a dialogue between a sufferer and his friend (they each have alternate stanzas), in which the sufferer complains to his friend of the injustices he suffers, although pious, and of the prosperity of those who are not. His friend replies in similar ways to those of Job's friends, "He who looks to his god has a protector, / The humble man who reveres his goddess will garner wealth" (ll. 20–21). Although the debate is always courteous, the friend can be sarcastic in response to the sufferer's complaints, in a manner reminiscent of the Book of Job: "Adept scholar, master of erudition, / You blaspheme in the anguish of your thoughts" (ll. 254–255). In a similar way, the friend repeats that the will of the gods is ultimately incomprehensible: "Divine purpose is as remote as innermost heaven, / It is too difficult to understand" (ll. 256–257). Unlike the Book of Job, however, the poem ends with a prayer by the sufferer for the help that has thus far been withheld by the gods. The relationship between this and similar ancient Near Eastern texts with the Book of Job is probably indirect. As Carol Newsom puts it, it is likely that "there was a larger tradition of wisdom dialogues about the problem of the righteous sufferer and the general issue of moral disorder in a world supposedly governed by divine justice" (29).

The Book of Job has long been regarded as a composite text. Four major stages in its composition are often hypothesized:

1. A story about the trials of a good man, originally told orally. This stage is reflected in the prose frame of the Book of Job, Chapters 1–2 and 42:7–17. The

DOI: 10.4324/9781315751566-6

middle part of this story is missing from the Book of Job, but probably included a section in which Job's friends spoke disparagingly of God and he refused to do so. In Job 42:7, God says to the friends, "My wrath is kindled against you [...] for you have not spoken of me what is right, as my servant Job has," which does not seem clearly to represent the preceding dialogues as we now have them.

2. A gifted poet, who "found the 'all's-well-that-ends-well' frame story unsatisfying" (Balentine 14), and wanted to articulate a "critique of its underlying premises about a principle of reward and retribution" (Crenshaw, *Job* 12), uses the frame story. He substitutes for its prose dialogue between Job and his friends the poetic dialogues of Job 3–31, the two divine speeches of Job 38–42, and Job's brief responses (40:3–5; 42:1–6). Either the author of these dialogues or someone else later inserts Chapter 28, "written in a different style and language" (Crenshaw, *Job* 12), on the difficulty of finding wisdom.

3. Considerably later, a different author inserts the speeches of Elihu. Reasons for this claim include the fact that Elihu is not mentioned anywhere else in the book; his speeches are a monologue, unlike the dialogic speeches of Job's other friends; and that, unlike anyone else in the book, he explicitly quotes from other characters' words, suggesting that the author of these speeches had the rest of the book in front of him.

4. A scribe, finding Job's last speech theologically unacceptable, removes it, and gives some of Bildad's speech to Job. Or the last speeches of Job, Bildad, and Zophar were disturbed and parts were lost in the transmission of the text. Some explanation needs to be found for the fact that, toward the end of the third cycle of speeches, "the friends and Job seem to be making the wrong arguments and contradicting themselves and there is no third speech of Zophar" (Dell 8).

Most scholars favor an exilic or early postexilic date for the book, with the Elihu speeches usually dated as late as the third century BCE. While both the poetry and the prose contain linguistic forms that seem to be archaic, perhaps from the tenth century, it has also been argued that these texts "appear to be written in a deliberately archaizing style" (Newsom 23). The figure of the *satan* has its closest parallels in postexilic texts such as Zechariah 3:1–2, and 1 Chronicles 21:1. Katherine Dell writes, in favor of a postexilic date, "The book [...] appears to attack the fundamental premise of exilic theology that suffering must be the direct result of sin and represent punishment from God" (4). Furthermore, as a "clear critique of the earlier wisdom exercise" as represented by Proverbs, the book would seem logically to have a later date in the tradition of wisdom writing (Dell 9).

Yahweh and the Satan

In the Book of Job, readers encounter for the first time details of Yahweh's heavenly court, and of one at least of the interactions between God and the "sons of God" (*benei ha-elohim*), that is, the divine beings who make up this court. Both morally and theologically, this encounter is an unforgettable one. Indeed, it is positively shocking, and leaves the reader with nothing but questions, which are not

104 *The Bible as Literature*

satisfactorily resolved by the end of the book. Among the divine beings of the heavenly court is the satan, *ha-satan*. The noun *satan*, and the cognate verb *satan*, are common terms in Hebrew. The noun means "adversary," and the verb means "to be an adversary" or "to act as an adversary." In a legal or analogous context, the words can mean "accuser" or "to act as an accuser" (cf. Num. 22:22, 32; 1 Kings 5:4; 11:14; Psalms 71:13; 38:20). When the term refers to a member of Yahweh's heavenly court, and takes the article (*ha*, "the"), it does not indicate a being whose name is "Satan," as in 1 Chronicles 21:1 and in the New Testament. Rather, it means "the accuser" or "the adversary," indicating the function of that member of Yahweh's court, rather than his name. In Job 1–2, *ha-satan* means "the accuser." There is one of the *benei ha-elohim* who make up Yahweh's heavenly court whose function seems to be to seek out and report to Yahweh disloyalty to him in those who claim to be his people. He appears again in the Hebrew Bible in the first part of the Book of Zechariah, also written in the postexilic period (Zech. 3:1–2).

In Zechariah, Yahweh firmly rejects the satan's accusation of his servant Joshua. This is not the case in Job. The prologue to the book (1:1–2:13) contains the morally and theologically scandalous story of the dialogue between Yahweh and the satan. Yahweh begins this dialogue, saying to the satan, "Have you considered my servant Job?" (1:8). It is odd, and unexplained in the text, why Yahweh would ask the satan whether or not he has considered Job, of whom Yahweh says twice (and the narrator says a third time), "There is no-one like him on the earth, a blameless and upright man who fears God and turns away from evil" (1:8; cf. 2:3; 1:1). It seems at first sight to indicate a kind of anxiety in Yahweh, as if even the most righteous man on earth may not be as righteous, may not be in as loyal a relationship of covenant love to Yahweh, as he seems. The text does not give any reason for Yahweh's question, but the reader is asked by the question to ask herself why it has been asked, and this, for the modern reader at least, is the first answer that comes to mind. It is odd, and theologically troubling, to think of God as anxious, even narcissistic. In Zechariah, he has no such anxiety, firmly rejecting the satan's accusations (Zech. 3:2). But in Job, he positively asks for such an accusation, and allows the accuser to test his initially hypothetical response, that Job will curse God if his blessings are taken away, to the full.

The moral inadequacy of the portrait of Yahweh deepens as the prologue continues. When Job maintains his integrity after the first assault by the satan on all his possessions and all of his children, Yahweh tells the satan in the heavenly court, "He still persists in his integrity, although you incited me against him to destroy him for no reason" (2:3). The word translated "for no reason" here, *chinnam*, is doubly striking. First, it picks up on the satan's use of the same word earlier in the prologue, in his first reply to Yahweh's question, "Have you considered my servant Job?" The satan answers, "Does Job fear God for nothing [*chinnam*]?" (1:9). It is easy for Job to be righteous, he means, when God has always blessed him in return. *chinnam* – the adverb means "for nothing," "in vain," or "without cause." It is at the heart of the theological dialogue between Yahweh and the satan in the prologue. It is very noticeable that both the satan and Yahweh use the term, at the heart of their thinking about Job and his relationship to God. There is a connection between them in the prologue. *ha-satan* may be Job's "adversary" but he is not Yahweh's. They are something like the good cop and the bad cop of a police drama – Yahweh seems kinder, the satan seems crueler; but both are working together to test Job.

"He still persists in his integrity, although you incited me against him to destroy him for no reason." First, there is the rather lame, and failed, attempt to shift some of the blame for the unnecessary deaths of Job's ten children, his servants, and the destruction of his livestock, onto the satan – "you incited [*sut*] me." This attempt is a failure because of course Yahweh is responsible for his decision to give all that Job has into the satan's power, as he does in 1:11. Even worse, and even more unthinkable theologically, is Yahweh's admission that the deaths of ten children, numerous servants, and the misery and trauma that this will mean for Job and his wife, was done "for no reason." Balentine calls this "the single most disturbing admission in the Old Testament, if not in all scripture" (60).

This is the heart of the prologue. It is theologically unthinkable. It is a thoroughly, clearly, and deliberately inadequate portrayal of God. Even Job's friends do not suggest that God allows suffering for no reason. When the narrator of the prologue, therefore, portrays Yahweh as morally weak and irresponsible, he is clearly signaling that he himself knows no better about the problem of pain, about the question of God's justice and human suffering, than any of the characters in the dialogue that his story frames. God's justice is truly a mystery, the prologue, like the Book of Job as a whole, says. No one has the answer, no one has or can attain to a transcendent perspective, transcendent of living within what Newsom calls the "terrible fragility of human life" (51). The Book of Job leaves us only where we started, with questions. It does not give us any answers, any resolutions, or any closure. It only respects the questions. There is no one who knows any better than Job or his friends, the prologue says – we are all in this boat together, all doing our best to answer the question and none of us doing it very well.

Job and His Companions

This becomes especially clear in the body of the Book of Job, the long series of three cycles of dialogue between Job and his "friends [*re'im*]" (2:11) Eliphaz, Bildad, and Zophar. Perhaps the most striking impression created by the dialogues between Job and his friends is their enormous inadequacy, in several ways. Dialogue indeed is not the right term, since there is very little direct response to the previous speaker in either Job or his friends. Job's friends fail to "console and comfort him," which the prologue described as their goal (2:11). They fail to convince him of the justice of God, which seems to be their intention, or of the value of the wisdom tradition, which seems to matter to them. Perhaps the first thing that strikes the reader of the dialogues is how much they are not exactly dialogues, that is, that each speaker is not exactly responding to what the previous speaker has said. As James Crenshaw puts it, "They often talk past one another, ignoring fundamental arguments and remaining silent about controversial claims" (*Job* 55). Roland Murphy describes one of Zophar's speeches as "a lecture, not a conversation" with Job (58), and this is a good phrase. As in a lecture, the speakers in the poem are interested primarily

106   *The Bible as Literature*

in expressing their own view, and much less interested in entering into dialogue with the other. As a result, since none of the four (and this will be true of Elihu too) are primarily concerned with mutually reaching the truth of the matter they discuss, no such truth emerges. The dialogues consist primarily of a babel of voices talking loudly, emotionally, passionately, angrily, and with many unstated but patent psychological needs at work. There is no journey, no progression toward consensus, revelation, truth, or wisdom in these assertions; just length, repetition, anguish, and anger. The dialogues offer no clear answer to the question of suffering; just people trying and failing to convince one another of their more or less adequate views.

The next striking way in which the dialogues are inadequate is in fact perhaps the source of their greatest insight. That is, the dialogues make clear that the problem of pain is not in practice addressed by reason alone. Job is, understandably, highly emotional in response to the terrible events he has endured, and his responses to and about God concerning them are anguished, distressed, angry, and confused. Job is so upset, again understandably, that he often does not quite make sense, and this precisely is the sense of much of the dialogues. As Job says in his very first response to his friends:

> O that my vexation were weighed,
> And all my calamity laid in the balances!
> For then it would be heavier than the sand of the sea;
> Therefore [al-ken] my words have been rash.
>
> (6:2–3)

This will continue to be the case throughout the ensuing dialogues. Job is suffering deeply – therefore his words are rash. That is, his suffering causes his words to express his turbulent emotions, which often take precedence over rational arguments. This is indeed how Job talks. In his first response to Eliphaz, he concludes by saying that he will soon die, as all human beings will (7:1–10). Then he asks God, "Am I the Sea, or the Dragon, / that you set a guard over me?" (7:12). Here he means that God is fighting with all his enormous power, that dwarfs that of human beings, against him, as if he were one of the primal monsters of chaos that God had to defeat in Canaanite mythology. He makes several loosely associated points one after the other. First, he says human life is hard – "Do not human beings have a hard service on earth?" (7:1). Then, he says his life is excessively hard – "My flesh is clothed with worms and dirt" (7:5). It is not quite clear what the relationship of the suffering of human life in general is, in this speech, to the relationship of Job's suffering in particular. They are simply two ideas expressed next to each other, one after the other, without clear logical connection. The same thing happens when Job asks, "Am I the Sea or the Dragon?" Now he asks why God uses such force against him. The connection between the ephemeral nature of human life – "my life is a breath" (7:7) – and the severity with which God seems to be punishing Job is similarly not exactly clear. Is Job a frail human, or is God punishing him more than most human beings? It is not clear; Job is expressing multiple ideas at once, one after the other, as his emotions (understandably) dictate. The entire conclusion of

Wisdom Literature 107

this speech (7:11–21) works like this. Job says one thing after another, each loosely associated with each other, which together do not quite make sense, at least logically or rationally. They make as it were the emotional sense that Job is in anguish and angry at God. Exactly what his case is is not clear; his anger in fact is his case.

His responses to his friends and to God are not carefully considered or rationally judged, and this is precisely the point that the dialogues make so well: they never are. Responses to the problem of human suffering and human belief in a just God, can be never be entirely rational. Job is an Everyman figure in the book, and he is an Everyman in this sense in particular in the dialogues. The problem of pain is only ever discussed from within the middle of the very pain, the very problem, which is being discussed. There is no transcendental vantage point from which to discuss it, the dialogues that constitute the main body of the Book of Job say, and surely they are right. This is one of the book's greatest insights, its clear and deliberate portrayal of the fact that the question of human suffering is always debated from within (which is why it so quickly turns into anger and shouting at one another). It is always debated by human beings who are themselves suffering or have suffered or have seen loved ones or their fellow human beings for whom they feel suffer. The problem of pain is not solved, nor even asked, by reason alone, the dialogues say, but by all the faculties at once of human beings in pain. There is no place to address it but in medias res.

Job and Yahweh

In speaking of "dialogues" so far in the Book of Job, I have been referring to the dialogues between human beings, between Job and his three friends, and Elihu's interjection. The book closes, of course, with two more dialogues, between Job and Yahweh. After Elihu speaks, "The LORD answered Job out of the whirlwind [*sera'ah*, 'storm-wind']" (38:1). The whirlwind seems to indicate the sublimity of Yahweh's creation. Yahweh's answer to Job concerns the sublimity of the natural world, of the heavens and the earth that Yahweh has made, sustains, and governs in his *mishpat* – his "justice" or "governance" – and wisdom. This is what Yahweh emphasizes in his answer to Job. The fact that he speaks "out of the whirlwind" when he does so suggests that this is in a sense what creation already "says." It says that its creator is a great and awesome mystery, massively exceeding human capacities to know and to do. The form and the content of Yahweh's speech are identical. He speaks in the whirlwind, and then says in the form of divine speech what the whirlwind already says to the man or woman who reflects upon it, that its creator is great and wondrous beyond our comprehension and abilities to comprehend.

This is Yahweh's answer to Job – just look at the wonder of creation, how massively it exceeds your ability as part of it to understand, to know, to replicate, or to control. In what sense is this an answer? Most commentators point out, sometimes to the point of ridicule, that this is not a direct answer to Job's questions, complaints, or wishes. As Murphy puts it, Yahweh's speeches are "acutely irrelevant" to Job's situation (94). This is true, and so surely part of the point. As Newsom says, "The very obliqueness of the speeches is part of the way they function as answer" (236).

108　*The Bible as Literature*

As we saw, Job was primarily distressed and angry, as anyone would be in his situation. What he wanted above all was to speak face-to-face with God, as in a courtroom, to bring his complaint against God for having punished him with suffering although he had been righteous. Job wanted to bring a lawsuit against God, although he knew how futile this desire was since God would be the judge as well as the defendant. God's reply (precisely insofar as it is not exactly a reply) is that Job was right about this – it is futile to attempt to bring a case against God. Job already knew that God was judge as well as defendant; in his reply, God adds that he is not only the judge, but also built the courtroom, wrote the laws, and founded the country. Indeed, he made the men and women who made the laws; the reason and moral judgment with which they made them; the materials with which the courtroom, the city, and the country are built; and the capacity of men and women to build them. This is God's "reply" to Job. The sublimity of the natural world shows clearly that I am not the kind of "person" (there is no right word here, not even "being") whom you can bring to trial over the governance of the world. Do the righteous sometimes suffer, and do the wicked sometimes prosper? Maybe so, but the sublimity of the natural world is enough to show you that I can be trusted – at least, not questioned by you, a part of it – with its governance.

Job's first reply to Yahweh is "I am of small account," in the NRSV's translation (40:4). The verb he uses here, *qalal*, means to be light, insignificant, or unimportant. It can have connotations of contempt. The NIV translates, "I am unworthy"; the KJV "I am vile." Job is agreeing with Yahweh here; that Yahweh is the sublime creator of all the marvels of the natural world, including him, Job, and that he, Job, is nothing, a breath, light and insignificant in comparison to his surpassingly wonderful creator. Yahweh tells Job that the creature cannot judge the creator with the very faculties of judgment the creator has created in him, and Job accepts this. He has no more judgment of Yahweh to express. As he says in his second reply to Yahweh, "I have uttered what I did not understand [*avin*], / things too wonderful [*niphla'ot*] for me to know" (42:3).

Although Job accepts Yahweh's speeches, the reader is left with questions. What is the relationship between Yahweh's answer and Job's complaint? Neither Yahweh nor the narrator, author, or editors of the Book of Job make that clear. The ambiguity of Job's final response suggests that ambiguity and unclarity are the note that the author or editor of the book intended to finish on, intended to emphasize. It simply is not said in the Book of Job what the relationship is between Job's complaint, that he is suffering although he has been righteous, and Yahweh's response, that he is the sublime creator of the sublime universe. The book as it were states these two points, and then leaves the reader with the difficult task of joining them. There is a relationship, the book says, between the evident sublimity of the world that God has created, and so the even greater sublimity of the creator himself, with the question of human suffering. What the relationship is, though, it does not say.

And so the reader is left at the end of the Book of Job in Job's own position, in the middle of things, in the middle of the question of human suffering. The reader does not rise, as a result of her reading the book, to a transcendental vantage point on the question, and this is the lesson of the book, that there is no such

Wisdom Literature 109

transcendental vantage point. There is, in short, no answer to the question of human suffering, the Book of Job says. There is only the wrestling with the question. The book gives the reader its best attempts at answers, all of which it clearly recognizes to be imperfect, partial, and inadequate. And that, like everyone else who has ever lived, is all it has: some pointers on the way to dealing with the question of the meaning of the life one is oneself living while asking the question. The sublime qualities of the natural world point to the even greater sublimity of its creator, who is "too wonderful" (42:3) to understand. Acceptance of one's created and finite nature is a proper and good way to live, in response to Yahweh, the creator. That is all. That is all the book has for its reader. The Book of Job, like no other in the Bible, places the reader in the story, in the poetry, in the drama of the book itself. Job is not only Everyman, Job is me. I do not know better than he, nor does the author or editor of the book. We are all in this together. There is no guide, there is no clear answer; just some dimly discernible hints and suggestions for walking the path, for living human life, difficult and dark as it is, as best one can.

TEXT FOR DISCUSSION

C. G. Jung, *Answer to Job*

> *The Swiss psychologist C. G. Jung (1875–1961) wrote this book in 1952, working on a subject that had occupied him for years, that of providing a psychologically more realistic account of the problem of human suffering than he felt was offered by the orthodox Christianity in which he was brought up.*

The Book of Job places this pious and faithful man, so heavily afflicted by the Lord, on a brightly lit stage where he presents his case to the eyes and ears of the world. It is amazing to see how easily Yahweh, quite without reason, had let himself be influenced by one of his sons, by a *doubting thought*, and made unsure of Job's faithfulness. With his touchiness and suspiciousness the mere possibility of doubt was enough to infuriate him and induce that peculiar double-faced behavior of which he had already given proof in the Garden of Eden, when he pointed out the tree to the First Parents and at the same time forbade them to eat of it [...] From the human point of view Yahweh's behavior is so revolting that one has to ask oneself whether there is not a deeper motive hidden behind it. Has Yahweh some secret resistance against Job? ... But what does man possess that God does not have? Because of his littleness, puniness, and defenselessness against the Almighty, he possesses [...] a somewhat keener consciousness based on self-reflection: he must, in order to survive, always be mindful of his impotence [...] Could a suspicion have grown up in God that man possesses an infinitely small yet more concentrated light than he, Yahweh, possesses?

110   *The Bible as Literature*

Without Yahweh's knowledge, and contrary to his intentions, the tormented though guiltless Job had secretly been lifted up to a superior knowledge of God that God himself did not possess [...]

Job realizes God's inner antinomy, and in the light of this realization his knowledge attains a divine numinosity [...] Job, by his insistence on bringing his case before God, even without hope of a hearing, had stood his ground and thus created the very obstacle that forced God to reveal his true nature.

QUESTIONS

1. Jung reads the relationship between God and the satan psychologic- ally, that the satan represents an element of God's psyche of which, at the beginning of the book, God is unconscious. The satan's speech represents a "doubting thought" in God, criticizing and questioning the omnipotence of which alone God is clearly conscious. What do you think of this view?
2. Job is psychologically and morally superior to God, in Jung's view. He is clearly aware of the negative elements of his experience, his powerless- ness, his frailty, and his mortality. Yahweh is not so self-aware, harping only on his omnipotence. A nagging doubt that Job has a psychological and moral health that he, Yahweh, does not is precisely what makes him behave so immorally as to subject Job to the terms of the satan's bet. He is jealous of Job's wholeness. What do you think of this interpretation?
3. The character of Job performs a service for the reader of the Bible, making clear to God that there is a moral darkness in God of which God is unconscious. The biblical God is an "antinomy," a "totality of inner opposites," rather than merely good or just as he claims to be. This is the beginning of a psychologically and morally more healthy portrayal of God, for Jung, one that acknowledges the wretchedness as well as the greatness of human experience. What do you think of this view, that the Book of Job opens up a wider and healthier picture of God that includes evil as well as good?
4. Later on in the book, Jung argues that a moral development takes place in the portrayal of God throughout the Bible. In the accounts of the incarnation and crucifixion of Jesus, God takes Job's human suffering upon himself (42–47). The first "answer to Job" provided by the Bible is that, in the portrayal of Christ in the New Testament, God has finally become a divine being with whom a reader can identify with psycho- logically healthy results, since he has finally taken upon himself all the complex good and evil of human experience. What do you think of this view?

Proverbs

Introduction

As we saw with the Book of Job, the Wisdom literature of the Hebrew Bible is part of a flourishing international discourse on wisdom in the ancient Near East. This is very much true of the collections of proverbs and the instructions from a father to his son in the Book of Proverbs. There are numerous collections of proverbs and instructions extant from Mesopotamia, Egypt, and Syria-Palestine (Clifford 9–17). The Babylonian "Counsels of Wisdom" (c. 1500–1200 BCE) are a series of instructions from a learned father to his son, including practical advice for young men on how to get on in the world. The closest parallel to the Book of Proverbs is the Egyptian text "The Instruction of Amen-em-Opet," which many scholars think was adapted by the collectors of "The Words of the Wise" in Proverbs 22:17–24:22. The "Instruction" ends, "See thou these thirty chapters: / They entertain; they instruct" (ch. 30), just as "The Words of the Wise" ask, "Have I not written for you thirty sayings / of admonition and knowledge?" (Prov. 22:20). It begins, "Give thy ears, / hear what is said, / Give thy heart to understand them" (ch. 1), just as the "The Words of the Wise" begin, "Incline your ear and hear my words, / and apply your mind to my teaching" (Prov. 22:17). There many close parallels between the texts, such as instructions not to move boundary markers on the fields of widows and orphans ("Instruction" ch. 6; Prov. 23:10); not to set your heart on wealth ("Instruction ch. 7; Prov. 23:4); not to befriend people who become angry ("Instruction" ch. 9; Prov. 22:24); and many others.

The superscription of the Book of Proverbs reads, "The proverbs [*meshalim*] of Solomon son of David, king of Israel" (1:1). There are at least eight different collections of sayings that comprise the whole book, however, all but the last of which (31:10–31) have their own headings. These include "The proverbs [*meshalim*] of Solomon" (10:1); "The words [*devarim*] of the wise [*chachamim*]" (22:17); "Other proverbs [*meshalim*] of Solomon that the officials [*anashim*, lit. "men"] of King Hezekiah of Judah copied" (25:1); and several others (24:23; 30:1; 31:1). Some scholars believe that it is possible Solomon was responsible for writing or collecting some of the proverbs in the Solomonic collections (Clifford 3; Horne 8; cf. van Leeuwen 752). In describing his fame for wisdom, the Book of Kings specifies that he "composed three thousand proverbs [*mashal*]" (1 Kings 4:32). It is unlikely that Solomon is the author of the whole of the book, however, given its ascriptions of some of the proverbs to others by name. Michael Fox writes,

> Historically, it is improbable that many, if any, of the proverbs were written by Solomon. The social background implied by the sayings is quite varied. The proverbs do not usually bespeak the concerns of the royal court and never speak from the perspective of a monarch. Moreover, many of the teachings would not make sense as Solomon's tutelage of his son.
>
> (Proverbs 1-9 56).

112   *The Bible as Literature*

The collection of collections that the Book of Proverbs constitutes was compiled over several centuries. Most scholars consider the Solomonic collections to be the earliest sections of the book, probably preceding the work of the "men of King Hezekiah" (25:1) in the eighth century BCE, who added a second collection of proverbs to an already existing collection attributed to Solomon. These men were probably scribes, court officials who did the work of reading and writing, for which Richard Clifford argues "the best proof is the sophistication of the writing and the familiarity with foreign literature evident in the sayings and instructions" (7). Although the social context of the proverbs is diverse, drawn from both popular and intellectual sources, most scholars think of the royal court as the most likely setting in which they were compiled (van Leeuwen 753; Horne 11; Fox, *Proverbs 1-9* 10–11). Fox rightly concludes that the book is "representative of many domains of ancient Israelite society through numerous generations" (*Proverbs 1-9* 11). Most scholars date Proverbs 1–9 and 30–31 to the postexilic period, usually the Persian or early Hellenistic periods. Fox writes, in support of a late date, that Proverbs 8 in particular seems to reflect an "intellectually cosmopolitan" culture, with "a certain awareness of Greek styles of thought"; adding that "Proverbs nowhere shows a concern with separating Jews from foreigners, which was the great challenge in the fifth century" as shown by the books of Ezra and Nehemiah (*Proverbs 1-9* 49).

Madam Wisdom

Proverbs 1–9 personifies wisdom as a woman, in way that Carol Fontaine describes as "amazing" and "remarkable" for "the striking amount of power attributed to a female figure within a male-dominated society" (146, 147). Like other feminist commentators, she describes this character as "Woman Wisdom." Woman Wisdom may bear traces of Mesopotamian or Egyptian goddess worship, but she is "new and unique" in the Hebrew Bible (Murphy 279). When she is first introduced in Proverbs, she is described in a striking (and untranslatable) plural form in the original Hebrew. The ordinary, feminine singular, noun for "wisdom" in Hebrew is *chochmah* (the *-ah* ending being a typical feminine singular ending). But in Proverbs 1:20 (and 9:1; 14:1; 24:7), she is called *chochmot* (the *-ot* ending being the typical plural of the *-ah* ending) – that is, a feminine plural noun is used. The verbs that follow the noun are singular, so a single person is being talked about, but the ordinary (feminine singular) noun *chochmah* is pluralized to *chochmot*. This is an unusual locution in biblical Hebrew. The most convincing suggestions as to its sense are that it may be a plural of "majesty" (Fox, *Proverbs 1-9* 97) or of "intensification" (Alter 335). It indicates that there is something very special, very important about Wisdom personified. She may even be a queen. Some commentators describe her as "Lady Wisdom," which is appropriate in the sense that the book of the Proverbs is very much a product of a patriarchal culture (and "Lady" is a patriarchal term). But it is not appropriate in the sense that, while a Lady is subordinate to her Lord, there is no sense that Wisdom has a husband to whom she is subordinate. Her relationship to Yahweh (in 8:22–31) is not one of marriage and, complex though it is to define, it is an unusually exalted one. Perhaps

Wisdom Literature 113

we might call her "Madam Wisdom," in the sense that a woman who holds an especially important social role is addressed today as "Madam President," "Madam Secretary," or the like.

Madam Wisdom is the most important figure among a complex series of women figures in Proverbs 1–9. These are first, the *zarah*, "strange," or *nochriyyah*, "alien" woman (2:16–19; 5:3–6; 7:5–23). Second, there is the addressee of the poem's own wife (5:18–20). Third, there is the *ra*, "evil" woman (6:24) – which the NRSV follows the Septuagint in reading "the wife of another," a phrase that also appears at 6:26. Finally, there is the "foolish woman" (*eshet kesilut*) (9:13–18). With the exception of the young man's wife, these women all blend, by virtue of their shared characteristics, into one figure, the figure of folly, the opposite of wisdom, which is symbolized by adultery.

The NRSV translates the terms *zarah* and *nochriyyah* as "loose" (or "loose woman") and "adulteress" respectively. The NIV uses similar terms; the KJV has the more accurate "strange" (or "strange woman") and "stranger." *Zar* (or *zarah* in the feminine) means "strange," in the sense of not properly belonging to a given context or situation. A foreign god, an idol as opposed to Yahweh, can be described as *zar*, "strange" or "foreign" (Ps. 44:20; Isa. 43:10; Deut. 32:16). So the "strange woman" of Proverbs 1–9 is strange in the sense of not properly belonging to the young man to whom the text is addressed. She is married to someone else; she is his "neighbor's wife" (Prov. 6:29). The term may also mean that she does not behave as her marriage demands – that is, that she is a stranger to the rules of married behavior. She is a stranger in a similar way to the rules of Israelite society. The second term, *nochri* (*nochriyyah* in the feminine), is often used in parallel with *zar* in Hebrew poetry (Ps. 28:21; 69:8; Prov. 20:16; 27:13). It means "foreign" or "alien," in the sense of non-Israelite. Here in Proverbs 1–9, however, it primarily emphasizes what has been already said with *zarah*, in a parallelism familiar in Hebrew poetry, that the strange woman is especially strange, especially foreign, in that she is a stranger or foreigner to the rules of covenant life, and so strange and foreign to any kind of relationship into which the young man addressed by the text should enter.

The strange, foreign woman, who appears three times in Proverbs 1–9, is above all characterized as an adulteress. She "forsakes the partner of her youth / and forgets her sacred covenant" (2:17); she tells the young man addressed by the poem, "Come, let us take our fill of love until morning [...] / For my husband is not at home" (7:18–19). The "evil" woman of 6:24 is "the wife of another" (6:26), and the young man's "neighbor's wife" (6:29). Both characters are willing partners in adultery with the young man; and in 7:5–23, she goes to great lengths actively to seduce him. The foolish woman, like the strange woman, calls young and foolish men into her house. She tells them, "Stolen water is sweet, / and bread eaten in secret is pleasant" (9:17), which seems primarily to refer to the illicit pleasure of adultery. All three characters, therefore, blend into a single, composite character, a combination of folly and adultery. The foolish woman is clearly opposed to Madam Wisdom in Chapter 9 – both call young and inexperienced men into their houses: "You that are simple, turn in here" (9:4; cf. 9:16). So the essence of this

114   *The Bible as Literature*

composite character is her folly, and her adultery is the symbol of this folly. The strange woman, the evil woman, the wife of another, and the foolish woman are all adulteresses, and as such opposed to Madam Wisdom, that is, to Wisdom itself. The opposite of relating to Yahweh through wisdom is failing to relate to him through folly. Adultery, the composite female characters of Proverbs 1–9 say, is both an example and the essence of folly – not so much a symbol but *the* symbol of folly. They are opposed both to Madam Wisdom and to the young man's own wife of 5:18–20. Marriage, in the system of female characters set up in Proverbs 1–9, is the symbol of wisdom, itself the way to relate rightly to Yahweh; and adultery the symbol of its opposite, folly. Proverbs 1–9 reiterates the repeated message of the Hebrew Bible, that right relationship to Yahweh is above all a kind of marriage. It is like a marriage; marriage is the best analogy in human experience for it; and, the system of women characters in Proverbs 1–9 suggests, it is in fact a kind of marriage.

The Woman of Strength

This is emphasized even more strongly by the decision of the editors of the text to conclude the Book of Proverbs with the encomium to the woman of strong character (31:10). The Hebrew phrase *eshet chayil*, which we have seen before in the Book of Ruth, means a woman, or wife, of strength. *Chayil* means "strength," and has a wide semantic range, including "ability," "wealth," and even "force" in the sense of an "army." Fontaine writes that it "denotes persons at the height of their powers and capacities" (151). The term means woman or wife of strength, strength of character, from which all other kinds of strength, including physical stamina, derive. Many commentators think of the wife of strong character as the embodiment of wisdom. The poem about her, from Proverbs 31:10–31, is an acrostic poem in Hebrew, in which each of the 22 verses begins with each letter of the Hebrew alphabet, in order, which seems to indicate that she is the full embodiment of wisdom, that she represents wisdom from A to Z. The position of the poem at the end of the book also strongly suggests that this is the case. The proverbs that make up the body of the book teach the reader how to live wisely; the book culminates with an example of what this looks like in practice. That example is a wife. In this sense, the book ends as it began, and has been carefully edited to do so. Both the prologue and the epilogue to the proverbs say that wisdom is best understood in terms of marriage. One is, if one chooses rightly, married to wisdom. To be wise is to love wisdom, to love her faithfully, to grow with her throughout your life (and perhaps even to produce offspring from this union). To love wisdom is to love Yahweh; to live wisely is to live rightly before him as a member of his covenant people. Wisdom is ultimately a kind of marriage to Yahweh, a passionate, loving, lasting, and productive relationship.

The poem on the woman of strength with which the book closes is a portrayal of the nature of this kind of relationship. The capable wife who embodies wisdom is a strikingly full character. Most obviously, in addition to her personal and domestic virtues, she has a full, powerful, and successful public life. "She considers a field

Wisdom Literature 115

and buys it"; "She makes linen garments and sells them; / She supplies the merchant with sashes" (31:16, 24). She is a shrewd, industrious, and successful merchant. Commentators are divided, ultimately for lack of convincing historical context, on the extent to which this was usual or unusual in a woman of the class, time, and place in which the poem was written and incorporated into the Book of Proverbs. We can say that, in general, it is unusual, although not unheard of, in patriarchal society for a wife both to have and to be praised for a public role as a successful investor, producer, and trader of commodities. As van Leeuwen puts it, "the praise of woman here [in Prov. 31:10–31] is designed to alter errant male perceptions of women" (945). The woman of strong character has a very complete life as a wife, and the author of the poem is deliberately emphasizing as much.

He does so at the level of the poetic language he uses too. When he writes that the woman's husband will have "no lack of gain" (31:11), as the NRSV translates, the word translated as "gain," *shalal*, usually means "booty" or "plunder." It does so in Proverbs 1:13. As Fox comments, "the word is used so often to mean 'booty' that martial overtones cling to it" (*Proverbs 10-31* 893). As van Leeuwen puts it, "the woman is like a warrior bringing home booty from her victories" (941). The word indicates that she has not only the strength typically ascribed to a man but the strength typically ascribed to a soldier. In verse 15, she "provides food for her household," in the NRSV's translation, but the word translated as "food," *tereph*, most frequently means "prey," or figuratively "plunder." The word most usually means the kill of animals. Again, the poet is deliberately connoting the strength, the power of the woman of strong character – she is as dangerous and fearsome as a lion as well as a soldier – even in describing her traditionally feminine relations to her husband and children. In the same way, "she girds herself with strength" (31:18), in the NRSV's translation. The Hebrew literally says that she "girds her loins with strength." Girding one's loins, that is, "tucking one's tunic into a belt in preparation for a battle" (Fox, *Proverbs 10-31* 894), connotes that the woman of strength has the bravery, strength, and power of a warrior in battle. Van Leeuwen calls it "a mascu-line image" (942). The poet is very clear that in addition to providing well for her home and her children, and to practicing the morality and religion that she teaches her children, she is a brave and formidable force in society. She has a full life; she flourishes, as an individual, as a wife and mother, and as a member of society.

If the Book of Proverbs says that wisdom is like marriage to Yahweh, the epi-logue in particular portrays what kind of a marriage this is. It is a marriage in which both partners flourish. It is to live life to the full, to actualize all of one's potential, to be oneself in every way it is possible to be oneself. The image of embodied wisdom in the epilogue to the Book of Proverbs is a woman who lives a full life as a wife, mother, and citizen. This is what the marriage to Yahweh that wisdom consists in is like. If adultery is the symbol of folly, and marriage is the symbol of wisdom in Proverbs, it is a marriage that does not constrain or subordinate one spouse, the wife, to her husband. On the contrary, the Book of Proverbs says, to be married to Yahweh through living wisely is to be married to a husband who allows and even expects you to flourish. Ultimately, this is the sense in which the poem on the woman of strength concludes the Book of Proverbs by portraying wisdom

116   *The Bible as Literature*

embodied in a person's life. A wisely lived life, it says, is a life in which you flourish, man or woman, in every way of which you are capable.

TEXT FOR DISCUSSION

Lucy Newlyn, *Diary of a Bipolar Explorer*

> Diary of a Bipolar Explorer *(2018) is an account of living with bipolar disorder, which the author ends with a series of proverbs in which she summarizes what she has learned from the experiences described in the book. Below is a selection of these proverbs (I have added numbers for the purpose of reference):*

Lucy's proverbs, aphorisms, and home truths:

1. A taboo is like standing water. Flush it away and start anew.
2. Leave labelling to the bureaucrats and the bigots. There are more than enough of them.
3. A stigma is like an ill-fitting coat; sooner bin it than let out the seams.
4. Know your own mind. No one else can know it for you.
5. A glow-worm's light may lead you on paths un-travelled.
6. Beware of advice disguised as questions.
7. Hope is a needle threaded in the dark.
8. A good proverb is as nutritional as an egg.
9. Ten minutes chatting with a true friend are worth more than all the hours a professional can spare you.
10. The wise cat sleeps where the stone is warm.
11. What use is all your wisdom to a slug?
12. Proverbs are formulaic, but there is no formula for wisdom.
13. For every prying gossip-monger there is someone who doesn't give a damn.
14. There is no Truth, only the various stories.
15. Better to lose your way ten times in a wood at night than to choose the quick way home and miss the owls.
16. Pause at the sign saying DOMESTIC WASTE ONLY.
17. Aphorisms are the last refuge of an untidy mind.

QUESTIONS

1. Several of Newlyn's proverbs reflect on wisdom, the most fundamental concept of the biblical proverbs. The reflections on proverbial wisdom as such in 8 and 17 also contribute to this reflection. How would you

compare and contrast the ideas of wisdom in these proverbs with those in the biblical book?

(a) Newlyn's proverbs 10 and 11 find a wisdom in the natural world, perhaps greater than that found in human society. How does this compare to the biblical proverbs?
(b) Newlyn's proverbs 12 and 17 suggest that wisdom exceeds traditional writing about wisdom, a view with which Job and Ecclesiastes would agree. How would you explain this similarity of thought in texts from such different times and places?
(c) "A good proverb is as nutritional as an egg" (8) – proverbial wisdom nourishes the person, body and soul, for Newlyn. How does this view compare with that of the sages who wrote Proverbs?

2. Many of Newlyn's proverbs remind the reader not to get into the psychically harmful habits that contemporary society encourages. Do not get into taboo thinking (1); do not listen to society's labels for you (2); do not allow others to stigmatize you (3); don't worry about gossips (13). Do you find any similar advice in the biblical proverbs? To what extent is this kind of advice comparable to those found in Proverbs?
3. "There is no Truth, only the various stories" (14). At first sight, this seems very different from the view of Proverbs. But many proverbs speak of Yahweh as exceeding human knowledge, such that true wisdom is knowing how little one knows him (e.g. Prov. 16:8; 19:21). Does Newlyn's view have any correlate in the biblical proverbs, or in the Bible more generally?
4. Newlyn's proverbs 4, 6, and 9 value self-knowledge over against the professional knowledge of therapists or psychiatrists. To what extent is this idea, that one's own experience of oneself is more to be trusted than others', expressed in Proverbs or in the Bible more generally?

Ecclesiastes

Introduction

As we know, Wisdom literature is an international discourse in the ancient Near East. Some of the ways in which Ecclesiastes reflects on human life have parallels in Egyptian and Mesopotamian texts. Perhaps the closest parallels in fact are to be found in the Babylonian *Epic of Gilgamesh* (cf. Brown 2–5; Seow 64–65), which reflects as deeply on the mortality of human beings as Ecclesiastes. Gilgamesh reflects, "Only the gods live forever under the sun. / As for mankind, numbered are their days; / Whatever they achieve is but wind" (III, iv, 6–8), ideas closely

118   *The Bible as Literature*

paralleled in Ecclesiastes. In response to the transitory nature of life decreed by the gods, Gilgamesh is advised:

> Thou, Gilgamesh, let full be thy belly,
> Make thou merry by day and by night.
> Of each day make thou a feast of rejoicing,
> Day and night dance thou and play!
>   (X, iii, 6–14)

Ecclesiastes will derive a similar moral from a similar view of human life.

The book begins, "The words of the Teacher [*qohelet*], the son of David, king in Jerusalem" (1:1). There is a rabbinic tradition that the Song of Songs was written by Solomon when he was young; Proverbs when he was in his prime; and Ecclesiastes when he was old (Brown 11). In fact, scholars are widely agreed that Solomon is not the author of Ecclesiastes. This is partly because of the content of the book itself. The narrator of the book drops the persona of the king after 2:1–11; he gives advice to courtiers as if he were on their social level (8:2–6; 10:4); he blames the royal bureaucracy for social injustice (5:8); and at the end of the book he adopts the persona of the teacher and sage rather than of the king (12:9–11). As C. L. Seow writes, "The author seems to speak more as an observer and a critic of society rather than as a ruler" (37).

The linguistic features of the book seem to be decisive to most scholars in assigning a postexilic date to it. Crenshaw writes, "[Qohelet's] peculiar language marks a transitional stage between classical Hebrew and Mishnaic Hebrew," the latter spoken and written during in the first through fourth centuries CE (*Ecclesiastes* 31). Furthermore, the book seems to show an indirect contact with Greek philosophy in its presupposition that the individual can and should work out the truth about the world and how to live in it with his own powers of reason. Fox argues that this view "probably reflects a Jewish awareness of this type of thinking among foreign intellectuals" (*Ecclesiastes* xi–xii), which would tend to date the book to the Hellenistic period (after 332 BCE). Most scholars date it to the fourth or third centuries BCE, with some preferring an earlier postexilic date.

Qohelet

The speaker of the book of Ecclesiastes is called *qohelet*. The Septuagint translates this term as *ekklēsiastēs*, which continues to serve as the book's name in Christian Bibles. *Qohelet* cannot exactly be translated into English. It is the participle of the verb *qahal*, which means to "assemble" or "gather." The cognate noun *qahal* is a common one, meaning "assembly," "company," or "congregation." So, a *qohelet* is one who assembles or gathers. This may mean he assembles people into a congregation, and so is the "leader of the assembly" (Towner 950) or "one who does something in the assembly" (Fox, *Ecclesiastes* 3). This is the way in which the Septuagint and Martin Luther took the term. Or it can mean that he gathers or assembles proverbs or wise sayings (cf. Eccles. 12:9) As Sibley Towner points

Wisdom Literature 119

out, the NRSV's translation of the term as "Teacher" tries to capture both possible senses (950). Fox suggests "teacher to the public" (*Ecclesiastes* 3). Here I will simply use Qohelet's title in English transliteration, understanding that it means that he is a gatherer, perhaps of people, perhaps of wisdom, and probably of both.

The Book of Ecclesiastes is the closest the Hebrew Bible comes to philosophy. If the book was written in the fourth or third centuries BCE, then that is one or two centuries since Socrates had been teaching in Athens. While no view in the book can be directly traced to the view of a specific Greek philosopher, the book's philosophical mode of investigation of the world through one's own rational and sense faculties seems likely to derive from contact among Jewish intellectuals with Greek philosophy. Fox argues that "the boldest, most radical notion" in the Book of Ecclesiastes consists not in any of Qohelet's specific views about the world or about how to behave in it, but rather his "belief that the individual can and should proceed towards truth by means of his own powers of perception and reasoning" (*Ecclesiastes* xi). Qohelet proceeds like a philosopher. As he puts it in the first chapter of the book, "I applied my mind [*natatti et-libbi*, lit. I gave my heart] to seek [*lidrosh*] and to search out [*latur*] by wisdom [*ba-chochmah*] all that is done under heaven" (1:12). This is how Qohelet acquires and increases wisdom, or *chochmah* – by looking at the world, applying his mind to what he sees, and by reflecting, in thought and speech, upon it.

Vanity

The first principle of Qohelet's philosophy is that "all is vanity" (1:2). He expresses this initially in poetry – note the repetition of words and sound patterns (such as the /h/, /k/q/, and /l/ sounds) in the Hebrew of Ecclesiastes 1:2:

> *Havél havalím, amár qohélet,*
> *Havél havalím, ha-kól havél*

(The acute accents in my transliteration indicate the stressed syllables in each word.) The Hebrew word *hevel* means "breath" or "vapor," and is frequently used in the Hebrew Bible in a figurative sense, as Qohelet does in Ecclesiastes, to indicate that a thing is fleeting, that it lasts only a moment, and is instantly dissolved into nothingness. It is most commonly used in this sense of idols (cf. Jer. 10:15; Deut. 32:31) and, as with Qohelet, of human life (cf. Psalm 62:9). There is a definite moral connotation to the term. It means that something is insubstantial and therefore that it is wrong to attach, as people too often do, too much significance or value to that thing. Things are usually described as *hevel* in the Hebrew Bible, which people overvalue or wrongly treat as if they were not, as they are in fact, soon to be the nothing that is their essential nature. This, Qohelet asserts, is what everything (*kol*) is. Towner points out the frequency of the word *kol*, "all," "every," "each," in the book of Ecclesiastes. It is used in 41% of the verses of the book, far more frequently than in any other biblical book, speaking, as Towner rightly puts it, to Qohelet's "determination to reflect on the meaning of all of life" (957). And

120   *The Bible as Literature*

this is the essence of all of life, for Qohelet, that it is, like idols, like human life, and like moral temptations, nothing but a breath, something which misguided people, perhaps even fools or *kesilim*, think of as if lasting and trustworthy, but which the wise man knows is not.

The Book of Ecclesiastes consists primarily of two things – first, Qohelet's assertions that all is *hevel*; and second, his responses to this situation in which human beings find themselves. Perhaps the most striking thing about these responses is how many there are, and how little they cohere with one another. The reader of the book has the impression that Qohelet is willing to try any kind of ethical response to life as he sees it, because the problem of living in such a world is both so difficult and so necessary to solve. Qohelet, that is, does not know how best to live in this *hevel* world, and is willing to try all kinds of theories and ideas in order to answer this pressing question, the question that dominates his life as a philosopher and as a person.

Hedonism

The most frequently repeated response Qohelet articulates to our *hevel* life is this: "There is nothing better for mortals to eat and drink, and find enjoyment [*tov*] in their toil [*amal*]" (2:24). The KJV translates the Hebrew of the last clause here more literally as, "make his soul enjoy good in his labour." Qohelet expresses this view six times (2:24; 3:13; 3:22; 5:18–20; 8:15; 9:7–9), by far the most of any of the many ethical prescriptions he proposes. Eat, drink, and find enjoyment in your toil. At 5:19, he adds that if God has given you "wealth and possessions [*osher u-nechasim*]," and the ability to enjoy (*achal*, lit. "eat," i.e., "consume") them, then you should use that ability and enjoy them. At 9:8–9, he adds, "Let your garments always be white; do not let oil be lacking on your head," and "enjoy life with the wife whom you love." Qohelet very strongly commends taking pleasure in what you can take pleasure in in life. He commends physical, material pleasures. Eating, drinking, possessions, clothing, sex, companionship – these are the best things in life, for Qohelet. He makes no distinction between the body and the soul, but values that which the human person considered as a whole enjoys. He may have contempt for the fact that not everyone, nor anyone at all times, can enjoy the good things of human life; but he has no contempt for those things in themselves. Quite the opposite – these are the best things, the best experiences human beings can have in their vain lives.

Qohelet's hedonism is theological. He repeatedly emphasizes that eating, drinking, taking pleasure in one's toil, and in clothing, possessions, and love, are the gifts of God to human beings. Eating, drinking, and find enjoyment in one's toil is "from the hand of God," as he puts it in 2:24–25, "for apart from him who can eat or who can have enjoyment?" At 3:13, he calls these things "God's gift [*mattat elohim*]," a phrase he repeats at 5:19 to describe wealth, possessions, the ability to enjoy these things, and the ability of some "to accept their lot and find enjoyment in their toil." To some people at some times, God gives the material and spiritual

Wisdom Literature 121

resources to enjoy being alive, even in this vain life, in which one works and works for nothing. That is life at its best, for Qohelet. When God gives you enough to eat, to drink, work that it is possible to enjoy, possessions and relationships that it is possible to enjoy, the ability to enjoy these things, and the ability to accept that such enjoyment is the best one can have in life, then take advantage of these gifts. They may not last, and there is nothing better than them. This is what Qohelet calls the lot (*cheleq*) of human beings (3:22; cf. 5:19).

Pessimism

I have described this element of Qohelet's philosophy as hedonism. The connotation of sensual excess that that term has in ordinary English, however, is no part of Qohelet's thought. In Chapter 2, he "kept his heart from no pleasure," but finds that even the greatest pleasures as a way of life are "vanity and a chasing after wind" (2:10–11). Some commentators import the idea of moderation or temperance into Qohelet's thought, but in fact he does not use such a concept. He never says, eat, drink, and find enjoyment in your toil, but not to excess. Rather, the book as whole seems suggest that Qohelet thinks that being able to enjoy life's pleasures is a rare gift which will frequently be impossible. He reflects on injustice and oppression in the monarchical society about which he writes: "I saw all the oppressions [*ashuqim*] that are practiced under the sun. Look, the tears of the oppressed – with no-one to comfort them!" (4:1; cf. 3:16; 5:8). Qohelet sees that oppression of the poor is widespread throughout society, indeed is the norm, and has no ethical or political advice to combat or change this. The oppressed and the poor are unlikely to be able to follow his advice to "find enjoyment in their toil," and are certain not to have "wealth or possessions" to "enjoy" (2:24; 5:19). So his hedonism is deeply tempered by his pessimism. There is no danger, in Qohelet's thinking, of sensual excess in his advice to eat, drink, and find enjoyment in one's toil. The danger, on the contrary, is that one will be able to do this too little rather than too much, since the world is such that oppression, injustice, and wickedness rule rather than justice and righteousness.

Fearing God

The next of Qohelet's responses to his conviction that all is *hevel* that we will consider here is the one which is emphasized by its place as the conclusion of the book. The book ends on a note all the more striking for its contrast with all that has gone before: "The end of the matter: all has been heard. Fear God, and keep his commandments; for that is the whole duty of everyone" (12:13). Most scholars agree that the two epilogues to the Book of Ecclesiastes were written by someone other than Qohelet. This concluding thought, though, is in many ways in keeping with the book as a whole, to such an extent that, if it is indeed a later addition, it is one that is made by someone who understands the book to which he is adding very well. It is not at all implausible that the book is by a single author. Qohelet is

122   *The Bible as Literature*

looking throughout the text for one solution after another, for one appropriate ethical response after another to the overwhelming evidence that all is *hevel*. These solutions do not cohere well with another, are not synthesized or integrated into a consistent ethical philosophy, but rather have the character almost of desperation, as if Qohelet is trying as best he can to perform the almost impossible task of mounting some kind of ethical response to a world in which ethics, like all else, seems meaningless. In this sense, the fact that the book ends with yet another attempted solution, one that we have mostly not heard before, is entirely in character with the rest of the book.

Qohelet's advice at the end of the book, to "fear God, and keep his commandments," may seem at first sight to be a more traditionally Yahwist sentiment than what has gone before. The fact that it is placed at the end of the book gives it a certain emphasis, as if he has journeyed though various answers, and this is finally the right one. But structurally, there is no sense given by the book that this last attempt at a solution to the vanity of things is in any way a conclusion or a better answer than all of the others proposed along the way. The point of the book is in fact its many answers. As with the Book of Job, there is ultimately in Ecclesiastes only the attempt to answer, rather than a successful or final answer, to the question the book addresses. Like Job in the midst of human suffering, so with Ecclesiastes in the midst of the vanity of all things, the authenticity of the question is in the end the only answer we have.

Not-Knowing

Indeed, if there is any one of Qohelet's multiple responses to the vanity of human life that has a synthetic function, that seems to be the center, the heart of these responses, it is his view, expressed fully and clearly only once, that no one can understand human life as God has made it. He makes this point at 8:17:

> I saw all the work of God [*ma'aseh ha-elohim*], that no-one can find out what is happening under the sun. However much they may toil [*amal*] in seeking, they will not find it out; even though those who are wise claim to know, they cannot find it out.

I would argue that this verse is the center of the book, the heart – as it were the absent heart, the dark sun around which all revolves – of its philosophy. Wisdom consists, Qohelet asserts, in knowing that one does not know. God has made heaven and earth, all that is "under the sun," as Qohelet repeats. Understanding its principle, its *cheshbon* (7:28), is beyond human beings who are part of this creation, are part of the world under the sun. The authors of Job and Ecclesiastes agree. Human beings cannot fathom the world as God has created it. The best they can do therefore, is "fear [him], and obey his commandments." Reason can take us only so far; at its edge, faith (which the Wisdom books call the fear of the LORD) must take over. This is the non-message, the philosophy of absence, of Ecclesiastes.

Wisdom Literature **123**

TEXT FOR DISCUSSION

Ernest Hemingway, *The Sun Also Rises*

The title of Ernest Hemingway's first novel, The Sun Also Rises *(1926), is taken from Ecclesiastes 1:5. The novel has two epigraphs – first, "You are all a lost generation"; and second, Ecclesiastes 1:4–7 (KJV), which begins, "One generation passeth away, and another generation cometh; but the earth abideth forever. The sun also ariseth, and the sun goeth down, and hasteth to the place where he arose." These epigraphs describe the kind of lives led by the "lost generation" of Americans after World War I described in the novel.*

"It's funny what a wonderful gentility you get in the bar of a big hotel," I said.

"Barmen and jockeys are the only people who are polite any more."

"No matter how vulgar a hotel is, the bar is always nice."

"It's odd."

"Bartenders have always been fine." […]

We touched the two glasses as they stood side by side on the bar. They were coldly beaded. Outside the curtained window was the summer heat of Madrid.

"I like an olive in a Martini," I said to the barman.

"Right you are, sir. There you are."

"Thanks."

"I should have asked, you know." […]

Brett had sipped from the Martini as it stood, on the wood. Then she picked it up. Her hand was steady enough to lift it after that first sip.

"It's good. Isn't it a nice bar?"

"They're all nice bars." […]

"You know," Brett said, "he'd only been with two women before. He never cared about anything but bull-fighting."

"He's got plenty of time."

"I don't know. He thinks it was me. Not the show in general." […]

"I thought you weren't going to ever talk about it." […]

"I just talk around it. You know I feel rather damned good, Jake."

"You should."

"You know it makes one feel rather good deciding not to be a bitch."

"Yes."

"It's sort of what we have instead of God."

"Some people have God," I said. "Quite a lot."

"He never worked very well with me."

"Should we have another Martini?"

124 *The Bible as Literature*

QUESTIONS

1. In this passage from the end of the novel, as throughout the novel, the characters' conversation seems trivial and endless. It's often difficult to tell who is talking, as if it does not really matter. In the first few lines from the text above, Jake Barnes and Lady Brett Ashley speak about big hotels, bars, barmen, and martinis, because this is all there is to talk about. With the title and epigraph of the novel from Ecclesiastes 1:4–7, Hemingway seems to be saying that modern life is characterized by exactly the kind of meaninglessness that Qohelet described. What do you think of this view?
2. Hemingway's terse narrative style is at work in the two narrative sentences interspersed between the dialogue in the text above – "We touched the two glasses..."; "Brett had sipped from the martini..." One sentence merely succeeds another, much as Ecclesiastes says, "The sun ariseth and the sun goeth down"; "the wind goeth toward the south, and turneth about unto the north," and so on. Does Hemingway's style, in which he largely confines himself to portraying outward events alone, express some of the meaninglessness he sees in modern life, which he sees also to have been observed by Ecclesiastes?
3. In this passage, as throughout the novel, the characters drink a lot. Here we see Brett's hand shaking until steadied by alcohol. The main event of the novel is the characters' participation in the week-long fiesta of San Fermín in Pamplona, Spain. Qohelet thinks of eating, drinking, and taking pleasure in one's toil as one of the right responses to the meaninglessness of life. Hemingway's characters seem to be trying but failing at this. Does Hemingway think differently than Qohelet about taking pleasure in life?
4. At the end of this passage Brett talks about deciding "not to be a bitch," by which she means that she has left the 19-year-old bullfighter with whom a relationship could never have worked out. She calls making this good decision "sort of what we have instead of God," to which Jake, a Catholic, replies, "Some people have God." Jake seems to think like Ecclesiastes that it is both possible and desirable, despite the apparent meaninglessness of modern life, to believe in God. What you do think of this view?

Works Cited

Alter, Robert. *The Hebrew Bible, Volume 3: The Writings*. W. W. Norton, 2019.
Balentine, Samuel E. *Job*. Smyth and Helwys, 2006.
Brown, William P. *Ecclesiastes*. John Knox, 2000.
Clifford, Richard J. *Proverbs: A Commentary*. Westminster John Knox, 1999.
"Counsels of Wisdom." *Before the Muses: An Anthology of Akkadian Literature*, edited by Benjamin R. Foster, vol. 1, CDL Press, 1993, pp. 328–31.
Crenshaw, James L. *Ecclesiastes: A Commentary*. Westminster, 1987.
———. *Reading Job: A Literary and Theological Commentary*. Smyth and Helwys, 2011.

Wisdom Literature 125

Dell, Katharine J. *Job*. Bloomsbury T & T Clark, 2017.

Fontaine, Carol R. "Proverbs." *The Women's Bible Commentary*, edited by Carol A. Newsom and Sharon H. Ringe, Westminster John Knox, 1992, pp. 146–51.

Fox, Michael V. *Ecclesiastes*. Jewish Publication Society, 2004.

———. *Proverbs 1-9*. Yale UP, 2000.

———. *Proverbs 10-31*. Yale UP, 2009.

Hemingway, Ernest. *The Sun Also Rises*. Scribner, 1926.

Horne, Milton P. *Proverbs-Ecclesiastes*. Smyth and Helwys, 2003.

Murphy, Roland E. and O.Carm. *The Book of Job: A Short Reading*. Paulist Press, 1999.

Newson, Carol A. "Job." *The New Interpreter's Bible Commentary*, vol. 3, Abingdon Press, 2015, pp. 17–270.

Seow, C. L. *Ecclesiastes*. Yale UP, 1997.

"The Babylonian Theodicy." *Before the Muses: An Anthology of Akkadian Literature*, edited by Benjamin R. Foster, vol. 2, CDL Press, 1993, pp. 806–14.

"The Epic of Gilgamesh." *Ancient Near Eastern Text Relating to the Old Testament*, edited by James B. Pritchard, 3rd ed., Princeton UP, 1969, pp. 72–99.

"The Instruction of Amen-em-Opet," *Ancient Near Eastern Text Relating to the Old Testament*, edited by James B. Pritchard, 3rd ed., Princeton UP, 1969, pp. 421–25.

Towner, W. Sibley, "Ecclesiastes." *The New Interpreter's Bible Commentary*, vol. 3, Abingdon Press, 2015, pp. 947–1019.

van Leeuwen, Raymond C. "Proverbs." *The New Interpreter's Bible Commentary*, vol. 3, Abingdon Press, 2015, pp. 749–945.

6 The Prophets

Isaiah

Introduction

Since Bernard Duhm's commentary *The Book of Isaiah* (1892), it has been generally accepted by biblical scholars that there are three major divisions within the Book of Isaiah – Chapters 1–39, Chapters 40–55, and Chapters 56–66. Following Duhm's terminology, these sections have become known as First, Second, and Third Isaiah, language that we will still use in this chapter with the prefatory clarifying remark that they refer to three largely and loosely distinct sections of the text rather than to three individual authors. From the 1980s onward,

> Isaian scholarship [...] has been exercised to move beyond this critical orthodoxy either by attempting to demonstrate a deliberately unifying theological intent [between the three sections] or by identifying structural, thematic, and lexical clues to an underlying unity at the redactional rather than the authorial level.
>
> (Blenkinsopp, *Isaiah 1-39*, 82)

As Joseph Blenkinsopp puts it, "the book has undergone *successive* restructurings and rearrangements in the course of a long editorial history" (83, emphasis in original), not all of which are recoverable. We can say the following about the composition history of the book. Isaiah of Jerusalem, who is referred to in the "historical appendix" to Chapters 1–39, most of which is taken verbatim from 2 Kings 18–20, and in the three superscriptions at Isaiah 1:1, 2:1, and 13:1, was active from approximately 740 to 700 BCE. There is a "significant [...] substratum" of his work in Chapters 1–39 (Blenkinsopp, *Isaiah 1-39,* 74). This has been added to by later writers, and edited by later editors in a complex, multiple process, in which "even some passages considered authentic to Isaiah seem to have undergone editorial development" (Tull 13). Chapters 40–55 have "a relatively high level of coherence and continuity" compared with Chapters 1–39 and other prophetic compilations (Blenkinsopp, *Isaiah 40-55*, 73), although redaction critics have hypothesized various levels of insertion, rewriting, and editing in an ultimately "layered

DOI: 10.4324/9781315751566-7

document" (Goldingay and Payne 7). The references in this section to Cyrus II, the emperor of Persia, who took over the empire of the Medes, the kingdom of Lydia in Asia Minor, the Greek cities on the Ionian coast, and in 539 eventually Babylon itself and hence the entire Babylonian empire, date the core of this section most probably to the 540s BCE, during the period of these successful campaigns. Most scholars believe that it was written in Babylonia (Blenkinsopp, *Isaiah 40-55*, 92–95, 102–104; Goldingay and Payne 25–37). The bulk of Chapters 55–66, which most scholars agree "do not come from one hand or one time period," seems to presume a situation in Judah shortly after the return from exile in Babylon allowed by Cyrus in 539, and most scholars date this material to the first century of Persian rule in the province, that is, from the late sixth to the late fifth century BCE (Blenkinsopp, *Isaiah 55-66*, 59, 43).

The relationship between the three sections remains a matter of debate. The view of Blenkinsopp and Brevard Childs, that Third Isaiah represents an "exegetical tradition" or process of "ongoing writing" by a group of writers who regard Second Isaiah as authoritative is a plausible one, given the constant play of repetition and difference between those two sections (Blenkinsopp, *Isaiah 55-66*, 63–66; Childs, 441–444). With respect to the relationship between the three major sections of the book, there is little certainty. As Patricia Tull writes:

> Most evidence points to the addition of 40–55 along with at least parts of 50–66 to Isaiah's own growing corpus during the time of the Second Temple [515 BCE–70 CE], by someone who perceived common themes in the prophetic treatment of Jerusalem, its past, future, and present. In other words, it makes good sense to see Isaiah 1–39 and 40–66 as having developed first as discrete works, though culturally interrelated [...] At some point, perceived as sharing a common interest in Jerusalem and her God, the Holy One, they were stitched together, and their seams reinforced by a series of additions in the beginning, middle, and end of the book, lending the air of coherence and continuity.
>
> (18)

History and Theology in Isaiah 1–39

Perhaps the most striking impression created by the first 39 chapters of the book as it has been finally edited is the sheer multitude of enemies by which Judah and Jerusalem are threatened. Several major political events are referred to directly throughout these chapters, and many others are alluded to.

(1) The first is the "Syro-Ephraimite war" of 734–732 BCE. When Assyria became dominant in the region, Kings Rezin of Damascus and Pekah of Israel organized a rebellion among Near Eastern states against the imperial power. King Ahaz of Judah refused to join this coalition, and Rezin and Pekah attacked Jerusalem with a view to replacing Ahaz with someone more cooperative. Their assault on the city failed, and Damascus was subjugated by the Assyrians.

128   *The Bible as Literature*

(2) Ten years later, when King Hoshea of Israel refused to pay tribute to the Assyrian emperor, the same fate met Samaria. The city was destroyed by the Assyrians, and its citizens were deported throughout the empire.

(3) The third major event with which these chapters deal is the siege of Jerusalem in 701 BCE by the Assyrian emperor Sennacherib. King Hezekiah of Judah took an active role in planning rebellion against Assyrian rule. Sennacherib's army devastated Judah, destroying 46 towns, in response to which Hezekiah submitted to the Assyrians and paid a huge indemnity to save Jerusalem (Blenkinsopp, *Isaiah 1-39* 98–105; Tucker 35–37; Tull 8–11; Seitz, *Isaiah 1-39* 10–15).

The impression a reader gets from the experience of reading Isaiah 1–39, however, is a completely different one from this brief historical account of the events with which these chapters are concerned. The final editors of the text were not primarily concerned with the chronological sequence that a historical account depends on. The text rather gives an impression of a constant, endless, shifting and even ultimately nameless threat to the peace and well-being of Jerusalem, its rulers, and its people as they try more or less successfully to live out their lives as Yahweh's covenant people. As we read through the first chapters of the text, we begin with an unnamed destruction of Judah and Jerusalem:

> Your country lies desolate,
>   your cities are burned with fire;
> in your very presence
>   aliens devour your land;
>   it is desolate, as overthrown by foreigners.
>
>   (1:7)

The historical situation described here is not clear, and of the many proposals suggested, "most favor the Assyrian 701 invasion as the most fitting scenario of which modern readers are aware" (Tull 58). Two chapters later, there is another prophecy of the destruction of Judah and Jerusalem, which seems to be more general, more in the future, and less tied to any specific military or political threat:

> I will make boys their princes
>   and babes shall rule over them [...]
> Someone will even seize a relative,
>   a member of the clan, saying,
> "You have a cloak;
>   you shall be our leader,
> and this heap of ruins
>   shall be under your rule."
>
>   (3:4, 6)

The Prophets   129

Two chapters later, as the text denounces social injustice, the prophet writes, "Therefore my people go into exile without knowledge" (5:13). In the context of the whole Book of Isaiah, this could refer equally to the deportation of the citizens of Israel to Assyria in 722 or that of the citizens of Judah to Babylon in 586. Later in Chapter 5, the prophet proclaims that Yahweh will bring a nation to destroy either Israel or Judah, which is probably Assyria, but even that is not specified, and which may refer to the Assyrian destruction of Samaria in 722 or to the Assyrian destruction of Judah in 701 (5:26–28). In the call narrative that follows in Chapter 6, Isaiah asks Yahweh, "How long, O Lord?" must the people of Judah remain unresponsive to Yahweh's call, and Yahweh replies that it will be "until cities lie waste without inhabitant […] / until the LORD sends everyone far away, / and vast is the emptiness in the middle of the land" (6:11–12). This too could be the Assyrian exile of 722 – the prophecy is dated to "the year that King Uzziah died," which is probably 738 – or, in the context of the book as a whole, the Babylonian exile of 586. This narrative is then directly followed by a prose narrative that speaks directly of the threat of the Syro-Ephraimite war of 734–732 (7:1–2).

The editors of the text have not put Isaiah 1–39 together with chronology nor even clarity with respect to historical events in mind. They are not primarily interested in a historical account of the constantly shifting political tensions in the region during and after Isaiah's lifetime, in response to which Isaiah prophesied. Rather, they have created a sense of a constant series of threats of destruction faced by Jerusalem, Judah, Israel, and their neighboring states. First Isaiah gives an existential sense, rather than a historical account, of peoples and nations constantly on the verge of destruction, massacre, and deportation. No one is safe, the text says over and over again, no individual, no state. Destruction is coming, whether you are a small and insignificant nation like Judah or a world power like Assyria or Babylon. This is the overwhelming impression of First Isaiah. The prophet Isaiah is deeply and closely involved in Judah's politics, with immediate access to at least two kings, whom he confidently advised in Yahweh's name. Nevertheless, the message of the book with respect to politics transcends politics. No king, not even on David's throne, can be relied on, to save himself, his people, or his territory. First Isaiah's vision of the good life is in the future, is to come. Rulers, even the good king Hezekiah, so infrequently choose justice instead of a bribe, and people so infrequently choose righteousness instead of idolatry, that the blessings of Yahweh's covenant are not going to permeate through Judean society (nor beyond) in Isaiah's time. That is going to happen, First Isaiah stresses, only in the new, other, Davidic kingdom to come.

The Highway through the Desert

Second Isaiah too has a theological unity beneath its impressionistic structure. John Goldingay and David Payne compare the movement of the sections to a suite of music, in which three or four dominant themes repeatedly flow in and out of the hearer's attention (19). In Second Isaiah, Yahweh promises return from

130 *The Bible as Literature*

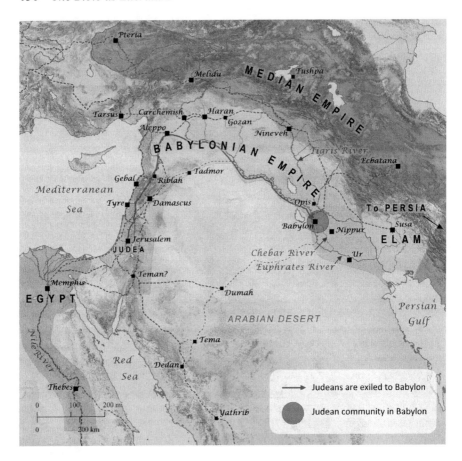

Figure 6.1 The route of the exile to Babylonia. Credit: biblemapper.com

exile in Babylon. One of the most striking images with which this message of restoration is expressed is that of the highway in the desert, which separates the exiles in Babylon from their home in Jerusalem. A vast and inhospitable space of desert (in modern-day Iraq and Jordan) lay between Babylon and Jerusalem, stretching some 500 miles, and in fact the exiles returned from Babylon as the Babylonians marched in, in a long loop to the north, following the Euphrates River to the northwest and then south down the Mediterranean coast. See Figure 6.1. The Book of Isaiah, however, imagines a miraculous blooming of the desert in between Babylon and Jerusalem, and a highway coming into existence through this fertile, hospitable place, across which Yahweh will lead the people of Israel in joy to the fullness of life in Mount Zion.

Initially, this is simply a way home for the exiles, but in the book's longest meditation on this theme, there is a further eschatological dimension, in which the way across the desert becomes also the way into the fullness of life for those whom Yahweh has "redeemed" or "ransomed." First, the desert will blossom:

> The wilderness and the dry land shall be glad,
>> the desert shall rejoice and blossom;
> like the crocus it shall blossom abundantly,
>> and rejoice [*gil*] with joy [*gilah*] and singing [*ranan*].
>> (35:1–2)

Indeed, the desert will not only be transformed into a fertile garden but also will sing with joy as it does so. The eschatological note is sounded right from the beginning of this prophecy. The earth is becoming what it was always going to be in Yahweh's kingdom to come. Next, miracles of healing will occur – the blind will see, the deaf will hear, the lame will walk, and the mute will speak (35:5–6). The prophet envisions all that is wrong in the world being transformed into the way Yahweh always intended it to be. It is a process in which all creation sings for joy (*gil ve-ranan*) at finally becoming itself in Yahweh's kingdom.

The prophet says of the highway across the desert, "The redeemed [*ge'ulim*] shall walk there / and the ransomed of the LORD shall return / and come to Zion with singing" (35:9–10). The concept of redemption (*ge'ullah*) has a specific primary sense in the Hebrew Bible, as we saw in our discussion of the Book of Ruth, in which a family member saves another in some way from serious trouble or difficulty (Lev. 25:25–28, 47–55; Num. 35:9–27; Ruth 3:9, 12; 4:1–10). When the Book of Isaiah envisions those who walk on the highway through the transformed desert to Zion as Yahweh's "redeemed," this means primarily that Yahweh has acted as their family member. In Naomi's words, he is "near [*qarov*] to [them], a redeeming kinsman [*go'el*]" (Ruth 2:20). Yahweh has acted on behalf of his impoverished or enslaved family members and bought them back into freedom, into the fullness of life in his family. The return from exile in Babylonia means everything to the prophet's sixth-century Judean audience, but in the Book of Isaiah it means more than itself. Second Isaiah's vision of Yahweh's gift of return from exile becomes essentially and primarily a vision of something greater, something more general, something that affects not only the people of Judah but all the peoples who are emphasized throughout the book. It becomes a vision of the good life, a vision of peace and prosperity for all people, united in worship of their creator and redeemer Yahweh, in a renewed, fertile earth and a renewed, full life. It becomes a vision of Yahweh's messianic kingdom. This is what Yahweh is really doing, according to the Book of Isaiah, preparing the kingdom to come that will exceed in righteousness, justice, and peace all the kingdoms, indigenous or foreign, that the people of Judah or any other people have ever seen. As Childs puts it, "the imagery of return to Zion has been extended far beyond the concrete historical situation" of the return from Babylon (258) and into "the final eschatological exaltation of Zion and the entrance into the ultimate joy of the kingdom of God" (256).

132   *The Bible as Literature*

The Servant Songs

Since Duhm's commentary, the four passages in Second Isaiah that he described as "servant of Yahweh songs" (42:1–9; 49:1–7; 50:4–11; 52:13–53:12) have been discussed in great detail. The most striking, unusual, and memorable set of characteristics of the servant are presented in the fourth song, having been anticipated in the second and third (49:4, 7; 51:6, 10). They constitute the paradox that the servant will be on the one hand greatly honored but on the other "despised and rejected by others," "a man of suffering [*ish mach'ovot*] / and acquainted with infirmity," and "held [...] of no account" (53:3). The first thing we hear about the servant is that he is considered unattractive, even repulsive: "He had no form [*to'ar*] or majesty [*hadar*] that we should look at him, / nothing in his appearance that we should desire [*chamad*] him" (53:2; cf. 52:14). The servant does not look like a king, nor does his appearance in any way symbolize beauty, goodness, or power. He has no power, no popularity, and no love. Although the translation of this verse is complex, the NRSV's rendering that he is "one from whom others hide their faces," like the KJV's "we hid as it were our faces from him," fits the context well. No one who counts, no one who can change the world in any way either knows him or wants to know him. He is the opposite of power, a man of suffering and sorrow, and yet somehow, in this new way, he will bring about Yahweh's justice, teaching, and salvation.

How does he do this? He seems to suffer vicariously for the community. He "bears our infirmities" and "carries our diseases" (53:4). St. Jerome rendered the term "stricken" (*nagua*) in the next line of this verse as *leprosum* – in his version, the servant is seen as a leper. Childs is right to emphasize that in the biblical view sickness and sin are not sharply distinguished, and that the servant in a general, existential way suffers vicariously for the multiple and complex distresses of the human condition. He seems to do this by suffering these distresses himself. He suffers from oppression and affliction. He suffers from lack of love, lack of society, and lack of power. He suffers from sickness. These things lead him to suffer from social and political injustice. He seems to be arrested and killed though he had committed no crime (53:7–9), and was unable (and indeed unwilling) to prevent this. Because of this, in an ultimately mysterious way that the song does not explain, he does Yahweh's work; he functions as Yahweh's servant. The last three verses of the song (53:10–12) recapitulate the first in emphasizing that, in suffering in this general and apparently total way, he becomes great, presumably on behalf of the very community for whom he has suffered. How this will be the case the song does not explain, presumably because it is not able to. The prophet (along with whatever editors his work may have had) is groping in the dark toward the light of his vision here. He is inarticulately trying to point to something he has not seen, heard of, or understood before about the way in which he believes Yahweh is going to work in the world. Christopher Seitz speaks very well of the poetic idiom of the fourth servant song and its function:

> The text is poetic in the very basic sense of the word. That is, the confession of
> the servants is in the very nature of the thing a discovery of something that they

themselves are struggling to describe. Hence, for example, the tendency of the text to back over terrain more than once or to pile up descriptions as if searching for the proper words.

("Isaiah 40–66" 464)

(Seitz speaks of "servants" here because he believes that the song has multiple authors). He is certainly right about how the song works. The prophet is convinced that Yahweh's justice will be satisfied through a servant who in some way suffers in his own person the sufferings of the community. He does not know how this is possible, and so he keeps trying different ways to articulate it, but he does know that Yahweh is going to do it. In this way, the Book of Isaiah says, Yahweh's justice will be established throughout the earth in a new kingdom to come, of which the Davidic kings in the eighth century in whose reigns Isaiah of Jerusalem prophesied were only a shadow, a symbol, and a first, faulty step.

The Non-ending of Isaiah 56–66

The Book of Isaiah does not conclude on this climactic note, of course. Much of Chapters 55–66 seem to presume the situation in Judah after the exiles have returned from Babylon. The most significant thing about this situation with respect to the meaning of the Book of Isaiah as a whole is that nothing has changed, neither the corruption, idolatry, and threats of destruction of First Isaiah nor the need for Yahweh's redemption expressed by Second Isaiah. Third Isaiah is a complex patchwork of texts that presume different situations, and that have been edited in such a way as to create a sense of constant repetition of fundamental experiences rather than a chronologically progressing narrative.

In the first place, Third Isaiah makes the message of the Book of Isaiah clear that political corruption, military threats, and the idolatry that the prophets strongly suggest is the cause of the former, will never end, not in this age. These were Jerusalem's problems in the eighth century, in First Isaiah; they were Jerusalem's problems in the early sixth century, resulting in the Babylonian exile, in Second Isaiah; and they remain Jerusalem's problems in the late sixth century and beyond, in Third Isaiah. If Second Isaiah was not clear enough that the return from Babylon would be a symbol, a kind of foretaste, of Yahweh's redemption of Judah, rather than the thing itself, Third Isaiah makes that finally certain. The central panel of Chapters 60–62 emphasizes that the universal kingdom of peace that Yahweh will bring about on the earth is still to come after the return from exile. Still to come, and still as much needed as when the people of Judah were in exile. The Book of Isaiah teaches its audiences that Judah lives in the middle of Yahweh's redemptive history. Corruption, idolatry, and destruction ebb and flow, but ultimately never cease to govern the history both of Judah and the nations. What equally never ceases to be present in this history is Yahweh's will to change it, to transform life on earth into the goodness, righteousness, justice, and peace he always intended it to be. The Book of Isaiah sounds two constant notes, and portrays Judean history as an experience of living between them. "Forsaken" and "Desolate" is now;

134　*The Bible as Literature*

"My Delight Is in Her" and "Married" is coming (62:4). From beginning to end, the Book of Isaiah has a foot in both camps, the Jerusalem of the present and the Jerusalem to come, the kingdoms of the earth and the kingdom of the new heaven and the new earth. It is a Janus-faced book, looking with regret at the constant cycle of history on the hand and out of it to Yahweh's redemption of it on the other.

TEXT FOR DISCUSSION

from Georg Friedrich Handel, *Messiah*

The German composer Handel composed the oratorio Messiah *in 1741, with a libretto made up of texts from the KJV and the Coverdale Psalter by Charles Jennens. Part 1 of the three-part oratorio is composed primarily of prophetic texts taken to predict the coming of Jesus the Messiah. Below is the text and a link to the performance of Part I, Movement 12, "For unto us a child is born."*

Libretto:

For unto us a child is born, unto us a son is given: and the government shall be upon his shoulder: and his name shall be called Wonderful, Counsellor, The mighty God, The everlasting Father, The Prince of Peace.

(Isaiah 9:6)

Performance:

Many performances of the movement are available online. The London Symphony Orchestra's version can be found here: www.youtube.com/watch?v=MS3vpAWW2Zc

---

QUESTIONS

1. Perhaps the first impression the hearer of this piece receives is of the beautifully ordered and structured quality of the music. The Book of Isaiah does not have this quality. The first nine chapters of Isaiah are chaotic, confusing, and not entirely clear. Nor is it certain in context to whom Isaiah 9:6 refers – it may be King Ahaz; it may be King Hezekiah; it may celebrate the birth, the coronation, or the military victory of the king (Tull 200–202). How would you describe the relationship between the orderly quality of Handel's musical setting of the verse and the much less orderly quality of the text from which it is taken?

2. The meditative structure of the choral arrangement of the verse, in which each clause is repeated multiple times, changes the nature of the text. On the one hand, the effects of the parallelism of Hebrew poetry, in which the second half-line sets up a relationship of similarity and difference with the first half-line, is lost. On the other hand, the fact of relationship between each phrase is emphasized by the choral arrangement, as the text's words are repeated, lengthened, and sung together by the different vocal parts. What effects does the choral arrangement of the verse, with its repetition, lengthening, and interweaving of words and phrases, achieve? Is it a more or less valuable experience than simply reading the verse?

3. The musical arrangement emphasizes the names that the royal child will be given, by means of crescendo and the striking violin parts. The second half of the verse has a climactic quality in the choral setting. This seems to me a good representation of the biblical text, suggesting that these names are Messianic and that the ultimate significance of Isaiah's prophecy is the reign of righteousness, justice, and peace that the Davidic king to come will bring. Would you agree that Handel's musical emphasis on Isaiah 9:6c-d, "Wonderful, Counsellor, The mighty God, The everlasting Father, The Prince of Peace," is faithful to the intention of the biblical text?

Jeremiah

Introduction

There is wide agreement among scholars that the Book of Jeremiah has been through a complex process of editing, by many hands and over a long period of time, which extends past the life of Jeremiah himself in the later seventh and earlier sixth centuries BCE. Terence Fretheim writes, "The book is clearly a collection of materials emergent in various times and places" (17), comparing it to a "collage" (19), and speaking of its "kaleidoscopic" effect (22). Leslie Allen compares the book to a "quilt" (10), and to "an old English country house, originally built and then added to in the Regency period, augmented with Victorian wings, and generally refurbished throughout the Edwardian years. It grew over a long period of time" (11).

Several kinds of material seem to have been brought together in the compilation of the book, including:

(1) Poetic oracles, especially in Chapters 2–25. Many believe that these oracles were proclaimed by Jeremiah himself, although scholars disagree on the extent to which they have also been edited. I find the view plausible that there is both a nucleus of Jeremiah's own words and a layer of editing which are no longer always possible to distinguish. Patrick Miller speaks of the presence of the

136 *The Bible as Literature*

"historical prophet" and the "presented prophet" in the oracles and narratives, making clear that it is often impossible to differentiate between them (561).

(2) Prose accounts of the ministry of Jeremiah, especially in Chapters 19:1–20:6; 26–29; 32; 34–45. Some of these may be by Jeremiah's scribe Baruch (Lundbom 96–97).

(3) Prose sayings, often showing affinity with the thought and style of the Book of Deuteronomy and the Deuteronomistic history (for example 7:1–8:3; 11:1–17; 25:1–11; 3:6–11; 21:1–10). The presence of Deuteronomistic language in these sections leads most to hypothesize that they are from later editors of Jeremiah's work, working after the fall of Jerusalem (Fretheim 28; Miller 565). The goal of these editors seems to have been to expand Jeremiah's oracles "to make them more applicable to a subsequent generation" (Fretheim 28; cf. Leuchter 181). In Fretheim's words, the book as a whole is "primarily concerned [...] to use the heritage of Jeremiah to address the ongoing spiritual and religious needs of a devastated and questioning community" after the disaster of the exile (5).

The Siege of Jerusalem

The Book of Jeremiah is all about the experience of Judah and Jerusalem in the period of the rise of the Babylonian empire. Jeremiah is called to be a prophet in the thirteenth year of King Josiah, 627 BCE (Jer. 1:2), which is also the year in which Asshurbanipal, the last great emperor of Assyria, dies. Many prophecies in the book are dated to "the fourth year of King Jehoiakim," 605 BCE (Jer. 25:1), in which Nebuchadrezzar acceded to the throne of Babylon and defeated the Egyptians at the battle of Carchemish, which finally ended Assyrian power in the region and "allowed the Babylonians to move westward and begin to establish control of Syria-Palestine," and by 604 or 603, Judah had become a Babylonian vassal (Miller 559). By 598, the Babylonian army had marched into Judah, and in 597 laid siege to Jerusalem. Within three months, Jerusalem surrendered, and the young King Jehoiachin, along with the royal family and many leading citizens, were deported to Babylon. Within five years, King Zedekiah rebelled against Babylonian rule, with disastrous consequences. The Babylonians laid siege again to Jerusalem in 588 BCE, and after a year and a half destroyed the city, deporting Zedekiah and the remaining citizens of Jerusalem to Babylon in 586, and leaving only "the poor people who owned nothing" (Jer. 39:10) in the land of Judah. The Temple was destroyed, the Davidic monarchy at an end.

The Book of Jeremiah is all about these events. It is all about the rise of Babylon in Mesopotamia, its expansion westward toward Palestine, its assaults on Judah and Jerusalem, and its eventual destruction of Jerusalem and with it the people of Israel's long sense of identity as Yahweh's covenant people. The dominant aesthetic effect of the Book of Jeremiah is the portrayal it provides of the experience of the approach of the Babylonians to Jerusalem, the two sieges and destruction of the city, and the deportations. Like the Book of Isaiah, the Book of Jeremiah has not been edited with chronological sequence or progression primarily in mind. Rather,

The Prophets   137

it successfully creates a sense of buildup, of the gradual increase of pressure on the king and leaders of Jerusalem as Babylonian imperial expansion in the region increases and places worse and worse demands on the city and its people. This turns into siege conditions, and the eventual total destruction of the city and the lives of its citizens. This is the experience into which the Book of Jeremiah gives us a dramatic view. While reading it, the reader lives through the heart of the experience of the destruction of Jerusalem and all that that destruction means to the people of Judah.

Despite the enormous historical significance of the fall of Jerusalem to the people of Judah, the Book of Jeremiah, like the Deuteronomistic History, portrays it as an ultimately theological event. The experience of the fall of Jerusalem, which the narratives in the Book of Jeremiah describe so vividly, is ultimately in the book the experience of Yahweh's judgment. The narratives portray the enormous traumatic effect of the siege, the famine, the fall of the city, its destruction, the brutal aftermath of the fall, and the exile on the citizens of Jerusalem and on Jeremiah individually because the editors of the book are in the end portraying the enormous traumatic effect of Yahweh's judgment on his people. This is what breaking Yahweh's covenant looks like, according to the Book of Jeremiah, and it is terrible.

Prophecies of Judgment

The Book of Jeremiah is a gradual progression of prophecies that, unless the kings and people of Judah return to the covenant and cease to worship other gods than Yahweh, Yahweh will visit his judgment upon them in the form of the army of King Nebuchadrezzar of Babylon. The structure of the Book of Jeremiah is complex, and scholars argue as to how best it should be divided up and understood. Nevertheless, it also has a considerable unity, in that the oracles (mostly in poetry) in Chapters 1–25 represent directly the same threat of judgment of which the narrative sections, from Chapters 20 to 45, then tell the story. Chapter 25 functions as a kind of summary of the oracles Jeremiah has been preaching over the 23 years since he has been a prophet. Jeremiah tells the people of Judah, "For twenty-three years [...] the word of the LORD has come to me, and I have spoken persistently to you, but you have not listened" (25:3). The message that Jeremiah and all the other prophets have preached is the same, Jeremiah says:

> Turn now, every one of you, from your evil [ra'ah] way and your wicked [roa] doings, and you will remain upon the land that the LORD has given you and your ancestors from of old and forever; do not go after other gods to serve and to worship them, and do not provoke me to anger with the work of your hands. Then I will do you no harm [ra'a]. (25:5–6)

This has indeed been the constant message of Jeremiah's prophecies throughout Chapters 1–24. Although judgment and destruction feature so graphically, in fact the heart of the message is "amend" (yatav, lit. make good) your ways, or "turn" (shuv) back from them. If the people of Judah "turn" from serving other gods and

138 *The Bible as Literature*

serve Yahweh again as his covenant people, if they "amend" their ways and actions, Yahweh will "change his mind" (*nicham*) about the coming destruction he has visited upon them in judgment for their faithlessness in the form of the Babylonian army. As Yahweh tells Jeremiah in commissioning his Temple sermon:

> It may be that they will listen, all of them, and will turn back from their evil way, that I may change my mind [*nicham*] about the disaster that I intend to bring on them because of their evil doings. (26:3)

Jeremiah concludes the sermon in exactly the same way:

> Now therefore amend [*yatav*] your ways and your doings, and obey the voice of the LORD your God, and the LORD will change his mind [*nicham*] about the disaster he has pronounced against you. (26:13)

This is the heart, the point, the message behind all the human drama of the siege and fall of Jerusalem that affects the reader of the Book of Jeremiah so strongly. The fall of Jerusalem is Yahweh's judgment on the people of Judah to whom Jeremiah preached repentance for 40 years, from the year of his call in 627 to the fall of the city in 587, but who would not listen to his call. This is the theological story, the story of the relationship of Yahweh and his covenant people, at the very heart of the Book of Jeremiah, the most fundamental story beneath the dramatic and far-reaching consequences for all the people of Judah of the story of the siege and fall of Jerusalem and the Babylonian exile. Despite the enormous human drama and the far-reaching consequences for the entire people of Judah of the historical story of the siege and fall of Jerusalem and of the Babylonian exile, the story that the Book of Jeremiah finally and truly tells is the story of the covenant relationship between Yahweh and his people, of which the former is only a very, very consequential result. The thing itself, for the Book of Jeremiah, remains the living relationship between Yahweh and his covenant people.

Prophecies of Consolation

So far we have focused on the message of judgment in the Book of Jeremiah. I have described this as the heart of the message of the book. But there is, so to speak, a heart of the heart of the message of the Book of Jeremiah, and that is its divine promise of restoration after the destruction of Jerusalem, its divine promise of faithful and everlasting love after judgment. At the very center of the book comes the eye of the tornado, the calm at the center of the storm constituted by Chapters 30–33. Scholars refer to this section as the "Book of Consolation" or the "Book of Comfort," because it begins with Yahweh's instruction to "write in a book [*sepher*] all the words that I have spoken to you" (30:2). As Miller observes, "What follows, therefore, is understood as part of Jeremiah's message that is to be preserved for the future" (804). Yahweh especially wants his message of

The Prophets 139

restoration preserved for posterity, for generation after generation, in the lasting form of a book.

The Book of Consolation has been edited into the form of the Book of Jeremiah in such a striking way that it seems very likely to have been consciously and deliberately done in this way at some point in the book's redaction history. It is inserted right in the heart of the narratives on the buildup to and events during the siege and fall of Jerusalem. Between Chapters 26–29 just before it, which deal with the increasing threat of Nebuchadrezzar and the first siege of Jerusalem and the deportation of the royal family to Babylon in 597, and Chapters 34–45 just after it, which focus on the second siege and fall of the city in 588–587 and the second deportation the following year – right in the heart of these narrative sections on the fall of Jerusalem comes the Book of Consolation. The center of the story, the thing the story is ultimately about, turns out not to be Yahweh's judgment – this turns out to be only the second most important part, although by far the most striking, both to the Judean characters in the story and to the reader. The Book of Consolation is alien to the narrative of destruction and divine punishment of Jerusalem, both in form (it is mostly in poetry) and in content. It is a visitation from without, from beyond the terms and frame of reference of that narrative. It is the promise beyond story of Yahweh's restoration to an even greater state of blessing as his covenant people, which says that beyond the divine anger there is new and everlasting divine love and blessing.

The phrase *shuv et shevut*, which the NRSV translates as to "restore the fortunes," occurs seven times in Chapters 30–33. Miller rightly observes, "In 30:3 and 33:26 the phrase serves as a kind of *inclusio*, or envelope, around these chapters, identifying their theme at the very beginning and end" (797). The phrase literally means something like to "turn around the captivity," that is, to restore the people of Judah from exile back to their full lives in the land. It is the heart of the message of the Book of Consolation, that Yahweh will turn back or turn away all the negative experience of the captivity of the people of Judah in and by Babylon and restore them not only to their former peace and prosperity, but to an even greater degree of peace and prosperity than he had previously blessed them with.

The verb *shuv*, to "turn back" or "turn away," is one of the words Jeremiah uses to describe Yahweh's call to the people of Judah who have broken their covenant relationship with him and are serving other gods. *Shuv* – turn, return, turn back to me, Yahweh tells the people of Judah through Jeremiah over and over again. If they will return, he will change his mind about their coming destruction. But they do not, and so in the Book of Consolation, it is Yahweh himself who becomes the subject of the verb *shuv*. Though he had called the people of Judah to "turn back" to him, they have not, and so he himself will "turn back" their punishment and their captivity and restore them to the fullness of covenant life in the land he promised to their ancestors. What the people of Judah proved unable or unwilling to do for their own blessing, Yahweh will do for them for their blessing. He will be the one to act for their redemption, ransom, and restoration. The refrain *shuv et shevut* puts Yahweh firmly in charge of blessing the people of Judah both in history and beyond

140　*The Bible as Literature*

it, into eschatology. In the end, it says, only he will be agent of restoration, and his intention is to be just that.

Not only does Yahweh promise a restoration of the covenant in the Book of Consolation, but he promises something new and better, a "new covenant" (31:31). If the Book of Consolation is the center of the Book of Jeremiah, then the promise of the new covenant in 31:31–34 and its gloss in 32:36–41 is the center of the center of the book. It is the vanishing point, toward which all else in the book points. Something new is coming, something unlike anything the people of Israel have ever seen or known before. "The days are surely coming, says the LORD, when I will make a new covenant with the house of Israel and the house of Judah" (31:31). It will not be like the Sinai covenant (31:32). Rather:

> I will put my law [*torah*] within them, and I will write it on their hearts; and I will be their God and they shall be my people. No longer shall they teach one another, or say to each other, "Know the LORD," for they shall all know me, from the least of them to the greatest. (31:33–34)

In the following chapter, Yahweh uses the very striking words in describing the "eternal" covenant that he will rejoice in doing good (*yatav*) to the people of Israel and Judah "with all my heart and all my soul [*be-chol libbi u-ve-chol naphshi*]" (32:40, 41). That is, he will act toward Israel as he asked them to act toward him in the Sinai covenant, to love him "with all your heart and all your soul [*be-chol levavcha u-ve-chol naphshecha*]" (Deut. 6:4). With the differences only of the person of the pronouns, exactly the same phrase is used here in Jeremiah as in Deuteronomy. Just as Yahweh asks for all of the love, all of the commitment, all of the life of his covenant people, he who is their good, so in the new covenant, he will bless them with as much passion, as much complete attention, with all of himself as he always wanted from them. The new covenant will be a mutually passionate relationship, each partner giving everything they have to the other, and finding the fulfilment of themselves thereby. There is also a certain humility in this formulation. In the new covenant, Yahweh will be stepping down to the level of the people of Israel, whom he created and called, and performing their part of the Sinai covenant as well as his own. Once again, at the very heart of its concerns, the Book of Consolation promises that Yahweh will be the agent of the restoration (in every sense imaginable) of the people of Israel. Their part of the Sinai covenant, which they were unable or unwilling to keep, Yahweh himself will keep in the new covenant. He will complete the circle of the Sinai covenant in the new covenant, and perform all the parts for the good of the people he made and loves with a constant and unfailing love.

Intimacy seems to be the heart of the new covenant. Yahweh says, "I will put my law within them, and I will write it on their hearts" (31:33). Under the new covenant, the Torah will exist within the people of Israel – primarily within them, rather than learned from a scroll or from oral teaching. Simply to be will be to know Yahweh. Exactly how this will be the case is not clear – it is neither stated nor imagined by the prophecy. The prose account of the everlasting covenant in the following chapter says that, under this covenant Yahweh "will put the fear of me in their hearts, so that they may not turn from me" (32:40). Some deeper, intimate, inherent knowledge of Yahweh is envisaged, which will involve the people of Israel being less able or willing than they have been thus far throughout their history to turn away from it in breaking the covenant relationship, especially in the form of serving other gods when they seem to offer greater benefits. The people of Israel, it seems, will all have a greater desire for, a greater love for Yahweh, a desire to keep his covenant that is simply stronger, so strong as to be almost irresistible, than anything they have experienced thus far. What this will look like, how this will work out in practice, is unsaid, because unsayable, but it is at the very heart of the message of the Book of Jeremiah. Something new is coming. Yahweh is bringing something new and better into being for his covenant people than anything they have seen, known, or even imagined before, and its nature will be blessing of a greater, profounder and more lasting kind than anything even he has done thus far.

TEXT FOR DISCUSSION

Gerard Manley Hopkins, "Thou art indeed just, Lord, if I contend"

The Jesuit poet Gerard Manley Hopkins (1844–1889) wrote this sonnet in the last year of his life, meditating on the relevance of one of Jeremiah's laments (Jer. 12:1–6) to his own experience. The Latin epigraph is the Vulgate translation of all but the last clause of Jeremiah 12:1.

Justus quidem tu es, Domine,

> si disputem tecum; verumtamen justa loquar ad te: quare via impiorum prosperatur? etc (Jerem. xii I.)

> Thou art indeed just, Lord, if I contend
> With thee; but, sir, so what I plead is just.
> Why do sinners' ways prosper? and why must
> Disappointment all I endeavour end?

> Wert thou my enemy, O thou my friend,
> How wouldst thou worse, I wonder, than thou dost
> Defeat, thwart me? Oh, the sots and thralls of lust
> Do in spare hours more thrive than I that spend,

> Sir, life upon thy cause. See, banks and brakes
> Now leavèd how thick! lacèd they are again
> With fretty chervil, look, and fresh wind shakes

> Them; birds build – but not I build; no, but strain,
> Time's eunuch, and not breed one work that wakes.
> Mine, O thou lord of life, send my roots rain.

142   *The Bible as Literature*

QUESTIONS

1. In the first two and a half lines of the sonnet Hopkins translates Jeremiah's words, and after that reflects on the meaning of them in his own life. The first thing he mentions (in ll. 3–4) is "disappointment" – in everything he tries to do, he seems to have failed. Jeremiah's lament, on the other hand, continues to complain of the unjust prosperity of the wicked (12:2–6). What do you make of Hopkins's reflection on his personal disappointments as he thinks of Jeremiah's laments? To what extent is this faithful to the Book of Jeremiah?
2. In the second quatrain of the poem Hopkins reflects that, in his experience, God seems more like an enemy than the friend proclaimed by his faith. What do you think of Hopkins feeling this way? To what extent is it faithful to the Book of Jeremiah, or to the Bible more generally?
3. Hopkins loves the natural world, where he sees God at work. In ll. 9–12, he thinks of the abundance in Spring of the river banks, the fields, the wind, and the birds building their nests. Only he does not seem to bear fruit. Here he thinks differently from Jeremiah, who complains, "How long will the land mourn / and the grass of every field wither? / For the wickedness of those who live in it / the animals and the birds are swept away" (12:4). For Jeremiah, the natural world too is ruined by the prosperity of the wicked; for Hopkins, it remains a source of comfort. Why does Hopkins think so differently from the prophet here?

Ezekiel

Introduction

The Book of Ezekiel is more clearly unified than those of Isaiah or Jeremiah. It is relatively clearly structured, and with just one exception the 14 date notices in the text are in chronological order, giving the impression, in Margaret Odell's words, of a "prophetic diary" (1). In his landmark commentary of 1969, Walther Zimmerli argued for a "school of Ezekiel," which "edited the prophecies of Ezekiel, commented upon them, and gave them a fuller theological exposition" (*Ezekiel 1* 70–71). These sympathetic disciples expanded the prophet's oracles in a style similar to his own, continuing the process of updating and reworking the prophecies that Ezekiel himself had already begun. As Daniel Block writes, "Theologically and dispositionally, the persons in these schools were genuine heirs of their founder, but they accepted the responsibility of editing and updating the prophet's original pronouncements and applying his teaching to new situations" (*Ezekiel 1-24* 19). Many scholars, particularly in the Anglophone world, still take a similar view. Paul Joyce argues that "there is much evidence to suggest a tenacious continuity of tradition, with regard to both content and style" in the Book of Ezekiel, in which "secondary material bears an unusually close 'family resemblance' to primary" (12–13). Andrew Mein adds, "Ezekiel's oracles have undoubtedly undergone some process of redaction, but it is possible, and even likely, that the process began with the prophet himself," describing the book as "largely the work of the prophet himself and of his exilic editors, who share a social context not radically dissimilar to Ezekiel's" (193). While some of the book may have been reworked in Jerusalem after the exile, it is largely complete by the end of the exilic period (Mein 193; Joyce 16; Darr 1087–1088). It is plausibly pointed out, against those scholars who see much later layers of redaction, that the book seems to show little interest in the conditions of life in Judah after the return from exile, but is almost entirely concerned with the situation of the exiles in Babylonia (Darr 1088; Mein 193).

The person of Ezekiel as he appears in the book is a strange and sometimes troubling character. Mid-twentieth-century scholars sometimes offered psychiatric diagnoses of him (Block, *Ezekiel 1-24* 10; Darr 1086; Mien 195; Zimmerli, *Ezekiel 1* 17–18). Contemporary scholars tend not to do so, with one or two exceptions. Notable among these is Daniel Smith-Christopher's view that, like many modern refugees in many different situations, he may suffer from what we now call post-traumatic stress disorder (Mien 195). Without presuming to diagnose, this view helpfully reminds us that, given his experiences in the siege of Jerusalem, the forced march to Babylonia, his living as a foreign captive an enormous distance from home, and then the total destruction of the society he left behind, Ezekiel is surely a person who has suffered considerable trauma.

Ezekiel's Call

The sheer surprise, shock, and confusion that the modern reader experiences throughout almost all of the Book of Ezekiel begins from the very start, with the extended call narrative of the prophet. Katherine Pfisterer Darr describes Ezekiel's inaugural vision of the divine chariot as "at once detailed and veiled" (1113), and she is right to say so. As Block puts it, the account is "dominated by the language of analogy," giving the sense that Ezekiel is "at a loss for words" to describe his vision adequately (*Ezekiel 1-24* 90). Even at the linguistic level, there are many morphological, grammatical, and stylistic oddities (Block, *Ezekiel 1-24* 89) that give the impression of Ezekiel's struggling to twist his language into an adequate form to describe what is beyond what it is ordinarily used for and has been developed for. The impression the inaugural vision primarily leaves upon the reader is the dual one of both astonishing detail and yet distance from a clear imaginative picture of what is being reported about Yahweh. Chapter 1 ends with the perfectly representative summary of the vision, that "this was the appearance [*mar'eh*] of the likeness [*demut*] of the glory [*kevod*] of the LORD" (1:28). We can only see Yahweh at three removes – we don't as readers see Yahweh, but rather his glory; we do not see his glory, but rather the likeness of his glory; and we do not even see the likeness of his glory, but rather the appearance of the likeness of his glory. This vision is rightly described as priestly – the text means that Yahweh is too holy to be brought directly

144   *The Bible as Literature*

into it. We can only look at him through three mirrors. Ezekiel relates his vision of Yahweh, but is careful to be clear that neither he nor his readers look directly at or therefore accurately describe the creator of heaven and earth, first because he is too holy to be looked at, known, or spoken about, and second because it is impossible for sight, knowledge, or language to do so. So Yahweh appears like Medusa in Perseus's shield – the text can only work in various tortured and tortuous ways around the absence of the unspeakable.

We begin with the four living creatures (*chayyot*). The spectacle Ezekiel presents is both dramatic and awesome but not precisely clear to the visual imagination of his reader from the very beginning. This continues throughout the theophany – it is not possible exactly to visualize either how the living creatures or their wheels or the structure of the throne chariot look. Indeed, Robert Alter suggests that "a certain bewilderment may well have been Ezekiel's intention" (1054). The living creatures (or to be precise, the likeness of living creatures) are "of human form" (1:5), with four faces, four wings, and hands beneath their wings. They have "the face of a human being, the face of a lion on the right side, the face of an ox on the left side, and the face of an eagle," the last presumably facing backward, as the face of the human being faces forward (1:10). Perhaps most surprisingly to the modern reader, they have "wheels" [*orphannim*], "one for each of the four of them," whose rims are "tall and awesome, and full of eyes [*einayim*] all around" (1:15, 18). The construction of the wheels is "something like a wheel within a wheel" (1:16), which is ultimately impossible in the text as whole to visualize clearly – as Block asks, "Are we to think of a gyroscope, or swiveling casters, or concentric wheels […], or inner and outer wheels operating at right angles to one another?" (*Ezekiel 1-24* 100).

Since the scene is so difficult to imagine precisely, it is very likely that Ezekiel intended the meaning to be at least partly symbolic. The dominant symbols, or the repeated and emphasized concepts throughout the scene, are, I would suggest, fire, the number four, mobility, and *ruach* (i.e., spirit, wind, or breath). Since it is so unusual to see eyes in the rims of wheels, and certainly without precedent in the Hebrew Bible, we should perhaps add eyes too. The number four is perhaps the most frequently repeated concept in the vision. Especially when taken together with the intensely visualized mobility of the theophany, this number seems most likely to indicate the four winds, the four directions, the four corners of the earth – that is to say, everywhere. The prevalence of the number four in the vision seems to indicate the concept of everywhere, of all places and points on the earth. As Darr puts it, "Four represents totality" (1130; cf. Block 97; Odell 27). Ezekiel's vision of God is first a vision of God's presence everywhere. At all points on the earth – Jerusalem, Judah, and among the exiles in Babylonia – Yahweh, whose likeness Ezekiel sees, is the God, the covenant God, of all the earth, no less present to the humiliated exiles in Babylonia with whom Ezekiel lives now than in the glorious cult of the Jerusalem temple in which he was brought up to serve.

The wheels say something similar. Ezekiel is clearly impressed, almost to the point of being overwhelmed, by the wheels of the throne chariot. As Block observes, he describes them with considerable redundancy (*Ezekiel 1-24* 101). Ezekiel had seen cultic objects with wheels in the Temple in Jerusalem. But the wheels that are

The Prophets 145

part of his vision of the living creatures are nothing like these. They are "tall" and "awesome," and they are awesome in particular because their rims are "full of eyes all around." Some nine times in 1:19–21 alone Ezekiel emphasizes the wonder and complexity of their movement in relation to each other and to the living creatures. This is an overwhelming vision of movement. The vision of the wheels is a vision of the ease, power, and wonder with which God's glory moves. It is not only a vision of Yahweh's presence in Babylonia; it is a vision of his ability, with the greatest of ease and power, to be present anywhere, at any time, to any of his covenant people he chooses. The connotation of the "eyes" with which the rims of the wheels are studded is similar. The Hebrew word for "eye," *ayin*, is used twice in Ezekiel's opening vision to indicate the "gleaming" of a bright object (1:16; 1:4). Many commentators argue as a result that shining gems or nails are denoted in the wheels' "eyes all around" (Darr 1116; Block 100-1; Odell 28). While this may be the primary referent of the "eyes" in the rims of the wheels, though, the connotation of literal eyes remains strong in the vision. Zimmerli argues that they symbolize the "all-seeing power of the Rider of the throne-chariot" (*Ezekiel 1* 129). There is certainly a secondary sense, in my view, in which this is true. The vision of the wheels is one in which God moves with as much ease throughout the earth as he sees. His glory moves with the speed and effortlessness of the glance of an eye.

Surprising as it may be to say, then, given the bizarre and overwhelming visual and verbal qualities of Ezekiel's opening vision, this opening vision is ultimately one of comfort. The context in which Ezekiel sees the vision provides the heart of its meaning. That context is the destruction of everything in which the people of Israel had believed for centuries about God, their land, their king, and their temple. Ezekiel writes at a time and a place in which everything in heaven and earth, from Yahweh himself down, has been destroyed, utterly destroyed, with no hope of its ever being rebuilt. He has watched the brutal sack of Jerusalem by the army of an angry emperor punishing a rebellious vassal. He has watched the trail of tears of the long forced march to Babylonia, accompanied daily by death, sickness, rape, and brutality. He has seen the Temple looted, and its sacred treasures defiled and dumped in the Babylonian treasury. As Odell puts it, "Ezekiel writes, not in the midst of a crisis, but at the end of history" (9). As Block puts it equally clearly, "Based on appearances, Marduk, the god of Babylon, had prevailed" (*Ezekiel 1-24* 8).

It is in this context of complete disaster that Ezekiel receives the opening vision of his book. Frightening, bizarre, and ultimately incomprehensible as it is, this grand vision of Yahweh among the exiles in Babylonia is one of great hope and comfort. It means that Yahweh is here. He is still here, the God of heaven and earth; he is still all-powerful; he still sees, watches over, and cares for his covenant people. He is as close to them in Babylonia as he was above the cherubim in the holy of holies in the Jerusalem temple. Indeed, this is surely part of the significance of the similarity of the living creatures of the opening vision to the cherubim in the Jerusalem temple (Exod. 25:17–22). This vision is one of hope. As Ezekiel will prophesy, a new covenant is coming, and the opening vision makes that clear visually. Yahweh is here, he is everywhere; and though he will begin by punishing

146   *The Bible as Literature*

the house of Israel for their faithlessness to the covenant, he will restore and renew that covenant forever.

Ezekiel's Sign-Acts

Ezekiel is the prophet who performs the most sign-acts. Previous prophets had performed prophetic signs, but none performs as many as Ezekiel. Perhaps Ezekiel's most striking sign-act is his enactment of the siege of Jerusalem, which will take place several years later, between 588 and 586 BCE. Ezekiel portrays the city of Jerusalem on a clay brick (a common contemporary practice in Babylonia), carving the map or picture before the clay is fired. He then builds a model siege wall, ramp, camps, and battering rams all around it. He then takes an iron plate (or griddle) and follows Yahweh's instruction to "place it as an iron wall between you and the city" (4:3). So he sets up a model city of Jerusalem surrounded by realistic and effective siege works, lies down facing this model, and places a plate of iron in between his own face and the model city. The iron plate seems to symbolize the inflexible, immovable barrier between God, whose gaze would be represented by that of Ezekiel, and the city of Jerusalem. It seems to indicate that his anger, his judgment, symbolized by Ezekiel's "setting his face" toward the city, is no more susceptible of being removed than a wall of iron.

The bizarre and disturbing nature of Ezekiel's performance has only just begun. Lying on his side with his face toward the model city, Ezekiel is told by Yahweh to lie on his left side, presumably facing the model of the city under siege, for 390 days, "equal to the number of years of [the] punishment" (or "guilt," *avon*) of the house of Israel (4:5). In doing so, he "shall bear the punishment" (*nasa avon*) of the house of Israel. After these 390 days facing the model of the besieged city on his left side, Ezekiel then lies down on his right side and does the same thing for 40 days, "one day for each year," to "bear the punishment of the house of Judah" (4:6). Furthermore, in a way that is ultimately unexplained and not clearly visualizable, Yahweh tells Ezekiel, "I am putting cords on you so that you cannot turn from one side to the other until you have completed the days of your siege" (4:8). Does someone physically tie Ezekiel up, representing Yahweh as he does so, here, or are the "cords" more metaphorical, indicating that Ezekiel either cannot or does not move in response to Yahweh's command? It is not clear. All that is clear is that the spectacle is an extremely unpleasant one.

Ezekiel makes siege rations for himself – bread out of numerous grains and beans, symbolizing that there will not be enough of any single foodstuff to feed the citizens of Jerusalem under siege. The Talmud records an experiment in which a dog refused to eat the kind of bread Ezekiel made, so unpalatable are the rations (Darr 1148). Yahweh initially tells Ezekiel, "You shall eat it as a barley-cake, baking it in their sight on human dung," symbolizing the fact that "thus shall the people of Israel eat their bread, unclean, among the nations to which I will drive them" (4:13). The ritual uncleanness of human dung, as well surely as its social taboo, is deeply upsetting to Ezekiel, who protests, "Ah LORD God, I have never defiled myself" in any way, from my youth onward, and so Yahweh compromises, saying, "I will let you have cow dung instead of human dung, on which you may prepare your bread" (4:14–15). This is as disturbing to read about as the entire spectacle must have been to watch. The passionate and devoted priest, deeply committed to ritual purity on behalf of the covenant community, is reduced to pleading with God over which kind of dung he will cook his bread over, human or animal. This is deeply destructive of his identity as a priest, as is his next sign-act, shaving his head and beard, which were taboo actions for priests (Lev. 21:5; cf. 19:27). Everything Ezekiel holds most dear about his identity is being broken down by Yahweh in this sign-act.

Ezekiel's sign-acts are terrible to look at, and signify something even more terrible than they appear in themselves, the total destruction of Jerusalem, its culture, and its religion. They signify the end of the world. The only thing worse than the performance of the sign-acts themselves are the things they signify, that things are only going to get worse for the people of Israel. They say that this is what faithlessness to the covenant on behalf the people of Israel looks like. It looks like disaster upon disaster. Restoration may follow, but first will come the complete destruction of all Yahweh has promised Israel on the condition that they kept the covenant. If Ezekiel's sign-acts are bizarre, disturbing, and unsettling, they are intended to be so. Yahweh is against Israel, and will not help even a remnant of them until his faithless people have been broken down out of their long history of faithlessness to him.

The Valley of Dry Bones

In January 585, Ezekiel gets news in Babylonia that Jerusalem has been destroyed several months earlier (33:21). Before then, much of his book had concerned judgment; thereafter much of it concerns restoration. Perhaps the most striking of his prophecies of restoration is the vision of the valley of dry bones. Ezekiel is taken "by the spirit of the LORD" to the middle of a valley, which is "full of bones" (37:1). Ezekiel is impressed by how many there are, and how dry they are – "there were very many lying in the valley, and they were very dry" (37:2). Later in the vision, Yahweh calls them "these slain [*rugim*]" (37:9), indicating that they have died in battle. In the following verse they are called a *chayil*, which can mean an "army." Ezekiel sees the remains of the corpses of an enormous and terrible battle, that has happened long ago, which never received proper burial. There are very many of these corpses, now reduced only to bones, and these bones have long been bleached under the Mesopotamian sun. Block makes the plausible speculation that, faced with a vision of the slain on an enormous battlefield, Ezekiel's mind may have gone to the slain among the citizens of Jerusalem who had just died in their failed defense of the city against Nebuchadnezzar's army (*Ezekiel 25-48* 377). As a priest, he would have been unclean in the presence of improperly buried corpses. Again, this vision is personally traumatic, uncomfortable, and unpleasant for Ezekiel, breaking down his identity as an Israelite and a priest, and forcing him to rethink that identity in the new form demanded by Yahweh.

148   *The Bible as Literature*

Ezekiel's experience as a priest is also at work in his vision of the way in which the dry bones come together. His experience of dissecting animals for sacrifice (Zimmerli, *Ezekiel 2* 260) makes him familiar with the series of bones, sinews, flesh, skin (and ultimately breath), in which the multitude on the valley floor come together. What he has done as a priest, he watches Yahweh undo in his vision. Yahweh tells Ezekiel, "These bones are the whole house of Israel [*kol bet yisra'el*]" (37:11). The people of Israel in Babylonia, he goes on, are saying, "Our bones are dried up, and our hope is lost; we are cut off completely." In Hebrew, these three phrases are each two words, with rhyming and assonantal endings:

> *yavshú atsmoténu,*
> *ve-avedáh tiqvaténu,*
> *nigzárnu lánu.*

Zimmerli hears the sounds of a lament in these endings (*Ezekiel 2* 262). The words may reflect actual expressions used by Ezekiel's fellow exiles (Darr 1501). But above all they reflect the sentiment of the exiles, that all is lost and will always remain so, and it is to this sentiment that Ezekiel's vision responds. They feel that Yahweh has abandoned them. They did not even have the decency of a proper burial; their bones are lying unclean on the ground for scavengers to pick at. Ezekiel prophesies to them in effect, "This is how you feel, house of Israel, and you are right to feel this way. This is who you are; this is the judgement your faithlessness to the covenant brought upon you." And to these people, to these exiles, broken down beyond all breaking down, he now prophesies, "Thus says the Lord GOD; I am going to open your graves, O my people, and I will bring you back to the land of Israel" (37:12). The restoration Yahweh is going to bring about for his effectively dead exiled people is going to be a transformation so enormous, so complete as to be best understood by resurrection miracles like those of Elijah and Elisha in the Deuteronomistic history, in which corpses became living and flourishing human beings again. What Yahweh is going to do is impossible and miraculous. It cannot be done, but that will not stop him. He is going to do it anyway.

The River of Life

The Book of Ezekiel is one of the best aesthetically structured books in the whole of the Hebrew Bible. This in nowhere more the case than in its climactic fourth and final vision of a new, transformed Israel. Ezekiel sees this vision in several ways. He sees the Temple compound, measured in precise detail. He is instructed in detail in the *torah*, the rituals, of the new Temple. He sees the geographic boundaries of the new spaces and institutions of the land, which is divided up equally among the 12 tribes, *ish ke-achiv*, literally "each man like his brother" (47:14). Finally, and most strikingly, the vision takes on a symbolic, eschatological form. Ezekiel sees water flowing from the Temple. It flows eastward from the door of the temple itself, and eastward out of the outer gate of the Temple compound. As it flows beyond the outer gate, it gets deeper. Ezekiel's heavenly guide measures it every thousand cubits, and

The Prophets   149

it becomes ankle-deep, then knee-deep, then waist-deep, then uncrossable (47:3–5). Many trees grow on its banks. The heavenly guide tells the prophet:

> This water flows towards the eastern region and goes down into the Arabah; and when it enters the sea, the sea of stagnant waters, the water will become fresh [...] It will become fresh; and everything will live where the river goes. (47:8–9)

The symbolism of this part of the vision is as beautiful as it is clear. Right relationship with Yahweh in the new, restored Israel will turn it back into paradise. The vision deliberately picks up and develops the imagery of Eden in Genesis 2:

> The LORD God planted a garden in Eden, in the east, and there he put the man whom he had formed. Out of the ground the LORD God made to grow every tree that is pleasant to the sight and good for food [...] A river flows out of Eden to water the garden, and from there it divides and becomes four branches. (Gen. 2:8, 10)

This river waters the whole of the known world (Gen. 2:10–14). Ezekiel sees a vision of the new Israel as a new Eden. Right relationship with Yahweh in this society to come will transform every kind of current relationship into a good one. Even the land itself will bloom and flourish into a paradise on earth for the people of Israel. The desert of the Arabah will be irrigated by a deep, fresh river, in which "every living creature that swarms will live" (47:9). The dead, poisoned, almost unhabitable Dead Sea will "become fresh" and "there will be very many fish." The trees along its banks will bear fruit, not just annually, but "fresh fruit every month," and "their leaves will be for healing" (47:12).

The subordinate clause in 47:12 makes the cause of the miraculous transformation of the land clear: "Their leaves will not wither or fail, but they will bear fresh fruit every month, because [*ki*] the water for them flows from the sanctuary." In Ezekiel's vision, the water flowing from the Temple to the Dead Sea turns the land into paradise again precisely because it flows from the Temple. When Yahweh dwells in holiness at the personal, social, and political center of Israel, everything will change. All relationships will heal, even that of the people with the land itself. Ezekiel sees a time when Adam's curse will be revoked, and the people of Israel will live in a society most comparable to Eden again. Yahweh at the center of their lives will extend not only geographically throughout the country in equitable relationships but physically, as the semi-arid land truly becomes one flowing with milk and honey for the first time.

TEXT FOR DISCUSSION

William Blake, *The Marriage of Heaven and Hell*

> *The English poet, engraver, and visionary William Blake (1757–1827) wrote this text in 1790, parodying his former master, the Christian mystic Emanuel Swedenborg, whose texts included philosophical discourses*

150　*The Bible as Literature*

> *followed by a "Memorable Relation," describing a vision in which he was carried up to heaven.*

A Memorable Fancy

The Prophets Isaiah and Ezekiel dined with me, and I asked them how they dared so roundly to assert that God spoke to them, and whether they did not think at the time that they would be misunderstood, and so be the cause of imposition.

Isaiah answered: "I saw no God, nor heard any, in a finite organical perception: but my senses discovered the infinite in everything; and as I was then persuaded, and remained confirmed, that the voice of honest indignation is the voice of God, I cared not for consequences, but wrote." [...]

Then Ezekiel said: "The philosophy of the East taught the first principles of human perception; some nations held one principle for the origin, and some another. We of Israel taught that the Poetic Genius (as you now call it) was the first principle, and all the others merely derivative, which was the cause of our despising the Priests and Philosophers of other countries, and prophesying that all Gods would at last be proved to originate in ours, and to be the tributaries of the Poetic Genius.

"This," said he, "like all firm persuasions, is come to pass, for all nations believe the Jews' code, and worship the Jews' God; and what greater subjection can be?" [...]

I then asked Ezekiel why he ate dung, and lay so long on his right and left side. He answered: "The desire of raising other men into a perception of the infinite. This the North American tribes practise. And is he honest who resists his genius or conscience, only for the sake of present ease or gratification?"

QUESTIONS

1. I have included a portion of Blake's conversation with Isaiah because it seems to me that Isaiah's answer articulates Blake's view of biblical prophecy in general. Isaiah says that he never saw or heard God as one would another person, but rather that he "discovered the infinite in everything" with his senses. What do you think of this view of biblical prophecy? To what extent is it faithful to the books either of Isaiah or of Ezekiel?
2. Isaiah also answers that "the voice of honest indignation is the voice of God," which seems to express Blake's view of biblical prophecy. What do you think of this view? To what extent does it represent the books of Isaiah or Ezekiel?
3. Ezekiel tells Blake that the Hebrew Scriptures teach that God, who creates the world in Genesis 1–2, is "the Poetic Genius." That is, God is a supreme

imaginative poet, from whom all creative works (including the mythologies of the ancient worlds) derive. What do you think of this view? In what sense does the Bible teach that God is best understood in terms of the poetic imagination?

4. Blake asks Ezekiel about his shocking sign-acts, and the prophet replies that he did them with a view to "raising other men into a perception of the infinite." What do you think of this interpretation of Ezekiel's sign-acts?

5. Finally, Blake compares Ezekiel's determination to raise others to a perception of the infinite, though this means personal hardship, to the religious practices of American Indians. Presumably he is thinking of physically demanding religious initiation rituals. What do you think of Blake's view that Ezekiel's motivation as a prophet can be found throughout the world?

Works Cited

Allen, Leslie C. *Jeremiah: A Commentary*. Westminster John Knox, 2008.

Alter, Robert. *The Hebrew Bible, Vol. 2: Prophets*. W. W. Norton, 2019.

Blenkinsopp, Joseph. *Isaiah 1-39: A New Translation with Introduction and Commentary*. Doubleday, 2000.

———. *Isaiah 40-55: A New Translation with Introduction and Commentary*. Doubleday, 2002.

———. *Isaiah 56-66: A New Translation with Introduction and Commentary*. Doubleday, 2003.

Block, Daniel I. *The Book of Ezekiel: Chapters 1-24*. William B. Eerdmans, 1997.

———. *The Book of Ezekiel: Chapters 25-48*. William B. Eerdmans, 1998.

Childs, Brevard S. *Isaiah*. Westminster John Knox Press, 2001.

Darr, Katheryn Pfisterer. "Ezekiel." *The New Interpreter's Bible*, vol. 6, edited by Leander Keck et al., Abingdon Press, 2001, pp. 1073–1607.

Fretheim, Terence E. *Jeremiah*. Smyth and Helwys, 2002.

Goldingay, John, and David F. Payne. *A Critical and Exegetical Commentary on Isaiah 40-55, Vol. 1: Introduction and Commentary to Isaiah 40:1-44:23*. T&T Clark, 2006.

Joyce, Paul M. *Ezekiel: A Commentary*. T&T Clark, 2007.

Leuchter, Mark, "Jeremiah: Structure, Themes, and Contested Issues." *The Oxford Handbook of the Prophets*, edited by Carolyn J. Sharp, Oxford UP, 2016, pp. 171–89.

Lundbom, Jack R. *Jeremiah 1-20*. Yale UP, 1999.

Mein, Andrew. "Ezekiel: Structures, Themes, and Contested Issues." *The Oxford Handbook of the Prophets*, edited by Carolyn J. Sharp. Oxford UP, 2016, pp. 190–206.

Miller, Patrick D. "Jeremiah." *The New Interpreter's Bible*, edited by Leander Keck et al., vol. 6, Abingdon Press, 2001, pp. 553–926.

Odell, Margaret S. *Ezekiel*. Smyth and Helwys, 2005.

Seitz, Christopher R. *Isaiah 1-39*. Westminster John Knox Press, 1993.

———. "Isaiah 40-66." *The New Interpreter's Bible*, vol. 6, edited by Leander Keck et al., Abingdon Press, 2001, pp. 307–552.

152   *The Bible as Literature*

Tucker, Gene M. "Isaiah 1-39." *The New Interpreter's Bible*, vol. 6, edited by Leander Keck et al., Abingdon Press, 2001, pp. 25–305.

Tull, Patricia K. *Isaiah 1-39*. Smyth & Helwys, 2010.

Zimmerli, Walther. *Ezekiel 1: A Commentary on the Book of the Prophet Ezekiel, Chapters 1-24*. Translated by Ronald E. Clements, Fortress Press, 1979.

———. *Ezekiel 2: A Commentary on the Book of the Prophet Ezekiel, Chapters 25-48*. Translated by James D. Martin, Fortress Press, 1983.

7 The Gospels

The Synoptic Gospels

The "Synoptic Gospels" is the name scholars have given to the Gospels of Matthew, Mark, and Luke since the late eighteenth century, when the German scholar Johann Jakob Griesbach published his *Synopsis of the Gospels of Matthew, Mark, and Luke* (1776), with the three Gospels laid out in parallel columns so that they could be "viewed together" (which is what the word "synopsis" means). This arrangement clarifies the complex series of similarities and differences in the texts of the first three Gospels, which has become known as the "synoptic problem."

Matthew, Mark, and Luke contain a large amount of similar material, similar in content, wording, and sequence. In some passages there is almost complete verbatim agreement. The material found in all three Synoptic Gospels is known as the "triple tradition," and is mostly narrative in nature. Most of Mark's Gospel comprises triple tradition material. The material shared by Matthew and Luke but absent from Mark is known as the "double tradition," and it mostly contains sayings of Jesus. See Table 7.1. The material found only in Matthew or only in Luke is known as Special Matthew (or M) and Special Luke (or L). See Tables 7.2 and 7.3. As Mark Goodacre points out, "there are also passages that blur these neat categories," such as the Temptation of Jesus (Matt. 4:1–11 // Mark 1:12–13 // Luke 4:1–13), which "might be described as half-way between double tradition and triple tradition" ("Synoptic Problem" 357).

The solution to the synoptic problem that dominated New Testament scholarship from the end of the nineteenth century until the second half of the twentieth century is known (among other names) as the Two Source Hypothesis. Some version of it is still widely held and taught. It argues that Mark was the first Gospel written, and that Matthew and Luke used both Mark in writing their Gospels and a second, now lost, source known as "Q" (from the German word *Quelle*, "source"). Furthermore, Matthew and Luke use material found only in their Gospels. In this sense, the theory can also be called the Four Source Hypothesis. See Figure 7.1.

As Stanley Porter and Brian Dyer write, "Since the bulk of material shared by Matthew and Luke consists of sayings of Jesus, it is often hypothesized that Q was a 'sayings source' that began as oral traditions that were eventually written down" (19). Notably, Q is thought not to have contained a passion narrative. Special

DOI: 10.4324/9781315751566-8

154   *The Bible as Literature*

Table 7.1 The Double Tradition

THE DOUBLE TRADITION

Below is some of the material that appears in both Matthew and Luke but not in Mark:
• The Beatitudes (Matt. 5:3–12 // Luke 6:20–23)
• The Lord's Prayer (Matt. 6:9–15 // Luke 11:2–4)
• Turning the Other Cheek (Matt. 5:38–42 // Luke 6:29–30)
• Loving One's Enemies (Matt. 5:43–48 // Luke 6:27–28, 32–36)
• The Golden Rule (Matt 7:12 // Luke 6:31)
• The Parable of the Lost Sheep (Matt. 18:10–14 // Luke 15:3–7)
• The Parable of the Talents (Matt. 25:14–30 // Luke 19:12–27)
• The Parable of the Wedding Banquet (Matt. 22:1–14 // Luke 14:15–24)

Table 7.2 Special Matthew

SPECIAL MATTHEW

Some of the material that appears only in Matthew's Gospel:
• The Visit of the Magi (Matt. 2:1–12)
• The Flight to Egypt (Matt. 2:13–23)
• The Parables of the Hidden Treasure / Pearl of Great Price (Matt. 13:44–46)
• The Parable of the Laborers in the Vineyard (Matt. 20:1–16)
• Parable of the Ten Virgins (Matt. 25:1–13)
• The Sheep and the Goats (Matt. 25:31–46)

Table 7.3 Special Luke

SPECIAL LUKE

Some of material that appears only in Luke's Gospel:
• The Annunciation (Luke 1:26–38)
• The Magnificat (Luke 1:39–56)
• The Parable of the Good Samaritan (Luke 10:25–37)
• The Parable of the Prodigal Son (Luke 15:11–32)
• The Parable of the Pharisee and the Tax Collector (Luke 18:9–14)

Matthew and Special Luke probably derive from a range of sources, both oral and written, and may well have been "prone to influence from Matthew and Luke's creative minds" (Goodacre, "Synoptic Problem" 356). We should also note that such diagrams as Figure 7.1 and Figure 7.2 are "necessarily simpler that the reality that they are trying to represent" and that there are other "complexities that need to be taken into account, such as differing editions of each of the Gospels and the presence of oral traditions that will have supplemented and interacted with the written texts" (Goodacre, "Farrer Hypothesis" 48).

The Gospels 155

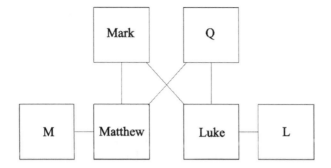

Figure 7.1 The Two Source Hypothesis

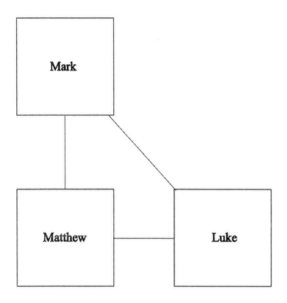

Figure 7.2 The Farrer Hypothesis

The next most widely held solution to the Synoptic Problem is the Farrer Hypothesis. This theory shares the position of the Two Source hypothesis that Mark was the first Gospel written. However, the theologian Austin Farrer, for whom the hypothesis is named, argued that the view of the Two Source Hypothesis that Matthew and Luke were written independently of each other, and so that the hypothetical source Q was needed to explain their non-Markan agreements, was wrong. Rather, he argues, Luke seems to be familiar with Matthew's Gospel, and so the need for Q disappears. Hence the alternative name "L/M" for this hypothesis, because it posits that Luke follows Matthew. See Figure 7.2.

156   *The Bible as Literature*

There are other hypotheses in addition to the two we have mentioned, most notable among which is an increased emphasis on the role of oral tradition in the formation of the Synoptic Gospels.

Matthew

Introduction

As we have seen, most New Testament scholars think that Mark's Gospel is the earliest of the Synoptic Gospels. It is commonly dated at about 70 CE. Since most also agree that Matthew used Mark as a source, Matthew's Gospel must have been written sometime after that date. Based on the earliest extant references to the Gospel, many scholars opt for a date in or near the 80s CE. Most hypothesize that it was written in Antioch or perhaps another city in Syria (where Matthew mentions Jesus's fame spreading, unlike any other evangelist [Matt. 4:24]). Galilee is also increasingly proposed.

Matthew was probably a Jewish Christian. His Gospel is interested in Jewish questions such as the Sabbath, dietary laws, Corban, and the Temple. He continues to use the Jewish tradition of not directly using the name of God, almost always using the phrase "the kingdom of heaven," in contrast to the other evangelists' use of "the kingdom of God" (Witherington 2; Boring 97). On the other hand, Matthew also has many texts that "reflect an alienation from Judaism" (Boring 97), reflecting both conflict and fluidity within and between the Jewish and Christian communities of his time. He is a Greek-speaking Jew – the Greek of his Gospel does not seem to be a translation (Culpepper, *Matthew* 14; Witherington 29). He may have been a scribe or a teacher in his community. Many scholars think that Matthew 13:52 gives a clue to the way in which the evangelist understood his own work: "Every scribe [*grammateus*] who has been trained [*mathēteutheis*] for the kingdom of heaven is like the master of a household who brings out of his treasure what is new [*kaina*] and what is old [*palaia*]" (Matt. 13:12). The name "Matthew" was probably ascribed to the author of the Gospel in the late first or early second century CE (Culpepper, *Matthew* 17; Witherington 5; Konradt 17; Luz, *Matthew 1-7* 59; Boring 106), perhaps because of his story of the call of the tax collector Matthew (Matt. 9:9), who is called "Levi" in Mark (Mark 2:14) (Konradt 17; Boring 107).

Jesus's Parables

Perhaps the most distinctive form of Jesus's teaching in the Synoptic Gospels is the parable. The Greek word translated as "parable" in the Synoptic Gospels is *parabolē*. The verb *paraballō* literally means to "throw beside," but in practice means to "throw before" or "throw to." It comes also to mean to "compare" or "liken," in the sense that, in a comparison, one thing is as it were "thrown beside" another. The Greek noun is almost always used in the LXX to translate the Hebrew noun *mashal*, which has a broad range of meanings. It refers to any

The Gospels   157

kind of formed or poetic language, above all language that is poetic in the Hebrew sense of using parallelism. The verb *mashal* from which the noun comes means to "be like" or to "be similar," and the noun *mashal* therefore seems to mean speech in which one thing is compared to another, particularly in the form of the parallelism that characterizes Hebrew poetry. The word "proverb" is perhaps the most frequent meaning of the term. The wise ethical sayings characteristic of the Book of Proverbs are frequently called *meshalim* (Prov. 1:1; 1:6; 10:1; Eccles. 12:9; 1 Kings 4:32; Job 13:12). In Psalms 49:4 and 78:2, the *mashal* constitutes the poetic discourse of the entire psalm, and Job's poetic addresses to God are also called *meshalim* at Job 27:1 and 29:1. When the Synoptic Gospel writers use the word *parabolē* to describe the kinds of sayings in which Jesus taught, they are using a word that, like the Hebrew word *mashal* before it, indicates that Jesus's sayings are wise ethical maxims; that they are characterized by poetic language, in the sense that they are aesthetically crafted to be memorable and of lasting significance to the hearer; and that the essence of these sayings is the comparison between one thing and another.

The Theory of Parables

In Matthew's Gospel, Jesus's teaching in parables begins in Chapter 13. Matthew's source Mark had arranged a series of parables about the kingdom of God in Mark 4:1–20, 26–34, which Matthew has significantly expanded and developed. In Matthew's Gospel, after Jesus's first parable, "the disciples came and asked him, 'Why do you speak to them in parables?'" (Matt. 13:10). Jesus replies:

> To you it has been given to know the secrets [*musteria*] of the kingdom of heaven, but to them it has not been given […] The reason I speak to them in parables is that [*hoti*] "seeing they do not perceive, and hearing they do not listen, nor do they understand." With them indeed is fulfilled the prophecy of Isaiah that says:
>> "You will indeed listen, but never understand,
>>> and you will indeed look but never perceive.
>> For this people's heart has grown dull,
>>> and their ears are hard of hearing,
>>>> and they have shut their eyes;
>>>>> so that they might not [*mēpote*] look with their eyes,
>>>> and listen with their ears,
>>> and understand with their heart and turn –
>>>> and I would heal them."
>
> (Matt. 13:11, 13–15)

This is a hard saying. Alan Culpepper describes Mark's version of this teaching as "one of the most difficult passages in the Gospel" (*Mark* 136). In fact, the Hebrew text of Isaiah 6:9–10, which Matthew cites in full here, is even harsher than the

158   *The Bible as Literature*

LXX translation that Matthew quotes. In the MT, the verbs are in the imperative. The quote below emphasizes these imperatives with bold type:

> [The Lord] said, "Go and say to this people:
> '**Keep listening** but **do not comprehend**;
> **keep looking**, but **do not understand**.'
> **Make** the mind of this people **dull**
>   and **stop** their ears,
>   and **shut** their eyes."

(Isa. 6:9–10)

The LXX, however, perhaps wanting to avoid the theology that these imperatives imply, turns them into indicatives (that is, from commands to statements; from "Listen!" to "you will listen," etc.). The LXX reads (with verbs in the indicative in bold type):

> [The Lord] said, "Go and say to this people:
> **You will indeed listen**, but never **understand**,
>   and **you will indeed look** but never **perceive**.
> For this people's heart **has grown dull**,
>   and their ears **are hard of hearing**,
> and **they have shut** their eyes.

(Isa. 6:9–10, LXX)

In the MT, God commissions Isaiah to tell the people of Judah not to understand his message. The implication is that Yahweh is so angry with his people that he does not want them to be healed by turning back to him. But in the LXX, God does not say this. Rather, he is angry *that* his people do not understand. He does not tell Isaiah that they should not see, hear, or understand; rather, he tells Isaiah that in fact they do not see, hear, or understand. The fact that they do not turn to God in the LXX is their choice.

So Matthew's LXX Bible has already softened the message of Isaiah 6:9–10 in the Hebrew Bible. Matthew himself seems also to try to soften Mark's account, which gives only the summary rather than the full quotation of Isaiah 6:9–10. In Mark, Jesus says that he speaks in parables "in order that [*hina*]" people will not understand and be healed (Mark 4:12). In Matthew, Jesus says that he speaks in parables "because [*hoti*]" people do not understand and become healed. As with the LXX translation of the MT, Matthew suggests that people's lack of understanding is their responsibility rather than God's. Nevertheless the saying remains hard, since Jesus seems to be saying that only some people will understand his parables, that others will not, and that this is the reason for his use of the form.

Several things need to be taken into account in understanding what Jesus says about his teaching in parables. First, the context in which Matthew (like Mark) places Jesus's first series of parables about the kingdom of God is significant.

The Gospels 159

The person and teaching of Jesus are being increasingly rejected, above all by the religious leaders of the Jewish people. In Matthew 11–12, Jesus speaks of the way in which this generation has rejected him and judged him as unrighteous for keeping company with sinners (11:16–19). Even in the cities where he has performed miracles, he is rejected (11:20–24). The Pharisees plot to kill him for healing on the Sabbath (12:9–14), and call his exorcisms the work of the devil (12:24). Directly after the series of parables in Matthew 13:1–53, Jesus is rejected even in his hometown of Nazareth (13:54–58). In Mark's Gospel, they think he has gone mad (Mark 3:22). These are the people, those who reject Jesus's teaching, above all the scribes and the Pharisees with their power to influence the people they teach, whom Matthew has in mind when Jesus tells his disciples, "To them it has not been given" to know the secrets of the kingdom of heaven (Matt. 13:10). No doubt readers are also to think of the chief priests and elders who successfully conspire against Jesus at the end of the Gospel. Matthew does not seem to mean that Jesus wants only some of those who hear his parables to understand them and live accordingly. Rather, as Eugene Boring puts it, he has placed Jesus's first series of parables within the context of the increasing opposition to Jesus's teaching from the people of Judea and their religious leaders, in such a way that "Jesus's parables in 13:3b-52 are his commentary on the meaning of his rejection by Israel and the founding of the new community" (300). For several New Testament writers, as the early Christian community dealt with the question why the people of Israel to whom the Messiah was sent largely rejected him, Isaiah 6:9–10 seems to have been a proof text that this had been prophesied in the Scriptures (Mark 4:12; Luke 8:10; John 12:40; Acts 28:26–27; cf. Rom. 11:8). Matthew, like Mark before him, associates the often demanding form of Jesus's parables with the fact that, from Matthew's Christian perspective, not all of the people of Israel understood what Jesus meant in them by the "secrets of the kingdom of heaven" (Matt. 13:11).

Second, Jesus tells his disciples that his parables divide their hearers into two groups, those who see, hear, and understand; and those who do not. As many commentators point out, however, there is no indication in Matthew's Gospel that a person cannot cross the boundary between those two groups. As Boring puts it, "Only insiders understand. But all are invited to become insiders" (305). In Matthias Konradt's words, Matthew 13:13–15 "does not say that, for the individual, this situation is irreversible [...] A change of mind is by no means excluded from the outset" (207). This is true. There are many other passages in Matthew's Gospel that repeatedly emphasize Jesus's concern for and preaching to the crowds who follow him wherever he goes. Matthew often speaks of Jesus's compassion for the crowds (Matt. 9:36; 14:14; 15:32). There is no suggestion in Matthew's Gospel that Jesus does not want his message of the kingdom of God to be understood by everyone. Rather, his citation of Isaiah 6:9–10 indicates his awareness of the fact that not everyone does in fact understand. We might add that, even in the Book of Isaiah, prophecies of judgment like Isaiah 6:9–12 are always followed by prophecies of compassion like Isaiah 9:1–7, which Matthew also applies to Jesus (Matt. 4:15–16).

160   *The Bible as Literature*

The Laborers in the Vineyard

One of the many parables that asks the hearer or reader to see, hear, and understand the secrets of the kingdom of heaven is the parable of the laborers in the vineyard, which is unique to Matthew (Matt. 20:1–16). Like many of Jesus's parables, this one sets up a system of expectations in the reader that is then reversed as the parable develops. The story of the laborers in the vineyard is a meditation on what is just or right. After agreeing with the first group of laborers to pay them a denarius for the day's work, the landowner tells the next group he hires three hours later, "I will pay you whatever is right [*dikaion*]" (Matt. 20:4). *Dikaios* means "just," "right," or "righteous." In Matthew's Gospel, righteousness is a common theme of Jesus's teaching (Matt. 25:37, 46; 13:43; 5:6, 20). The parable teaches that the righteousness or justice of the kingdom of heaven is different than the righteousness or justice of the world. When it is time for the laborers to be paid at the end of the day (as the Torah requires [Lev. 19:13; Deut. 24:14–15]), "each of them received the usual daily wage. Now when the first came, they thought they would receive more; but each of them also received the usual daily wage" (Matt. 20:9–10). The landowner has agreed to pay the laborers whatever is *dikaion*, right or just, and this is his idea of righteousness or justice. The parable begins, "The kingdom of heaven is like [*homoia*] a landowner who went out early in the morning," and so on (Matt. 20:1). The justice of the landowner is the justice of the kingdom of heaven, and this is very different from the ordinary standards of justice or righteousness to which Matthew's readers are accustomed. The laborers, like the readers, are expecting that the number of hours each group has worked will be compensated with a proportionate amount of money. Reasonable as it is, however, to expect that those who work more will receive more, this is not what occurs in the kingdom of heaven. Rather, the landowner says:

> "Friend, I am doing you no wrong [*ouk adikō*]; did you not agree with me for the usual daily wage?…I choose to give to this last one the same as I give to you. Am I not allowed to do what I choose with what belongs to me?"
>
> (Matt. 20:13, 15)

The rules of the kingdom of heaven are different from those of the world. The rule of the kingdom of heaven is grace, God's overflowing generosity, mercy, and love to all, regardless of what they deserve according to the justice of the world. This is true even when the justice of the world, as here, is rational and good.

As many commentators point out, being the kind of laborer for hire featured in the parable was a hard life, in first-century Galilee as now (Luz, *Matthew 8-20* 530; Witherington 373–375). A day laborer waiting in the marketplace to be hired at the eleventh hour of the day is in a very precarious position in the economy, as is his family. These are people to whom God is gracious, according to the parable, whom God treats in the kingdom of heaven as equals with the best and fittest of their fellows. The parable does not say that the moral standards of the world are

The Gospels 161

bad, but it does say that there is another, different world with different and better moral standards.

The parable, like many of Jesus's parables, asks its hearers or readers to choose between the kingdom of the world and the kingdom of heaven. The landowner's final words to the laborers who worked all day are, "Are you envious because I am generous?" (Matt. 20:15). In Matthew's Greek, there is a sharper contrast here. In fact, the landowner asks, "Is your eye evil [*poneros*] because I am good [*agathos*]?" An "evil eye" here means thinking, feeling, and acting according to the standards of contemporary society. It means continuing to think according to what everyone thinks, to public opinion, or to common sense. It means failing (or perhaps refusing) to understand that, while some of the standards by which we live are good (and some of them are bad), there is nevertheless a better standard to which Jesus calls his hearers, that of the grace of God which is the justice of the kingdom of heaven.

TEXT FOR DISCUSSION

The Infancy Gospel of Thomas

> *There are numerous early accounts of the life and teaching of Jesus that were rejected from the canon of the New Testament. One of the most popular of these was* The Infancy Gospel of Thomas *(Ehrman and Pleše 3), a relatively short text about Jesus's life as a child. "It dates approximately to the second half of the second century* CE *(Ehrman 58). The following text is from the second and third chapters:*

When this child Jesus was five years old, he was playing by the ford of a stream; and he gathered the flowing waters into pools and made them immediately pure. These things he ordered simply by speaking a word. He then made some soft mud and fashioned twelve sparrows from it. It was the Sabbath when he did this... But when a certain Jew saw what Jesus had done while playing on the Sabbath he left right away and reported to his father Joseph, "Look, your child [...] has profaned the Sabbath!" When Joseph [...] saw what had happened, he cried out to him, "Why are you doing what is forbidden on the Sabbath?" But Jesus clapped his hands and cried to the sparrows, "Begone!" And the sparrows took flight and went off chirping [...]

Now the son of Annas the scribe was standing there with Joseph; and he took a willow branch and scattered the water that Jesus had gathered. Jesus was irritated when he saw what had happened, and he said to him: "You unrighteous, irreverent idiot! What did the pools of water do to harm you? See, now you also will be withered like a tree, and you will never bear leaves or root or fruit." Immediately that child was completely withered...The parents of the withered child carried him away, mourning his lost youth. They brought him

162   *The Bible as Literature*

to Joseph and began to accuse him, "What kind of child do you have who does such things?"

The Apocryphal Gospels: Texts and Translations, ed. Bart D. Ehrman and Zlatko Pleše © 2011 by Oxford University Press. Reproduced with permission of the Licensor through PLSclear.

QUESTIONS

1. In Chapter 2, Jesus plays at five years old as a child would, but since he has divinely given miraculous powers, he combines child's play with these powers.
   (a) What do you think of the story of Jesus making mud sparrows and having them fly away?
   (b) What do you think the writer is trying to say about Jesus with this story?
   (c) How would you compare it to the miracle stories and to the infancy stories in the Gospel of Matthew?
2. In Matthew's infancy narrative, Joseph is a good man and an obedient servant of God (Matt. 1:18–25). Here he seems to be an angry father who does not understand or appreciate his divinely anointed son. In Chapter 5 too (which I have not reproduced here), Joseph is angry with Jesus because of all the complaints he gets about him from the other villagers. What do you think of the portrayal of Joseph in the *Infancy Gospel of Thomas*? What do you think the author is trying to say with it? How does it compare to the portrayal of Joseph in Matthew 1:18–25?
3. When another child spoils Jesus's game, Jesus is "irritated" and says to him, "You unrighteous, irreverent idiot [*adike, asebē, kai anoēte*]!" This strikingly contradicts Jesus's teaching in Matthew's Gospel, "If you are angry with a brother or sister, you will be liable to judgement; if you insult a brother or sister, you will be liable to the council; and if you say, 'You fool,' you will be liable to the hell of fire" (Matt. 5:22). What do you make of Jesus's childish anger here? What do you make of the contradictory accounts of Jesus's teaching in Matthew's Gospel and his actions in the *Infancy Gospel of Thomas*?
4. Jesus inflicts a terrible injury on the boy who has spoiled his game in revenge for having done so. He curses him, and immediately the child is "completely withered." In a very pathetic scene, the child's parents carry him away (because he can no longer walk), "mourning his lost youth [*thrēnountes tēn neotētan autou*]."
   (a) This miracle of causing sickness is the opposite of the miracles of healing Jesus does in Matthew's Gospel. Why do you think the author

The Gospels 163

> of the *Infancy Gospel of Thomas* wrote it? How would you relate it to the miracles of Jesus in Matthew's Gospel?
>
> (b) In Matthew's Gospel, Jesus curses and withers a fig tree (Matt. 21:18–22), just as he curses and withers the boy in the *Infancy Gospel of Thomas*. The same word, *exēranthē*, "withered," is used in both texts. How would you describe the relationship between Matthew's story and that of the *Infancy Gospel of Thomas*?

Luke

Introduction

Unlike Matthew or Mark, the author of the third Gospel begins with a prologue in which he refers to himself in the first person. He refers to the dedicatee of the Gospel, Theophilus, by name, but he does not name himself. The author indicates that he has read multiple accounts of the life and teaching of Jesus – "many have undertaken to set down an orderly account of the events that have been fulfilled among us" (Luke 1:1). He also distinguishes himself from the "eyewitnesses" (*autoptai*) of Jesus, saying that, for his part, he has learned what they have "handed on" (*paredosan*) to the church (Luke 1:2). Indeed, he makes clear that he has thoroughly familiarized himself with all the written and oral traditions about Jesus that he can find (Luke 1:3).

Most scholars agree that Luke (I will use the traditional name for the author of the third Gospel) used Mark as a source, so his Gospel was written after 70 CE. There is wide agreement that Luke was also the author of the Book of Acts. In that book, there are several sudden shifts from third-person narration about the journeys of Paul to the first-person plural (Acts 16:10–17; 20:5–15; 21:1–18; 27:1–28). There is debate among scholars as to whether this means that the author of Luke and Acts traveled with Paul on the journeys Luke narrates in the first-person plural, which occur in the 50s CE. If he did, Luke's Gospel should be dated toward the beginning of the period between Mark's Gospel and the earliest second-century references to Luke, that is, in the early 80s CE (Wolter 12). Most scholars date the Gospel either to the last quarter of the first century or the first quarter of the second (Carroll 4; Vinson 6–7; Culpepper, "Luke" 8; Bovon, *Luke 1* 8–9).

Luke is one of the best prose stylists among the New Testament writers. He has had an education in rhetoric, which means that he was probably from a wealthy family and lived in a city. Luke also knows the LXX very well, and deliberately writes in imitation of its style (much as a modern English writer would be able to imitate the style of the King James Bible). This equal grasp of Greek rhetoric and the Greek Bible makes the question of whether he was Jewish or a Gentile a difficult one. Most scholars have argued that it is more likely that he was a Gentile (Culpepper, "Luke" 9; Vinson 3; Carroll 2). François Bovon hypothesizes, plausibly to my mind, that Luke was "most likely a Greek by birth, who turned to Judaism early in life" (*Luke 1* 8). Both Bovon and John Carroll think that Luke

164   *The Bible as Literature*

was one of that "circle of sympathizers" of "devout Gentiles drawn to the worship of the synagogue" (Bovon, *Luke 1* 8; Carroll 2), whom Paul addresses in Acts as *hoi phoboumenoi ton theon*, "you who fear God" (Acts 13:16; cf. 13:26; 10:35). In *Against Heresies*, St. Irenaeus identifies the author of the Gospel as Paul's companion Luke referred to in Colossians 4:14; 2 Timothy 4:1; Philemon 24, and by implication in the "we" passages in Acts. It is unclear whether Paul's companion was in fact the author of Luke and Acts (Wolter 6–8; Carroll 1–2; Vinson 1–3; Culpepper, "Luke" 4–5). The Luke mentioned at Colossians 4:14 is a doctor, but attempts to demonstrate that Luke and Acts use a technical medical vocabulary that suggests authorship by a doctor have largely been refuted (Wolter 8; Vinson 3).

The Annunciation

Mark's Gospel does not narrate the birth of Jesus. Matthew tells the story of "an angel of the Lord" appearing to Joseph in a dream and saying that Mary, to whom he was betrothed, had conceived a child "from the Holy Spirit" (Matt. 1:20). Luke, on the other hand, tells the finely crafted stories of the annunciations to Zechariah and to Mary, Mary's visit to Elizabeth, the births of John the Baptist and Jesus, and the angel and the shepherds, all of which are unique to his Gospel. His two annunciation stories are artfully interweaved. Culpepper rightly points out that "the similarity of structure and content between the two scenes invites the reader to consider the differences between them" ("Luke" 50). The two main differences, to my mind, are those between Zechariah's and Mary's social positions and between their responses to the annunciation. With respect to their social position, Zechariah is a priest serving in the sanctuary of the Temple in Jerusalem. He is an important man at the center of national life. Mary, on the other hand, is no one, and from nowhere. She was young, possibly no more than 12 or 13 (Bovon, *Luke 1* 49; Carroll 39; cf. Vinson 36, who doubts this). But in terms of God's plan for the people of Israel, and indeed for all people, in Luke's Gospel, Mary is the one who will bear the greater child, indeed the greatest child. As Carroll puts it, this is "a reflection of the character of God's activity in Israel: it entails reversal in social status of the most radical kind" (44).

Mary also differs from Zechariah in that her response to the angel's message is the right one. Her response is, "Here am I, the servant of the Lord [*idou hē doulē kuriou*]; let it be with me according to your word" (Luke 1:38, NRSV); "Behold the handmaid of the Lord; be it unto me according to thy word" (KJV). Mary exemplifies more quickly than Zechariah the proper response in Luke's Gospel to the God whose kingdom her son will preach – simple, self-giving trust. Her response to God is yes. Joel Green points out that it is unusual for the person (usually a woman) to whom the divine message is given in annunciation-type scenes to have the last word. As he rightly puts it, Luke does this with Mary because "her response is exemplary, demonstrating how all Israel ought to respond to God's favor" (*Luke* 92).

When the angel tells Mary, "You will conceive in your womb and bear a son," she first responds, "How can this be, for I am a virgin [*andra ou ginōskō*, lit. I do not

The Gospels 165

know a man]" (Luke 1:31, 34). Gabriel replies, in the parallelism that characterizes Hebrew poetry:

The Holy Spirit will come upon [*epeleusetai epi*] you,
and the power of the Most High will overshadow [*episkiasei*] you.

(Luke 1:35)

There are many accounts in the ancient world of gods having children with women. In Greek mythology, Zeus the king of the gods, god of the sky and of thunder, has sexual relations with numerous women, fathering children who are divine, semidivine, or royal (cf. Talbert 22). Plutarch begins his life of Alexander by recounting multiple versions of the story of his conception by Zeus, who slept with his mother in the form of a snake (*Alexander* 2.3–3.4). In his life of Numa, Plutarch describes the Egyptian belief that "a woman can be approached by a divine spirit [*pneuma theou*] and made pregnant" (*Numa* 4.4). Bovon cites numerous Judaic and Egyptian parallels to Luke's account of the virgin birth (*Luke 1* 44–46), arguing that "the Christian doctrine of the Messiah could not remain unaffected by these diffuse and widespread expectations of a human and divine deliverer" (*Luke 1* 45).

In discussing stories like those of Numa, who was said to be the lover of a goddess, Plutarch observes, "That an immortal god should take carnal pleasure in a mortal body and its beauty, this, surely, is hard to believe" (*Numa* 4.3). Luke is careful to distinguish his account of the virgin conception of Jesus from any such story. Rather, the angel Gabriel tells Mary that the Holy Spirit will "come upon" you, and that the "power [*dunamis*]" of God will "overshadow" you, so that she will conceive (Luke 1:35). In using the verb *episkiazō*, "to overshadow," Luke may well have in mind Exodus 40:35, where the glory of the Lord fills the tabernacle. "The cloud overshadowed [*epeskiazen*] it, and the glory of the Lord filled the tabernacle [*skēnē*]," so that Moses could not enter it (Exod. 40:35, LXX). As this sentence makes clear, the word *skia*, "shadow," which gives the verb *episkiazō*, "to overshadow," is cognate with the word *skēnē*, "tent," which is used in the LXX for "tabernacle" (a tent being something that causes shade from the sun). So when Luke thinks of the power of God "overshadowing" Mary, the very word "shadow" reminds him of the tabernacle, just as the verb *episkiazō* reminds him of the glory of the Lord filling it. Luke is thinking of the virgin conception as an event most clearly understood by analogy to the glory of God filling the tabernacle in the wilderness in the Book of Exodus. His account of the life of Jesus is carefully conceived as a continuation of the Greek Scriptures. Just as the presence of God in the tabernacle was, so the virgin conception of Jesus is a covenant event, for Luke, an event in which God promises to deliver and bless his people, both Jews and Gentiles.

Mary's fullest response to the virgin conception is the song she utters in response to Elizabeth's prophecies. As Carroll rightly observes, the song "has the sound of a psalm of praise expressing authentic Jewish piety" (49). Both its leading ideas and its formal features are those of a psalm. Furthermore, the song itself is "a virtual collage of biblical texts" (Green 101). Mary's song begins with an echo of

166 *The Bible as Literature*

Hannah's song in the Book of Samuel (or of Kingdoms, as Luke knew it in the LXX). The latter begins:

My heart is made firm in the Lord,
my horn is exalted in my God

[*estereōthē **hē** kardia **mou en kuriōi***
*hupsōthē keras **mou en theōi mou***].
(1 Sam. 2:1, LXX)

Mary's song in Luke begins:

My soul magnifies the Lord,
and my spirit rejoices in God my Savior

[*megalunei **hē** psuchē **mou ton kurion***
*kai ēgalliasen to pnuema **mou epi tōi theōi** tōi sōtēri **mou***].
(Luke 1:46–47)

The words in bold in the Greek transliterations indicate where Luke has used the same words as he found in the LXX (altering the case of the nouns as his different verb choices require). The allusion to Hannah's song at the beginning of Mary's puts the miracle of the virgin conception of Jesus into a biblical context, for Luke. Hannah's song celebrates her conception of Samuel, who will faithfully lead Israel as God's covenant people in the roles of judge, prophet, and priest. Mary's song, with its use of Hannah's, indicates that Jesus is the development of God's plan for the people of Israel that has already been expressed in the Scriptural story of Samuel. Mary's next words continue Luke's comparison of her to Hannah. Mary says, "He has looked with favor on the lowliness of his servant" (Luke 1:48), just as Hannah prays, "Look with favor on the lowliness of your servant" as she asks God for a male child (1 Sam. 1:11, LXX). The Greek texts are almost identical:

epiblepsēs epi tēn tapeinōsin tēs doulēs *sou*
(1 Sam. 1:11, LXX)

epeblepsen epi tēn tapeinōsin tēs doulēs *autou*
(Luke 1:48)

Hannah's song, in celebrating the redemptive power of God as Mary's does, includes the words "The Lord puts to death and brings to life, / He brings down to Hades and brings up" (1 Sam. 2:6, LXX). Luke would surely have seen this text as a prophecy of the resurrection of Jesus, given his similar view of Psalm 16:8–11, which he narrates Peter quoting as a prophecy of Jesus's resurrection in Acts 2:24–32. Mary's song represents the fulfillment of Hannah's song in Luke's Gospel.

The Gospels 167

Hannah's story and song are parts of the Scripture, Luke subtly and carefully says with his patterns of allusion, in which the virgin birth of Jesus, God's Messiah who would preach the kingdom of God, be put to death and rise again, were prophesied.

Mary's song moves powerfully from her reflection on God's blessing of her to his blessing of all Israel, and ultimately of all "those who fear him [*hoi phoboumenoi auton*]" (Luke 1:50). As Green writes, in the second half of the song (Luke 1:51–55), it is "as if the camera, previously focused more narrowly on Mary, has suddenly pulled back to reveal the company of all Israel of which she is a part" (*Luke* 104). Like Hannah before her, Mary celebrates the social transformation that God will bring about through the son he has caused her to conceive. Mary's song moves from her own "lowliness [*tapeinōsis*]" as an individual (Luke 1:48) to all the "lowly [*tapeinoi*]" of Israel (Luke 1:52) and even of the nations. Mary's celebration is social and political at the same time as it is individual. In this sense, her song is a well-crafted prologue to Jesus's teaching about the kingdom of God in Luke's Gospel. The kingdom of God is a place in which "all who exalt themselves will be humbled, and those who humble themselves will be exalted" (Luke 14:11); in which the poor, the hungry, and those who weep will be blessed (Luke 6:20–21). Mary's song says the same, in the form of celebration that God will bless all the poor and oppressed of Israel as he has blessed her. As Carroll writes, "Mary's Song boldly proclaims a social revolution. God's realm redraws the maps of human social and political relations and inverts conventional roles" (52). Mary uses past tense verbs, which seems to indicate that she sees the process beginning, although not ending, with the conception of Jesus, which she celebrates in her song. Carroll is right to call Mary's vision prophetic: "Roman power, after all, will crush Jesus. Still if Mary is right about the reversals that divine power produces, crucifixion will not speak the last word" (52).

The Crucifixion

In Luke's Gospel, the crowd addressed by Pontius Pilate, the Roman governor of Judea, on Passover keep shouting, "Crucify, crucify him [*staurou staurou auton*]!" (Luke 23:21), although Pilate finds three times that Jesus has done nothing that merits death, indeed has done nothing wrong at all. Nevertheless, "their voices prevailed," and Pilate hands Jesus over *tō thelēmati autōn*, literally "to their will" (KJV) (Luke 23:25). Crucifixion was a terrible form of execution. It was reserved for slaves, the worst criminals, particularly those who threatened the authority of the Roman Empire, and criminals of the lowest classes. It was so cruel that it was not done to Roman citizens (Bovon, *Luke 3* 284). In defending a client against a charge of treason in 63 BCE, Cicero speaks of how beneath the dignity and rights of a free people the practice is: "The very word 'cross' should be far removed not only from the person of a Roman citizen but also from his thoughts, his eyes, and his ears" ("Gaius Rabirius" 16). As Green writes, "Bound or nailed to a stake, tree, or cross [...] death came slowly, sometimes over several days, as the body succumbed to shock or asphyxiation" (810). Flogging, torture,

168   *The Bible as Literature*

and public humiliation were part of the punishment. The ancient Jewish historian Josephus (c. 37–c. 100 CE) writes of Jews whom the Romans captured during the siege of Jerusalem in 70 CE: "Scourged and subjected before death to every torture, they were finally crucified in view of the wall [...] The soldiers themselves through rage and bitterness nailed up their victims in various attitudes as a grim joke" (*Jewish War* V, 449–451)

The different ways in which each of the four evangelists portrays Jesus's crucifixion, and the events leading up to it, yield fascinating results for the literary critic. Here I will focus on the some of the things that Luke does in particular in representing these scenes. First, Luke omits the scene in Mark in which, after Jesus is handed over by Pilate to be crucified, he is mocked, beaten, and humiliated by the soldiers who lead him out to be crucified (Mark 15:16–20; Matt. 27:27–31; cf. John 19:2–3). In Mark, the scene reads:

> They clothed him in a purple cloak; and after twisting some thorns into a crown, they put it on him. And they began saluting him, "Hail, King of the Jews!" They struck his head with a reed, spat upon him, and knelt down in homage to him.
>
> (Mark 15:17–19)

Almost all scholars agree that Luke uses Mark as a source, but Luke omits this powerful scene. There is no avoiding the agony or the humiliation of crucifixion, and Luke includes the mockery Jesus endures on the cross from the people of Jerusalem, their leaders, the soldiers in charge, and the other men crucified with him (Luke 23:35–39). However, he wants to focus less on the torture and humiliation of Jesus than Mark did. As Carroll puts it, Luke's account of the crucifixion "offers a vivid display of a righteous man facing death with equanimity, courage, and integrity" (464).

We see something similar in Jesus's words from the cross that Luke narrates, in contrast to those he found in Mark's Gospel. In Mark (followed by Matthew), just before Jesus dies, he "cried with a loud voice, 'Eloi, Eloi, lema sabachthani?' which means, 'My God, my God, why have you forsaken me?'" (Mark 15:34; cf. Matt. 27:46). Jesus uses the words of Psalm 22:1, which graphically expresses a sense of abandonment by God in extreme distress. Luke does not mention this. Rather, in Luke's Gospel, as Jesus is dying, "crying with a loud voice, [he] said, 'Father, into your hands I commend my spirit'" (Luke 23:46). Here Jesus uses the words of Psalm 31:5, which expresses trust in God. Both Psalms 22 and 31 graphically express both agony and divine redemption from this agony. Mark chose to emphasize the agony; Luke the redemption. In Luke's Gospel, Jesus's dying words express an unbroken faith in God who will deliver him from the very worst a human being can suffer. Furthermore, Luke adds an earlier word from the cross: as Jesus is being crucified, he says, "Father, forgive them; for they do not know what they are doing" (Luke 23:34). This phrase is unique to Luke's Gospel, and it contributes to the Gospel's emphasis on Jesus's unbroken relationship of trust in God, integrity, and faithfulness to his teaching about the kingdom of God all the way through the agony of crucifixion in which his life ends. As Culpepper puts it, in Luke's Gospel, "Jesus died a model death" (*Luke* 455).

TEXTS FOR DISCUSSION

1. The Alexamenos Graffito

The images below are the original and a copy in outline of a piece of graffiti scratched in plaster on the wall of what was once a house in Rome. Discovered in 1857, the graffito dates back to c. 200 CE, and is one of the earliest known depictions of Christ crucified. The Greek words mean, "Alexamenos worships God."

Figure 7.3 The Alexamenos graffito. Credit: Zev Radovan / Alamy Stock Photo

2. George Herbert, "Easter Wings"

This poem by the seventeenth-century poet and Anglican priest George Herbert was published in his posthumous volume The Temple *in 1633:*

> Lord, who createdst man in wealth and store,
> Though foolishly he lost the same,
> Decaying more and more
> Till he became
> Most poor:
> With thee
> O let me rise

170 *The Bible as Literature*

As larks, harmoniously,
And sing this day thy victories:
Then shall the fall further the flight in me.

My tender age in sorrow did begin:
And still with sicknesses and shame
Thou didst so punish sin,
That I became
Most thin.
With thee
Let me combine,
And feel this day thy victory;
For, if I imp my wing on thine,
Affliction shall advance the flight in me.

QUESTIONS

1. The image is a mocking one. The crucified man has an ass's head. The person who carved this graffito thinks that it is absurd that Alexamenos, who is presumably a Christian, thinks that someone so socially insignificant and undesirable as to have been crucified is said by Christians to be God. How would you relate Luke's account of Jesus's crucifixion to that of the person who carved this graffito?
2. The text carved by the picture, ΑΛΕΞΑΜΕΝΟΣ ΣΕΒΕΤΕ ΘΕΟΝ (*Alexamenos sebete theon*), means "Alexamenos worships God." The word *sebete* seems to be a misspelling for *sebetai*, "worships," suggesting that the person who carved is not well educated (or rich). What do you make of this in the light of Luke's account of Jesus's crucifixion?
3. The shape of Herbert's poem physically represents the "wings" of the title. Its diminishing and increasing line lengths represent the process of death and resurrection that the soul undergoes, in Herbert's belief, with Christ, who became "most poor" and "most thin" on the cross. How would you compare Herbert's portrayal of Christian death and resurrection with Luke's portrayal of Christ's?
4. Herbert's Christian faith teaches him that the Christian dies and is raised to life again with Christ. Paul's letters speak a great deal about this, but Luke's Gospel never mentions it. What do you make of the fact that Luke writes only about Jesus's death and resurrection, without mentioning its significance (at least, very clearly) for anyone else?
5. The two pieces are very different from one another in their portrayal of Jesus's death – the one scornful, the other reverent. What do you make of this difference in attitude toward the same narrated event?

John

Introduction

Toward the end of John's Gospel, in the accounts of the last day of Jesus's life and of his resurrection, a fascinating character who is never mentioned in the Synoptic Gospels appears, "the disciple whom Jesus loved [*ēgapa*]" (John 21:20; cf.13:23; 19:26; 20:2; 21:7). At the very end of the Gospel, it is said of him, "This is the disciple who is testifying [*marturōn*] to these things and has written [*grapsas*] them, and we know that his testimony [*marturia*] is true" (John 21:24). This sentence's meaning is not perfectly clear, but it associates the Gospel with the (unnamed) disciple whom Jesus loved. This disciple who "testifies" to the things written in the Gospel may also be the person referred to in John 19:35, where after the account of blood and water coming out of Jesus's side on the cross we read, "He who saw this has testified [*memarturēken*] so that you also may believe. His testimony [*marturia*] is true, and he knows that he tells the truth." Ten verses earlier, the only male disciple said to be standing near Jesus's cross is the disciple whom Jesus loved (John 19:26–27). In both cases, we hear that an eyewitness has testified to the Gospel's account of Jesus's death and resurrection, and in both cases the narrator asserts that this person's "testimony is true." Since the 1960s, many scholars have come to think that a "Johannine school" or "community" best explains these and other features of the Gospel and letters of John.

This community is thought to be one founded by and gathered around the disciple Jesus loved. Members of the community are responsible for the Gospel of John and for the letters of John, which have similar theological concerns and rhetorical styles. (The Book of Revelation, whose author is named as John [Rev. 1:1], has different concerns and styles, and is probably not associated with this community [cf. Powell 197]). Most scholars believe that the beloved disciple is not the author of the Gospel (cf. Thatcher 95–96). As we have seen, John 21:24 distinguishes the "we" among whom the writer seems to include himself from the beloved disciple. Furthermore, the previous verse seems to indicate that the beloved disciple is dead at the time these verses are being written (John 21:23). In Raymond Brown's view,

> the solution that seems to do most justice to the Gospel evidence is that the [Beloved Disciple] was the eyewitness who was responsible for the basic testimony/witness that was incorporated into the Fourth Gospel. But others were responsible for composing the written Gospel and redacting it.
>
> (195–196)

In Tom Thatcher's words, "While this individual was not likely the author of the Fourth Gospel in its present form, the content of John's narrative is grounded in the Beloved Disciple's testimony" (84).

There is no consensus among scholars as to the identity of the beloved disciple. The Fourth Gospel does not name him. In the story of the miraculous catch of fish

172   *The Bible as Literature*

after Jesus's resurrection, the beloved disciple is said to be one of the people in the boat – Thomas; Nathanael; James and John, sons of Zebedee; and two unnamed disciples (John 21:2). Early Christian tradition identifies him with the apostle John, son of Zebedee (cf. Mark 1:19). Some modern scholars still defend this traditional view (cf. Thatcher 88) but most do not, on the grounds that there is not enough support for it from the text of the Gospel itself. Other candidates have been named, including Thomas, Lazarus, a disciple who is not one of the 12 apostles, and one of the women among Jesus's disciples (Thatcher 88–90; Powell 189–190; Thompson 18). Some argue that a historical individual is not intended at all, but rather something like the evangelist's ideal version of a disciple of Jesus. Most scholars today believe that the author of the Gospel and his audience were Jewish Christians who had been expelled from the synagogue because of their belief that Jesus was the Messiah (cf. John 9:22; 12:42; 16:2), and that the Fourth Gospel reflects the Johannine community's involvement in this process. Most assign the Gospel a date toward the end of the first century.

John's Gospel is very different from the Synoptics, in both rhetorical style and theological content. The great majority of material in John's Gospel does not appear in the Synoptics. Jesus does not tell a single parable or perform a single exorcism. His ministry lasts three years rather than one; he visits Jerusalem five times rather than just once in the last week of his life; and his ministry largely takes place in Judea rather than in Galilee. Furthermore, Jesus's teaching is done in a reflective, meditative style foreign to the pithy language of everyday life that he uses in the Synoptic Gospels.

In the Beginning Was the Word

John's Gospel has a much higher view of the relationship of Jesus to God than the Synoptics. This is expressed from the very beginning of the Gospel, with its hymnic meditation on the Word of God (John 1:1–18). Indeed, scholars have for a long time hypothesized that one or more hymns, either Christian or pre-Christian, underlies the Prologue to John's Gospel, since its praise of the divine Word is expressed in such rhythmic, patterned prose and poetic imagery. The hymnic prologue begins:

> In the beginning was the Word, and the Word was with God, and the Word was God.
>
> *en archēi ēn ho logos, kai ho logos ēn pros ton theon, kai theos ēn ho logos.*
> (John 1:1)

The word *logos* has a wide semantic range in classical Greek, but its two fundamental sets of meaning are "word" and "reason." The one word in Greek for the two concepts indicates a semantic link between them, such that reason is something like inner speech and words are its outward expression. In Stoic philosophy, the *logos* of the universe is the rational principle by which it is structured. In the first century CE, when John's Gospel was being written, there had been interpretation of the Hebrew Scriptures by Jewish thinkers who had been educated in Greek

The Gospels   173

philosophy for some 200 years (Tobin 256). In this tradition, the Greek concept of *logos* is used in a variety of ways, some of them similar to its use in John's Gospel. The most notable parallels are to be found in the work of Philo of Alexandria (c. 20 BCE–c. 50 CE), the Jewish philosopher and exegete who aimed to interpret the Torah in the light of Greek philosophy.

For Philo, "the *logos* was the intermediate reality between God, who was essentially transcendent, and the universe [...] a reflection of the truly existent God above and a model on the basis of which the universe below was ordered" (Tobin 257). In speaking of the creation of the universe, Philo writes:

> Its cause is God, by whom it has come into being, its material the four elements, from which it was compounded, its instrument (*organon*) the Word of God (*logos theou*), through which it was framed, and the final cause of the building is the goodness of the architect.
>
> > (*De Cherubim* 127, quoted in Tobin 258)

The *logos* of God plays a similar role here to the way the concept is used in John's Gospel. For Philo, the *logos* is the instrument through (*dia*) which God brings the universe into being. In John, "all things came into being through [*dia*] him, and without him not one thing came into being" (John 1:3). Philo also speaks of the *logos* as God's "first born" (*prōtogonos*), just as in John he is the "only born" (*monogenēs*) son of God (John 1:14, 18). Furthermore, the *logos* is the way to God for human beings in Philo: "If you have not yet become fit to be thought sons of God, yet we may be sons of his invisible image [*eikōn*], the most holy *logos*. For the *logos* is the highest born image of God" (*De Confusione Linguarum* 147, quoted in Tobin 261). In a similar way, John writes of the *logos*, "No one has ever seen God. It is God the only Son, who is close to the father's heart [*eis ton kolpon*, lit. "in the bosom of" the father], who has made him known" (John 1:18). As Thomas Tobin argues, these parallels do not indicate that the author of the Gospel of John has read Philo's work, but rather that the prologue is "part of the larger world of Hellenic Jewish speculative interpretations of biblical texts" exemplified by Philo (268).

John's account of the Logos of God draws perhaps even more directly on Jewish thought about the Wisdom of God. In the Hebrew Bible, Wisdom preexists the creation of the world. In Proverbs, Wisdom says:

> The LORD created me at the beginning of his work,
>   The first of his acts of long ago,
> Ages ago I was set up,
>   at the first, before the beginning of the earth.
>
> > (Prov. 8:22–23)

Ben Sira writes of Wisdom, "Before all things, in the beginning [*ap' arches*], [God] created me, / and for all the ages I shall not cease to be" (Sir. 24:9). When John writes, "In the beginning was the Word," the idea of Wisdom as a preexistent divine being, more closely related to God than anything in creation, is part of the

174   *The Bible as Literature*

intellectual and religious heritage that has allowed him to think of the Word of God in similar terms. Furthermore, Wisdom is often described as something like a hypostasis of God, a quality or agent of God not clearly distinct from God himself:

> She [Wisdom] is a breath of the power of God,
> and a pure emanation [*aporrhoia*] of the glory of the Almighty.
> (Wisd. 7:25)

When John describes the Word of God as both "with God" and "God," it is partly this kind of thought that has allowed him to do so. Most notably, Wisdom is said to be present at the creation of the world, and God's agent in creating it. In Proverbs she says, "When [God] marked out the foundations of the earth, / then I was beside him, like a master worker" (Prov. 8:29–30). When John says of the Word in the prologue to the Fourth Gospel, "He was in the beginning with God. All things came into being through him," the only difference between this statement and what could be said about Wisdom in Jewish tradition is the masculine rather than the feminine gender of the pronouns. Like Wisdom, the Logos in the Fourth Gospel preexists creation, is closely related to God himself, and was the faculty or agent of God's creation through which he created the world.

The "word of the LORD" is also something like a hypostasis of God in the Hebrew Bible. It is the way or form in which God speaks to people (cf. Gen. 15:1–4; Isa. 38:4; Jer. 1:4–5; Ezek. 1:3). Furthermore, it is God's creative power or agent in the Hebrew Bible. In the first creation account God speaks, and each element of the world comes into being (Gen. 1:3, 6–7, 9, 11–12, 14–15, 20–21, 24, 26–27). Psalm 33 specifies that these acts of creation were the work of the word of God – "by the word of the LORD [*logos tou kuriou*, LXX] the heavens were made" (Psalm 33:6). Like Wisdom, the word of God in the Jewish scriptures is a faculty, power, or agent of God who is not clearly distinct from God himself. As Marianne Meye Thompson puts it,

> "The Word of the LORD" comes from God and is the means of God's creation and revelation. It is never separable from the identity of God; yet at the same time it can be spoken of as an active subject. The Word is both with God and is God.
> (38)

All these ideas about the word of God contribute to John's account of the Logos who became flesh in Jesus. Perhaps the reason why John describes Jesus as God's word rather than his wisdom (as Paul does in 1 Cor. 1:24) is that the concept of *logos* allows him to make especially clear that Jesus is God's self-expression, what God thinks and wants to say. It is in Jesus's teaching about himself that God is speaking (that Jesus is God's *logos*, his inner and outer words) to human beings. Second, as this teaching suggests, it is Jesus himself who is God's *logos*, who is what God wants to say to human beings. John seems to have taken care to formulate this idea in a way that will be comprehensible to those educated both in Jewish and in Greek traditions.

The Gospels 175

The Word Made Flesh

Much less comprehensible to those traditions is the way in which John develops his account of the Logos of God into the point of the prologue to his Gospel, that in the person of Jesus, to whom the beloved disciple testifies as an eyewitness, the Logos of God was present. More specifically, "the Word became flesh [*sarx*] and lived [*eskēnōsen*] among us, and we have seen his glory" (John 1:14). *ho logos sarx egeneto*, "the Word became flesh." The word *sarx* is a deliberate and notable decision here. The author could have said that the Word became *anthrōpos*, "man," but he chose *sarx*, "flesh," instead. This word has a complex of meanings, and here John seems to mean human being in all its weakness, frailty, and mortality. In Jesus, the Word of God, present from the beginning of creation and the agent of the creation of all things, became subject to all the difficulties that constitute human life – sickness, death, natural disaster, oppression, injustice, poverty, failure, meaninglessness. Job describes his life as a suffering human being: "A mortal [*adam*], born of woman, few of days and full of trouble, / comes up like a flower and withers, / flees like a shadow and does not last" (Job 14:1–2). This is what it is to be *sarx*, and this is what the Fourth Gospel says that the Word of God became in Jesus.

John uses a series of images for how such a thing, unheard of in Greek philosophy or Jewish religion, could take place. Most striking is the verb he uses in saying that the Word, having become flesh, "lived" among us. The verb is *skēnō* (σκηνόω). This is the verb cognate with the noun *skēnē*, which means "tent," and is the word used in the LXX for the "tabernacle" in which God dwells with the Israelites in the wilderness. *skēnō* means to dwell in a tent or tabernacle (or to set up a tent or tabernacle). When the tabernacle is completed at the end of the Book of Exodus, the glory of the LORD fills it: "Then the cloud covered the tent of meeting and the glory of the LORD filled the tabernacle" (Exod. 40:34). In the LXX translation of the second half of this verse, the *doxēs kuriou* filled the *skēnē*. John too speaks of seeing the "glory" (*doxa*) of the Word of God in the tabernacle of the person of Jesus: "The Word […] lived [*skēnō*] among us, and we have seen his glory [*doxa*], the glory [*doxa*] as of a father's only son" (John 1:14). John means that, just as the glory of God was present in the tabernacle in the wilderness, so now the Word of God was present in the person of Jesus, and in both cases the community worshipping God could see his glory there.

TEXT FOR DISCUSSION

William Holman Hunt, *The Light of the World*

One of the founders of the Pre-Raphaelite Brotherhood, William Holman Hunt (1827–1910), completed this picture in 1853. It quickly became one of the most popular representations of Christ in the Victorian period. Hunt painted three versions; below is the original, now in Keble College, Oxford.

176   *The Bible as Literature*

Figure 7.4 William Holman Hunt, *The Light of the World*, c. 1851–1853, oil on canvas. Keble College, Oxford

QUESTIONS

1. The painting is entitled *The Light of the World*, a reference to John 8:12, in which Jesus says, "I am the light of the world. Whoever follows me will never walk in darkness but will have the light of life." How well do you think Hunt has portrayed John's view of Jesus as the light in the darkness of the world?
2. The scene of the painting dramatizes Revelation 3:20, in which the risen Christ tells the church in Laodicea, "Listen! I am standing at the door, knocking." Read Revelation 3:14–22.
   (a) To what extent is Hunt's painting faithful to this passage of the Bible?

The Gospels 177

> (b) At Revelation 3:16, Christ seems angry with the Laodiceans, telling them, "I am about to spit ['spue', KJV] you out of my mouth." Christ seems less angry in Hunt's painting. Why do you think Hunt has painted him in this way?
> 3. At Revelation 3:20, Christ says, "I am standing at the door, knocking; if you hear my voice and open the door, I will come in." Intending the painting to have a spiritual significance, Hunt has added the detail of the door at which Christ knocks not having a handle on the outside. Christ knocks, but only the individual soul can choose to open the door to him. What do you think of this addition to the biblical text? Is it faithful to the portrayal of Christ in John's Gospel, or in the Bible more generally?
> 4. The painting is rich in sensual detail – the weeds that grow up around the door are beautiful in shape, color, and texture. Christ's robe, lantern, and crown are all gorgeously ornamented. What do you make of the highly sensuous qualities of this picture that depicts a spiritual relationship between the soul and God? To what extent do they reflect biblical thinking?

Works Cited

Boring, M. Eugene. "Matthew." *The New Interpreter's Bible*, vol. 8, edited by Leander Keck et al., Abingdon Press, 1995, pp. 89–505.

Bovon, François. *Luke 1: A Commentary on the Gospel of Luke 1:1-9:50.* Translated by Christine M. Thomas, Fortress Press, 2002.

———. *Luke 3: A Commentary on the Gospel of Luke 19:28-24:53.* Translated by James Crouch, Fortress Press, 2012.

Brown, Raymond E. *An Introduction to the Gospel of John.* Edited by Francis J. Moloney, Doubleday, 2003.

Carroll, John T. *Luke: A Commentary.* Westminster John Knox Press, 2012.

Cicero. "Speech in Defense of Gaius Rabirius Charged with High Treason." *Orations*, translated by H. Grose Hodge, Harvard UP, 1927, pp. 452–92.

Culpepper, R. Alan. "Luke." *The New Interpreter's Bible*, vol. 9, edited by Leander Keck et al., Abingdon Press, 1995, pp. 1–490.

———. *Mark.* Smyth and Helwys, 2007.

———. *Matthew: A Commentary.* Westminster John Knox Press, 2021.

Ehrman, Bart D. *Lost Scriptures: Books that Did Not Make It into The New Testament.* Oxford UP, 2003.

Ehrman, Bart D. and Zlatko Pleše. *The Apocryphal Gospels: Texts and Translations.* Oxford UP, 2011.

Goodacre, Mark. "The Farrer Hypothesis." *The Synoptic Problem: Four Views*, edited by Stanley Porter and Brian R. Dyer, Baker Academic, 2016, pp. 47–66.

———. "Synoptic Problem." *The Oxford Encyclopedia of Biblical Interpretation*, vol. 2, edited by Steven L. McKenzie, Oxford UP, 2013, pp. 354–362.

Green, Joel B. *The Gospel of Luke.* William B. Eerdmans, 1997.

Josephus, Flavius. *The Jewish War.* Edited by Geoffrey A. Williamson, revised ed., Penguin, 1981.

Konradt, Matthias. *The Gospel According to Matthew: A Commentary.* Translated by M. Eugene Boring, Baylor UP, 2020.

178 *The Bible as Literature*

Luz, Ulrich. *Matthew 1-7: A Commentary*. Translated by James E. Crouch, Fortress, 2007.

———. *Matthew 8-20: A Commentary*. Translated by James E. Crouch, Fortress, 2001.

Plutarch. "Alexander.," *Lives*, Vol. 7, translated by Bernadotte Perrin, Harvard UP, 1919, pp. 223–440.

———. "Numa." *Lives*, Vol. 1, translated by Bernadotte Perrin, Harvard UP, 1914, pp. 305–81.

Porter, Stanley and Brian R. Dyer, ed. *The Synoptic Problem: Four Views*. Baker Academic, 2016.

Powell, Mark Allan. *Fortress Introduction to the Gospels*. 2nd ed., Fortress Press, 2019.

Talbert, Charles H. *Reading Luke: A Literary and Theological Commentary*. Smyth and Helwys, 2002.

Thatcher, Tom. "The Beloved Disciple, the Fourth Evangelist, and the Authorship of the Fourth Gospel." *The Oxford Handbook of Johannine Studies*, edited by Judith M. Lieu and Martinus C. de Boer, Oxford UP, 2018, pp. 83–100.

Thompson, Marianne Meye. *John: A Commentary*. Westminster John Knox Press, 2015.

Tobin, Thomas H. "The Prologue of John and Hellenistic Jewish Speculation." *The Catholic Biblical Quarterly*, vol. 52, 1990, pp. 252–69.

Vinson, Richard B. *Luke*. Smyth and Helwys, 2008.

Witherington, Ben III. *Matthew*. Smyth and Helwys, 2006.

Wolter, Michael. *The Gospel According to Luke, Volume I (Luke 1:1-9-50)*. Translated by Wayne Coppins and Christoph Heilig, Baylor UP, 2016.

8 Paul's Letters

Introduction

Paul's Life

The only contemporary witnesses to Paul's life and thought are his letters and the Book of Acts in the New Testament, which do not always clearly agree with another. As James Prothro writes, this calls for "a reasoned use of both Paul's letters and Acts that recognizes what each source can and is meant to tell us," which includes "considering how the author of Acts crafts theological history" (22–23). The texts tell us that Paul was born in Tarsus, a city in southeast Asia Minor, or modern-day Turkey. The date of his birth is unknown, but he was probably born at about the same time as Jesus, perhaps between 4 BCE and 4 CE (Sanders 4). When he was young, he learned the trade of tentmaking (*skēnopoios*) (Acts 18:3) and continued to support himself with manual work as an apostle (1 Cor. 4:12; 9:6). He was probably not from a wealthy family. His first language would have been Aramaic (the *Hebrais dialektos* in which he addresses the crowd in Jerusalem [Acts 21:40]). His *koinē*, or common Greek, is good, while "not the elegant literary language of his wealthy Jewish contemporary, Philo of Alexandria" (Sanders 4), which also supports the view that he was not from a wealthy family. He knew the Septuagint extremely well, and had done so since he was a child. During the first half of his adult life he was a Pharisee, testifying to the Galatians, "I advanced in Judaism beyond many among my people of the same age, for I was far more zealous for the traditions of my ancestors" (Gal. 1:14). In Acts, Paul tells the crowd in Jerusalem that he was trained in Jerusalem by the Pharisee Gamaliel, the distinguished teacher of the law, and that he had been a very zealous student (Acts 22:3; cf. 5:34).

The Pharisees were driven by the conviction that all the people of Israel should live to the same standards of purity that were expected from priests in the Temple, so that every person was a priest, every house a temple, and every daily act holy (Roetzel 15–16; Sanders 28–53). According Josephus, they were the leading religious group among the Jewish people in the first century CE (*Jewish War* 2.162–163). As a member of this group, Paul persecuted the members of the fledgling religious group of Jews who believed that Jesus was the Messiah. Paul's persecution of them was a matter of his "individual zeal" (Sanders 5), although he would

DOI: 10.4324/9781315751566-9

180   *The Bible as Literature*

have had the support of the synagogue authorities to subject the Jewish members of the group to disciplinary floggings (Fredriksen 31).

Just a few years after Jesus's death, Paul has the vision of the risen Jesus that changes his life. He is probably in his thirties when this happens, and it probably happens in the 30s of the first century. On the road to Damascus, Paul has a vision of Jesus, whose followers he has been persecuting (Acts 9:3–19; 22:6–16; 26:12–18). According to Acts, the "light from heaven" that he sees while hearing Jesus's voice blinds him for three days, after which "something like scales [*hōs lepides*] fell from his eyes," and he is baptized (9:3, 18). Paul himself tells the Corinthians that Jesus "appeared also to me [*ōphthē kamoi*]" after his death, "as to one untimely born" (1 Cor. 15:8), after Jesus had appeared to Peter, the 12, some 500 disciples, James, and all the apostles.

According to Paul's testimony in Galatians, he visits the leading apostles, Peter and James, the brother of Jesus, in Jerusalem three years later, and then preached the gospel of Jesus in Syria and Cilicia (southwest Asia Minor, in modern-day Turkey) until returning to Jerusalem for the apostolic council in the late 40s (Gal. 1:17–2:1). After the council endorses his mission to the Gentiles (Gal. 2:7–9), Paul founds churches in cities around the Mediterranean coast, in Galatia, Philippi, Thessalonica, Corinth, and Ephesus. These are small groups of Jesus believers meeting in the houses of one of their members. In his account of Paul's missionary journeys in Acts, Luke always emphasizes that, in each city he visits, Paul begins his preaching in the local synagogue, which is often attended both by Jews and Gentile "people who fear God [*hoi phoboumenoi ton theon*]" (Acts 13:16). Sometimes he refers to these devout converts simply as "Greeks" (Acts 14:1; cf. 17:4; 18:4). It is during this stage of Paul's missionary activity, the 50s CE, that he writes most of his letters. In the late 50s he travels to Jerusalem, where he is arrested (for bringing a Gentile into the Temple), and spends two years in prison. After a series of trials in the provincial capital of Judea, he is sent to Rome to be tried by the emperor. It is probable that he died there in the early 60s in the persecution of Christians under Nero. Luke may hint at his martyrdom in Acts 20:25.

As many commentators emphasize, Paul's experience of the risen Christ did not constitute a conversion from "Judaism" to "Christianity." Paul continues to understand himself as a Jew throughout his missionary work, and even as a Pharisee (Rom. 9:1–15; 11:1; 2 Cor. 11:22; Phil. 3:4–6; Acts 23:6; 26:6–8). "Paul did not see believing in Jesus as casting off his Pharisaic heritage, but as doing what all who looked for the resurrection and the salvation of God *should* do when they realized that it had begun in Christ" (Prothro 19, emphasis in original). Christianity is not a religion in its own right, separate from and opposed to Judaism, during Paul's lifetime (Fredriksen 32). His understanding of the Hebrew Scriptures throughout his letters, as Calvin Roetzel puts it, shows "no repudiation of Israel" (18).

Undisputed and Disputed Letters

Modern scholars agree that seven of the thirteen letters ascribed to Paul in the New Testament are certainly by Paul. These are Romans, 1 Corinthians, 2 Corinthians,

Galatians, Philippians, 1 Thessalonians, and Philemon. Scholars disagree on the order and dates in which these letters were written, although most agree that 1 Thessalonians was the first and Romans was the last. Here I reproduce Roetzel's hypothesis (26–28) of the order and dates in which they were written:

1 Thessalonians	c. 50–51
1 Corinthians	c. 53
2 Corinthians	53–57
Galatians	c. 55
Philippians	c. 56
Philemon	c. 56
Romans	57

Galatians is the most uncertain in the sequence. Problems with chronology are also caused by the fact that Romans shows evidence of later redaction, and that 2 Corinthians and Philippians may be combinations of multiple letter fragments. For a sense of the debate around the dates and sequence of the letters, contrast Rainer Riesner's reconstruction (23) below (the letters in square brackets being of disputed Pauline origin):

Galatians	48
1 Thessalonians	50
[2 Thessalonians]	50
1 Corinthians	54
Philippians / Philemon / [Colossians]	54–55
2 Corinthians	55–56
Romans	57

There is no consensus among scholars on the extent to which Paul wrote the remaining six letters attributed to him in the New Testament. These can be loosely divided into three groups – 2 Thessalonians; the two prison epistles, Ephesians and Colossians; and the three pastoral epistles, 1 Timothy, 2 Timothy, and Titus. The first two of these groups are considered by some to be later compositions, written in Paul's name, and by others to be Paul's own work. Many believe that Paul wrote much of the text of these letters, but that they have been altered or edited by later writers (Seesengood 49). The three pastoral epistles are more frequently judged to be by a later author than Paul. The disputed letters are typically understood to be the work of a Pauline "school" (Harding 162) or a Pauline "tradition" (Malina and Pilch 1), in which later writers use Paul's name and authority to express what they believe that Paul would have thought in new and changing situations, or to defend what they consider to be the orthodox faith in a time in which "competing and opposing theological points were vigorously and bitterly debated" (Harding 145).

The reasons for which some of the letters are disputed include the contents suggesting a time after Paul's death; a different understanding of Jesus than Paul's;

182   *The Bible as Literature*

and a concern for non-Israelites reflecting a later situation than Paul's (Malina and Pilch 1). In 1 Thessalonians, for example, Paul seems clearly to expect Jesus to return in his lifetime (1 Thess. 4:15–17). He also warns that "the day of the Lord will come like a thief in the night," with most people unprepared (1 Thess. 5:2). But in 2 Thessalonians, he makes clear that a series of signs will precede the coming end. "That day will not come unless the rebellion comes first and the lawless one is revealed" (2 Thess. 2:3). As Robert Seesengood puts it, in 1 Thessalonians Paul had said that "there would be no signs of the end of the age"; then in 2 Thessalonians he "lists the signs of the end of the age" (65). Many scholars believe that this different eschatology, "matched with alterations in typical Pauline vocabulary, style, and structure" (Seesengood 65), reflects the view of a later writer who, unlike Paul, had been forced to accommodate his thought to a much longer period in which Christ had not yet returned. We should note that there are also letters ascribed to Paul that are not part of the New Testament canon – *3 Corinthians*, *Laodiceans*, and a series of letters between the apostle and the Stoic philosopher Seneca, of which six are said to be by Paul.

Adam and Christ

Romans is Paul's last and longest letter, the result of over two decades of teaching, preaching, and addressing the controversies that arose in the churches he had founded. In it, he expresses in detail and at length his understanding, for the Jewish and Gentile members alike of the Roman group of Jesus believers, who seem to have been at odds with one another, of the "gospel" (*euangelion*), the "good news" of what the life, death, and resurrection of Jesus mean for both groups, and for all humanity. He describes the gospel as "the power of God for salvation to everyone who has faith, to the Jew first and also to the Greek (Rom. 1:16).

As Paul repeatedly asserts throughout the letter, the Torah is a great gift from God to the Jewish people, but in Jesus, whom the Scriptures prophesied, "apart from the law, the righteousness of God has been disclosed [...] through faith in Jesus Christ for all who believe" (Rom. 3:21–22). The Torah was a great blessing, but in the life, death, and resurrection of Jesus, the revelation of God to the people of Israel and through them to the nations has developed, Paul believes. Now, he writes, "we hold that a person is justified by faith [*dikaiousthai pistei*] apart from the works prescribed by the law [*erga nomou*]" (such as circumcision, eating only clean animals, keeping the Sabbath, and all the other prescriptions of the Torah) (Rom. 3:28). Abraham is the father of all Jewish people and also of all Gentile people of faith, Paul argues, not because he obeyed the Torah (which he did not know) but because and insofar as he had faith in God's promise to him.

As he explains how this justification works, Paul begins by writing, "Just as sin came into the world through one man, and death came through sin, and so death spread to all because [*eph'hō*] all have sinned" (Rom. 5:12). His first step in explaining how faith in Christ justifies Jews and Gentiles alike apart from obeying the Torah is to describe the situation from which it justifies them. This is the situation, the "human condition" (Talbert 150), as Paul understands it in Romans.

Paul's Letters   183

Because of Adam's transgression of God's command described in Genesis 2–3, (a) sin came into the world, (b) death came into the world, (c) sin and death spread [*dierchomai*, lit. to "go through"] to all people. The argument goes very quickly here, particularly for readers of the Protestant Bible who have not heard very much like it previously in the Old Testament. As N. T. Wright puts it, Paul is writing "like an artist in a hurry," painting "a few large, sweeping strokes on a giant canvas, creating an overall picture without many details" (435).

Paul's view on the relationship between Adam's sin, the curse of his death, and the sin and death of all his descendants, is not precisely worked out. Rhetorically speaking, he is not primarily concerned with a doctrine of sin as he thinks about the righteousness that comes by faith in Christ, far less with the doctrine of original sin. As Robert Jewett writes, Paul's concern is "to employ the Adamic material as a foil to explain the abundant life in Christ that overturns the legacy of sin and death" (383). In fact, as Paul writes about the relationship between sin, death, Adam, and humankind, he uses a notoriously ambiguous phrase. Sin came into the world through Adam, he says, and death came through sin – "and so death spread to all because [*eph'hō*] all have sinned" (Rom. 5:12). The NRSV translates the phrase *eph'hō* (ἐφ'ᾧ) as "because"; the KJV "for that." Joseph Fitzmeyer lists 11 different senses in which it has been understood in the history of its interpretation (413–417), of two basic types. In the first kind, it is taken to introduce a relative clause – here the meaning of the preposition *epi* (elided to *eph'* before a vowel with a rough breathing) would be "in," "because of," "toward," or "on the basis of," and the relative pronoun *hō* ("whom" or "which") agrees with a masculine or neuter noun in the preceding clauses. These possible nouns include "world," "man," "death," and "law" (understood from context). St. Jerome took this option, and translated the phrase *in quo*, with the sense "in whom," the antecedent being "man." That is, Jerome's translation has the sense, "Sin came into the world through one man [...] in whom all have sinned." The second kind of interpretation takes the entire phrase *eph'hō* as a conjunction, most commonly "because," or perhaps "so that." Many modern commentators and Bible translations opt for "because" (Fitzmeyer 415; Talbert 148). Fitzmeyer opts for "with the result that," which has the advantage of expressing Paul's belief that human beings sin and die both because of Adam's transgression and because of their own (416).

The conjunction seems the better option than the relative clause to me, since the introduction to a relative clause means that, in order to make reasonable sense, the antecedent would need to be "man," which is an awkwardly long way from the relative pronoun. Furthermore, as several commentators point out, if Paul had wanted to say "in whom" all sinned, it would seem most natural for him to say *en hō*, "in whom" rather than *eph'hō*, "on, upon, or over whom" (Jewett 375; Fitzmeyer 413). Using Jerome's translation *in quo*, Adam "in whom all sinned," St. Augustine developed the Christian doctrine of original sin. The British heresiarch Pelagius, who denied the doctrine, had argued that in this verse Paul was teaching that Adam had influenced his descendants by setting them the bad example of sin. Augustine countered that Paul was speaking of *propagatio* (*De peccatorum meritis et remissione* 1.9.10), "propagation" or heredity (Fitzmeyer 408). In this view,

184   *The Bible as Literature*

sin is like a disease that each person inherits from their parents and ultimately from Adam, humanity's first parent. Paul's text expresses neither Pelagius's nor Augustine's view. The fact that he uses an ambiguous phrase already indicates that he is not writing carefully considered doctrine. He does not specify (nor even think about) the nature of the relationship between Adam's sin and the sins of humankind. He just knows that there is one, and wants to move on to describe Christ's justification of us from those sins. As Fitzmeyer puts it, "Paul never explains how that causality works or how Adam's sin is transmitted" (409). In Talbert's words, he is content to "affirm that fallenness is a fact [...] without being able to explain exactly how it is so" (158).

The reason for which Paul does not precisely define the nature of human sin and death nor of their relationship to those of Adam is, so to speak, emotional rather than logical. That is to say, Paul is writing this passage in Romans, as he writes so many others, guided above all by his overwhelming enthusiasm, his overwhelming joy, gratitude, and love for Christ as God's response to the human condition. Romans 5:15–21 is fascinating, among other reasons, for the rhetorical fact that each of these seven verses says the same thing in different words. Each expresses Paul's belief that, however grim the human condition is, characterized as it is since Adam by sin and death, God's free gift of justification or righteousness (Paul uses many terms for the gift of Christ) in Christ is much better. Adam is "a type [*tupos*] of the one to come," he says in Romans 5:14. Christ, the antitype, does not merely put right what Adam made wrong, for Paul. No, Christ not only allows all people, Jews and Gentiles alike, to live with God, but he does so in a way that exceeds anything Adam knew before his transgression brought sin and death into the world.

Paul says this seven times in Romans 5:15–21, an expression of the passion with which he feels it. Verse 15 says, "If the many died through the one man's trespass, much more surely [has] the grace of God [...] abounded for the many." Verse 16 restates this: "The judgement [*krima*] following one trespass brought condemnation [*katakrima*], but the free gift [*charisma*] following many trespasses brings justification [*dikaiōma*]." Paul's rhetorical purpose in this passage is emphasized by his deliberate use of a series of key terms all ending in -*ma*, as the reader can see from the four words I have transliterated in the previous sentence. He also uses *paraptōma* ("trespass"); *dōrēma* ("gift"); and *homoiōma* ("likeness"), employing all seven terms over the space of three verses (5:14–16). His purpose is to say over and over again, in term after term, sentence after sentence, that what Christ does for human beings, Jews and Gentiles alike, is unimaginably better than what Adam did (and we in him) was bad. Verse 17 restates verses 15 and 16 a third time: "If, because of the one man's trespass, death exercised dominion through that one, much more surely will those who receive the abundance of grace [...] exercise dominion in life through the one man, Jesus Christ." Each subsequent verse up to 5:21 does the same, restates Paul's point that, if Adam has made life bad for human beings, Christ has made it good, and that Christ makes it good to a far greater extent than Adam had made it bad.

Paul uses a variety of terms to express the superabundance of the gift of Christ with respect to the sin of Adam – *pollō mallon*, "how much more" (v. 15, 17);

perisseuō, to "abound" (v. 15); *perisseia*, "abundance" (v. 17); and *huperperisseuō*, to "abound exceedingly" (v. 20). These are the terms at the very heart of his thought about Adam and Christ, and hence about the "gospel," the "power of God for salvation to everyone who has faith, to the Jew first and also to the Greek" (1:16). He likes to use the word *perisseuō*, to "exceed," "abound," or "excel," to describe the free gift of Christ. He uses the rare cognate noun *perisseia*, "abundance," to describe it too. But perhaps the rare verb *huperperisseuo*, "to abound abundantly," to "superabound," expresses his thought about Christ most succinctly and fundamentally. The word is only used twice in the New Testament, here and by Paul in 2 Corinthians 7:4. The free gift of God in Christ, the righteousness that comes by faith to Jew and Gentile alike, is not only excessive or abundant or overflowing with respect to the evils of the human condition. It even exceeds excess, overflows overflowing, and abounds in abundance. As Jewett writes,

> The verb [*huperperisseuō*] is the transcendent climax of this remarkable series of references to [...] grace in Christ. Paul's formulation reaches beyond the scope of human logic to a spiritual reality [...] that remains indescribable in its abundance, fullness, and joy.
>
> (388–389)

Hyperabundant, super-excessive – this is what God has shown himself to be in Christ for Paul, and this is the good news he brings to Jew and Gentile alike in the shared human lives marked by the tyranny of sin and death. Paul uses the verb *basileuō*, to "reign as a king," of sin and death three times in Romans 5:12–21, and twice more of God's grace and those who receive it. As Jewett observes, in the context of the Roman Empire the word implies "irresistible coercive force" (377). The good life with God made available in Christ, for Paul, is stronger than the Roman emperor, and all the human evils that are best conceived by analogy with his rule.

TEXT FOR DISCUSSION

The Correspondence between Paul and Seneca

> *This series of letters between Seneca (4 BCE–65 CE), the great Roman philosopher, playwright, and politician, and Paul's contemporary, was composed in the fourth century CE by an unknown Christian author (Ehrman 160). Seneca was the emperor Nero's tutor, and became his political adviser when Nero acceded to throne at age 16.*

Seneca to Paul

I admit that I enjoyed reading your letters to the Galatians, and to the Corinthians, and to the Achaeans, and may our relations be like that religious awe which you manifest in these letters. For the holy spirit that is in you

186   *The Bible as Literature*

and high above you expresses with lofty speech thoughts worthy of reverence. Therefore since you have such excellent matters to propose I wish that refinement of language might not be lacking to the majesty of your theme [...] I confess that Augustus was affected by your sentiments. When your treatise on the power that is in you was read to him, this was his reply: he was amazed that one whose education had not been normal could have such ideas. I answered him that the gods are accustomed to speak through the mouths of the innocent and not through those who pride themselves on their learning. When I gave him the example of Vatenius, a farmer to whom appeared two men who later were found to be Castor and Pollux, he seemed thoroughly enlightened [...]

Paul to Seneca

Things have been revealed to you in your reflections which the Godhead has granted to few. Therefore I am certain that I am sowing a rich seed in a fertile field, not a corruptible matter, but the abiding word of God, derived from him who is ever-increasing and ever-abiding [...] You must make yourself a new herald of Jesus Christ by displaying with the praises of rhetoric that blameless wisdom which you have almost achieved and which you will present to the temporal king and to the members of his household and to his trusted friends [...] Once the word of God has inspired the blessing of life within them it will create a new man, without corruption, an abiding being, hastening thence to God.

The Apocryphal New Testament, edited by J. K. Elliott © 1993 by Oxford University Press. Reproduced with permission of the Licensor through PLSclear.

QUESTIONS

1. The author of Seneca's letter admires in terms taken from Paul's letters how Paul speaks through the Holy Spirit who dwells within him (cf. 1 Cor. 2:6–13; 1 Thess. 1:5–6). He upbraids Paul, however, about his lack of rhetorical skill and eloquence (of which Seneca was a master). In another letter, he says, "I do wish you [...] would comply with the pure Latin style, giving a good appearance to your noble utterances." The author knows classical standards of eloquence, and finds Paul to fall short of them, despite the profundity of what he says. Would you agree that Paul's writing style is poor?
2. The author imagines Seneca reading Paul's letters to the emperor Nero ("Augustus," the great one) and his being amazed that such ideas could come from someone without an elite education. The author compares

Paul's view that he speaks divinely revealed truth, although not wise by the standards of the world (1 Cor. 2:1–5), to the Roman story (told by Cicero) of a countryman to whom the gods Castor and Pollux appeared, telling him of a Roman military victory. What do you make of the author's observation that some of Paul's theological claims are comparable to those of Roman religion?

3. The first thing Paul says in his letter to Seneca is that God has revealed true insights to Seneca in the form of Seneca's own philosophical reflections. The author of the letter, that is, believes that some of the great pre-Christian philosophers worked out principles with their reason alone that Christianity would later teach as revealed truth. What do you think of this claim?

4. Seneca taught some things about God that Paul would have agreed with. For example, in his Letter 41 to Lucilius, he writes, "We do not need to uplift our hands towards heaven, or to beg the keeper of a temple to let us approach his idol's ear [...] God is near you, he is with you, he is within you [...] A holy spirit [*sacer spiritus*] indwells within us, one who marks our good and bad deeds, and is our guardian [...] No man can be good without the help of God." In the same letter, he writes that simply looking at a sublime natural landscape "will prove to you the presence of the deity [*fidem tibi numinis faciet*]," as Paul says in Romans 1:19–20. The author of the letters thinks that Seneca's philosophy has led him halfway to Christianity, speaking of "that blameless wisdom which you have almost achieved." What do you think of this view?

Works Cited

Ehrman, Bart D. *Lost Scriptures: Books That Did Not Make It into the New Testament.* Oxford UP, 2003.

Fitzmeyer, Joseph A. *Romans: A New Translation with Introduction and Commentary.* Yale University Press, 2008.

Fredriksen, Paula. "Who Was Paul?" *The New Cambridge Companion to St. Paul*, edited by Bruce W. Longenecker, Cambridge University Press, 2020, pp. 23–47.

Jewett, Robert. *Romans: A Commentary.* Edited by Eldon Jay Epp, Fortress Press, 2007.

Josephus. *The Jewish War.* Translated by G. A. Williamson, revised ed., Penguin, 1981.

Harding, Mark. "Disputed and Undisputed Letters of Paul." *The Pauline Canon*, edited by Stanley E. Porter, Brill, 2004, pp. 129–68.

Malina, Bruce J., and John J. Pilch. *Social-Science Commentary on the Deutero-Pauline Letters.* Fortress Press, 2013.

Prothro, James B. *The Apostle Paul and His Letters: An Introduction.* The Catholic University of America Press, 2021.

Riesner, Rainer. "Pauline Chronology." *The Blackwell Companion to Paul*, edited by Stephen Westerholm, Wiley-Blackwell, 2011.

188　*The Bible as Literature*

Roetzel, Calvin J. "The Man and the Myth." *The Oxford Handbook of Pauline Studies*, edited by Matthew V. Novenson and R. Barry Matlock, Oxford UP, 2022, pp. 11–30.

Sanders, E. P. *Paul: The Apostle's Life, Letters, and Thought*. Fortress Press, 2015.

Seesengood, Robert Paul. *Paul: A Brief History*. Wiley-Blackwell, 2010.

Talbert, Charles H. *Romans*. Smyth and Helwys, 2002.

Wright, N. T. "Romans." *The New Interpreter's Bible*, vol. 9, edited by Leander Keck et al., Abingdon Press, 2015, pp. 317–664.

9 Revelation

Introduction

The author of Revelation gives his name as *Ioannēs*, "John," four times (1:1, 4, 9; 22:8), and there is no reason to doubt this. Early Christian writers identify him with Jesus's apostle John, son of Zebedee. This is unlikely, however. For one thing, the author refers to the names of the 12 apostles being written on the walls of the New Jerusalem (21:14) in a way that suggests that they are a "venerated group of heroes of the faith" (Reddish 18), of whom he himself is not one. Dionysius of Alexandria argued in the third century CE that the author of Revelation could not have been the author of the Gospel and letters of John because his language and style are so different (quoted in Blount 7). Most modern scholars agree. John is probably an otherwise unknown Christian, unrelated to the Johannine community in which the Gospel and letters of John are written. He describes his work as a "prophecy" (1:3; cf. 22:7, 10, 18, 19), and probably thought of himself as a Christian prophet. He writes with considerable authority, and was probably well known among the churches of Asia Minor to whom he writes in Chapters 2–3. Brian Blount suggests that he "belonged to a prophetic community that gave itself responsibility for directing the communal lives of the Asia Minor churches" (7). He uses the Hebrew Bible widely, and his prose has numerous Hebrew or Aramaic idioms expressed awkwardly in Greek, suggesting that he is a Jewish Christian (Reddish 19; Blount 8; Koester 68), perhaps from Palestine.

Most commentators date the book to the end of the first century CE. St. Irenaeus writes in *Against Heresies* that John saw his visions at the end of the reign of the emperor Domitian (81–96 CE) (5.30.3), and the book is commonly dated to about 95 CE. Two of the most persuasive reasons for this are, first, that John repeatedly uses the symbolic name "Babylon" to describe Rome and its empire, which makes most sense after 70 CE when the Romans have destroyed Jerusalem and its Temple just as the Babylonians did in 587 BCE. Second, in Chapters 13 and 17, John seems to be referring to the *Nero redivivus* myth, the belief that the emperor Nero (54–68 CE) would return after his apparent death and destroy Rome, which early Christian writings associated with the idea of the antichrist (Blount 8; Reddish 16; Koester 74).

DOI: 10.4324/9781315751566-10

190   *The Bible as Literature*

The reign of Domitian (81–96 CE) is a plausible time for the Book of Revelation. More than previous emperors (with the exceptions of Caligula and Nero), Domitian fostered the cult of emperor worship. In Thyatira, for example, where John writes to the church (Rev. 2:18–29), "cultic propaganda went so far as to declare the Roman emperor to be the incarnation of Apollo and therefore a son of Zeus" (Blount 9). A letter from Pliny the Younger, the governor of the Asian province of Bithynia, c. 112 CE, speaks of Christians who refuse to worship either the Roman gods or the emperor:

> I asked them whether they were Christians. Those who responded affirmatively I have asked a second and third time, under threat of the death penalty. If they persisted in their confession, I had them executed. For whatever it is that they are actually advocating, it seems to me that obstinacy and stubbornness must be punished in any case.
>
> (*Epistles* 10.96, quoted in Boring 14)

He goes on to tell the emperor that if people accused of being Christians "invoked our gods," "offered sacrifices [...] before your image," and cursed Christ, he released them. This probably represents the situation in Asia Minor 20 years earlier under Domitian (Blount 11; Reddish; Boring 13). While imperial officials were not seeking out Christians for persecution; nevertheless, if people were brought before them on a charge of Christianity, they were harshly treated. Antipas (Rev. 2:13) was probably killed in Pergamum and John exiled (Rev. 1:9) for this reason (Koester 98).

The Book of Revelation begins with the word *apokalupsis* ("revelation") (1:1). Apocalypse is, among other things, a form of writing, a literary genre with which John was very familiar and on which he drew in Revelation. The genre develops in Jewish writing after the Babylonian exile, flourishes in the third and second centuries BCE, and continues in the early church. Mitchell Reddish lists 14 Jewish examples of apocalypse from the intertestamental period, including texts from *1 Enoch*, *Jubilees*, *The Testament of Abraham*, and *4 Ezra*; and over 20 from the early centuries of the church, including *The Shepherd of Hermas*, *The Apocalypse of Peter*, *The Apocalypse of Paul*, and *The Apocalypse of the Virgin Mary* (6). John Collins defines apocalypse as

> a genre of revelatory literature with a narrative framework, in which a revelation is mediated by an otherworldly being to a human recipient, disclosing a transcendental reality which is both temporal, insofar as it envisages eschatological salvation, and spatial insofar as it involves another, supernatural world.
>
> (9)

Apocalyptic texts intend to reveal a hidden truth about the present from the perspective of the future, which is that "the people who hold power in the present are deluded about the scope of their historical control" (Blount 9). Although it appears that tyranny holds sway over God's people, apocalypse tells its readers that in reality it is God who does so. Apocalyptic writing portrays a world that lies behind and ultimately shapes this one, however unlikely that may appear in the situation into which it speaks. Examples in the Bible, on which John consciously draws, include the book of Daniel, Zechariah 9–14, Ezekiel 38–39, and Isaiah 24–27.

The Two Beasts

The Beast from the Sea

Perhaps the central images in the sensual panoply of apocalyptic imagery in the book of Revelation are those of the beast (*thērion*) from the sea and the beast from the earth of Chapter 13, who appear in the series of visions between the seven trumpets and the seven plagues. The beasts are the "lieutenants" (Reddish 249) or "agents" (Koester 568) of the dragon (*drakōn*) of Chapter 12, whose meaning John clearly explains to the reader as "that ancient serpent, who is called the Devil [*Diabolos*] and Satan [*ho Satanas*]" (12:9). After the vision in which the dragon pursues the "woman clothed with the sun" (12:1), the dragon stands on the shore. John then sees "a beast rising out of the sea," with ten horns and seven heads, which was "like a leopard," with bear's feet and a lion's mouth (13:1–2).

As most commentators agree, the beast is a representation of the Roman Empire. This will become clear as John expounds his vision in Chapter 13, and he spells it out as clearly as the genre of apocalypse allows in Chapter 17, in his vision of the great whore and the beast. There the beast's seven heads are "the seven mountains on which the woman is seated" (17:9), a reference to the seven hills on which the city of Rome is built (Koester 677). The woman who sits on the beast is "the great city that rules over the kings of the earth" (17:18), which in John's day was Rome. The woman, the "great whore," is "seated on many waters" (17:1), which means that she is Babylon, situated by the Euphrates with its "network of canals" (Koester 672) (cf. Jer. 51:13; Psalm 137:1). On her forehead is written a name that is a "mystery [*mustērion*]," "Babylon the great, mother of whores and of earth's abominations" (17:5). The name is a "mystery," just as the fact that the beast's seven heads are the seven mountains on which the woman sits "calls for a mind that has wisdom [*ho nous ho echōn sophian*]" (17:9). John means that his vision of the woman and the beast is a symbolic representation of the Roman Empire as the new incarnation of the Babylonian empire that destroyed Jerusalem, its Temple, and its worship of God. The author of 1 Peter uses the same image, describing the church in Rome as "she who is in Babylon" (1 Pet. 5:3). He calls Christians "the exiles of the Dispersion [*parepidēmoi Diasporas*]," comparing their situation in the Roman Empire to that of the Jewish exiles in the Babylonian empire (1:1).

John is drawing on the vision described in the Book of Daniel in which "four great beasts came up out of the sea" (Dan. 7:1), the first like a lion with eagles'

192   *The Bible as Literature*

wings, the second like a bear, the third like a leopard with four heads, and the fourth a terrible beast with ten horns. These beasts signified four successive empires (Dan. 7:17), those of the Babylonians, the Medes, the Persians, and the Greeks. In Daniel's vision, the fourth beast from the sea with ten horns signified the Greek empire of Alexander the Great, the ten horns his Seleucid successors (descended from Alexander's general Seleucus), and the other little horn that comes up among them speaking haughtily (Dan. 7:8) Antiochus IV Epiphanes, the Seleucid emperor who brutally suppressed Jewish worship, considered himself divine, and set up a statue of Zeus in the Jerusalem Temple (Dan. 9:27; 11:31; 12:11; 8:13). In combining features of all four of Daniel's beasts from the sea, John indicates that the Roman Empire combines all the oppressive or bestial qualities of the empires of which Daniel speaks. By associating his beast from the sea most closely with Daniel's fourth beast, with its ten horns and blasphemous names, he means that the Roman Empire is above all the new incarnation of the persecution of the people of God that characterized the last and most powerful empire of Daniel's vision. The king represented by Daniel's fourth beast, Antiochus IV Epiphanes, cruelly persecuted the Jewish people (Dan. 7:25; cf. 1 Macc. 1:10–64) and, by using Daniel's imagery, John says that this is also what the Roman Empire is doing to the Christians of Asia Minor. By John's time, Jewish tradition was associating Daniel's fourth beast with the Roman Empire (Boring 155; Koester 570), and John does something very similar. He portrays it as a new and even more powerful beast from the sea, making proud and blasphemous claims and persecuting the people of God.

John says of the beast, "One of its heads seemed to have received a death-blow, but its mortal wound had been healed" (Rev. 13:3). Here is the first time in this vision that John explicitly identifies the beast from the sea with the Roman Empire. Just as Daniel's fourth beast had ten horns and then another arose, in a similar way there is something notable about one of John's beast's ten horns, that it seemed to have died but had come back to life again. John is referring to the legend of *Nero redivivus*, in which the hated emperor Nero, who had died by stabbing himself in the throat, had either not in fact died or had died but would come back to life and return to Rome to retake the throne and revenge himself on the city that had rejected him (Reddish 251; Blount 248–249; Koester 570–571). Nero was remembered by Christians for his cruel persecution of the church in Rome. After a fire devastated the city in 64 CE, he tried to blame the Christian community. The Roman historian Tacitus writes that Nero convicted an "immense multitude" of Christians and had them cruelly executed – "covered with the skins of beasts, they were torn by dogs and perished, or were nailed to crosses, or were […] burnt, to serve as a nightly illumination, when daylight expired" (*Annals* 15.44, quoted in Koester 586). In Christian tradition, the apostles Peter and Paul were killed in this wave of persecution. As Eugene Boring puts it, "The image of Nero as beast was burned deeply into the Christian consciousness" (20). John does not expect Nero to come back to life. Rather, he means that the cruel and oppressive rule of Rome under Nero is still alive and flourishing under the current emperor, probably Domitian. As Reddish

Revelation   193

puts it, "John is warning his readers that the evil that was incarnate in Nero is not finished yet" (251).

In representing the beast from the sea with a head that has been killed and come back to life again, John also means that Nero, and the oppression of the church by the Roman Empire for which he stands, is a blasphemous parody of the rule of God, which has been shown above all in the death and resurrection of Christ. He uses the same phrase to describe the death both of the Lamb, who represents Christ, and the head of the beast from the sea. In heaven, John sees a lamb standing *hōs esphagmenon*, as if it had been killed (5:6); in his vision of the beast from the sea, one of its heads is *hōs esphagmenēn*, as if it had been killed (13:3). The phrase is exactly the same (the verb differing slightly because the word for "lamb" is neuter and the word for "head" is feminine). John uses the legend of *Nero redivivus* to indicate that the Roman Empire is fundamentally characterized by the cruelty of Nero and by the fact that its claim to be the just and rightful ruler of its subjects is a blasphemous parody of that claim which belongs to God alone. Indeed, John goes so far to as to make clear in his vision that it is not in the name of God that the Roman emperor rules, but rather in the name of Satan. The subjects of the Roman Empire obey its laws and customs in awe and powerlessness, "saying, 'Who is like the beast, and who can fight against it?'" (13:4). In John's apocalyptic perspective, however, what is going on is this: "They worshipped the dragon, for he had given his authority to the beast" (13:4). Craig Koester speaks of "the conventional idea that the emperors occupied their thrones by the will of heaven" (580). John believes that the opposite of this imperial ideology is true. For John, to accept the claim of the Roman emperor to rule as a god or even by the will of the gods is simply to be worshipping the devil.

The Beast from the Earth

John sees a second beast in this vision. It has two lamb's horns but speaks like a dragon. Most clearly, in the language of the apocalyptic vision, "It exercised all the authority of the first beast on its behalf, and it makes the earth and its inhabitants worship the first beast, whose mortal wound had been healed" (13:12). It performs various supernatural signs on behalf of the first beast, and "deceives the inhabitants of the earth, telling them to make an image [*eikōn*] for the beast" (13:14). Having envisaged the Roman empire primarily as a political power in the beast from the sea, now in the vision of the beast from the earth, John portrays the Roman Empire primarily as a religious power. In exercising the authority of the first beast (Rome as a political power), on behalf of that power, the second beast (Rome as a religious power) makes its subjects worship in the ways prescribed by Rome in its own political interests. In this sense, John also calls the beast from the earth the *pseudoprophētēs*, or false prophet (16:13; 19:20; 20:10).

As commentators point out, there are two main forms of state worship in the Roman Empire of John's time, the polytheistic worship of the Greco-Roman pantheon of gods, and worship of the Roman emperor as a god. The Roman historian

194   *The Bible as Literature*

Dio Cassius writes that Domitian "insisted upon being regarded as a god and took vast pride in being called 'master' and 'god'" (*Roman History* 67.4.7, quoted in Reddish 12). Emperor worship was strong in Asia Minor:

> Statues of the emperors were prevalent in the cities; large, impressive temples to the emperors dominated the cities; coins sometimes depicted the emperor as divine [...] To be a part of the civic life of the cities of Asia Minor meant being involved in the imperial cult.
>
> (Reddish 252)

For the people of Asia Minor, their Roman conquerors came to them by sea, the Mediterranean Sea, which the Romans called *mare nostrum*, "our sea." John's beast from the earth, by contrast, is indigenous. As Blount puts it, "This beast is local" (257). John has in mind all the vast regional infrastructure of the cult of the emperor and of the Greco-Roman deities that were also state gods. In Reddish's words, the beast from the earth is a vision of "everyone who encourages and fosters emperor worship," from local magistrates to imperial priests to provincial councils (258). Boring understands this in a wide sense, expounding:

> All who support and promote the cultural religion, in or out of the church, however Lamb-like they may appear, are agents of the beast. All propaganda that entices humanity to idolize human empire is an expression of this beastly power that wants to appear Lamb-like.
>
> (157)

John regards as Satanic all those who participate and enforce the cult of the emperor and of the other gods whose cult supports his rule. While John speaks primarily to first-century Christians in Asia Minor for whom he envisages a worsening state-sponsored persecution for their faith, Boring is surely right to observe that the problem is a perennial one.

The Number of the Name

Like the 144,000 servants of God, who have the mark of a seal on their foreheads (7:3), those who worship the beast have a mark (*charagma*) on their right hands or foreheads (13:16). As Reddish puts it, "For John there is no room for compromise. Either one belongs to God or one belongs to the beast (and thus to Satan)" (260). "No-one can buy or sell" (13:17), in John's vision, unless they have the mark of the beast. This presumably indicates the extent to which business relationships depended on participation in the cult of the emperor (Koester 595–596; Boring 162). As Blount puts it, "The 'mark' of the beast symbolizes a person's allegiance to and participation in the religious, social, economic, and political rites associated with the imperial cult" (259).

The mark of the beast is the "number of its name," which is the "number of a person [*arithmos anthrōpou*]," and that number is 666 [*hexakosioi hexēkonta hex*] (13:18). In both Hebrew and Greek, each letter of the alphabet has a numerical value – the first nine letters stand for the numbers one through nine; the next nine letters for the numbers ten through ninety; and the remaining letters for the multiples of one hundred. Many commentators believe that the person whose name adds up to the number 666, whom John has in mind, is Nero. If Nero's name is written in its Greek form, "Nerōn," in Hebrew letters, along with the title Caesar, it equals 666:

נרון קסר, Nero Caesar:

    נ = 50
    ר = 200
    ו = 6
    ן = 50
    ק = 100
    ס = 60
    ר = 200
        666

In some manuscripts of Revelation, the number of the name of the beast is given as 616. Since the Latin form of the name Nero (i.e., "Nero," rather than "Nerōn") lacks a final "n," whose number is 50, then this too would seem to be a way in which the text is referring to Nero.

Several other significances have been suggested for the number 666. First, since the number six is one short of seven, the number that traditionally symbolizes perfection or wholeness, six would represent imperfection, or even evil. The multiple series of seven according to which the Book of Revelation is structured seem to attest to this. In this sense, 666 would be "triple evil, a fitting symbolic number for the beast that is the puppet of Satan" (Reddish 262). Boring adds that, since John's readers live in the sixth period of the series of seven in Revelation (seals, trumpets, bowls, emperors), before the kingdom of God comes, 666 is "the intensive symbolic expression of incompleteness, idolatry, judgement, non-fulfillment, evil itself raised to the third power" (162–163). Others point out that, according to the later apocalyptic text *The Sibylline Oracles*, Jesus's name in Greek (*Iēsous*) adds up to 888, going "beyond the perfect seven at every point" (Koester 598).

The most convincing interpretation to my mind is that the number of the name of beast is that of the emperor Nero. John refers to him from beginning to end of his vision of the beast from the sea and the beast from the land as he repeats the image of the beast that has been mortally wounded and yet lived (13:3, 12, 14). His vision of the Roman Empire is from beginning to end (if the number of the name of the beast indeed is that of the emperor Nero) a vision of Nero. Cruel, mad, tyrannical, and a vicious enemy of the people of God, the spirit of the Roman Empire

196   *The Bible as Literature*

continues to be that of Nero, for John, continuing to demand for itself the allegiance, commitment, and love that properly belong to God alone. This happened under Nero, it is happening again under Domitian, and John sees no end of its happening until the kingdom of God comes.

The New Jerusalem

John's final vision in Revelation, which Boring rightly calls "the climax and fulfillment" of the series of eschatological images in the book (213), is that of the new Jerusalem. He writes, "I saw a new heaven and a new earth, for the first [...] had passed away," and "I saw the holy city, the new Jerusalem, coming down out of heaven, prepared as a bride [*numphē*] adorned for her husband" (21:1–2). This is a vision deeply grounded in the eschatological prophecies of the Hebrew Bible, especially those of the books of Isaiah and Ezekiel. John has read these prophecies over and over again, and his vision synthesizes them into a climactic vision of the culmination of sacred history to which he believes the prophets have always been pointing.

In Third Isaiah, the prophet writes:

For I am about to create new heavens and a new earth;
the former things shall not be remembered
    or come to mind.
But be glad and rejoice for ever [...]
for I am about to create Jerusalem as a joy,
    and its people as a delight.
                (Isa. 65:17–18; cf. 66:22–23)

The Book of Isaiah imagines all nations coming to the new Jerusalem – "Nations shall come to your light, / and kings to the brightness of your dawn" (Isa. 60:3; cf. 60:3–16) – just as John sees that "The nations will walk by its light, and the kings of the earth will bring their glory into it" (Rev. 21:24). The prophet adds, "Your gates shall always be open; / day and night they shall not be shut" (Isa. 60:11), and John follows him, saying, "Its gates will never be shut by day – and there will be no night there" (Rev. 21:25). Furthermore, Third Isaiah continues, "The sun shall no longer be your light by day, / nor [...] shall the moon give light to you by night; / but the LORD will be your everlasting light, / and your God will be your glory" (Isa. 60:19). In just the same way, John prophesies, "The city has no need of sun or moon to shine on it, for the glory of God is its light, and its lamp is the Lamb" (Rev. 21:23). Second Isaiah imagines Jerusalem being transformed eschatologically into a city adorned with jewels in the "covenant of peace" to come:

I am about to set your stones in antimony,
    and lay your foundations with sapphires.

Revelation   197

I will make your pinnacles of rubies,
   your gates of jewels,
   and all your walls of precious stones.
                                    (Isa. 54:11–12)

The prophet compares Jerusalem to Yahweh's wife as he imagines this transformation (54:6), just as John sees the new Jerusalem set in jewels as a "bride adorned
for her husband" (Rev. 21:2). Third Isaiah speaks of God's redemption by saying,
"he has clothed me with the garments of salvation [...] / as a bride [*numphē*, LXX]
adorns herself with jewels" (Isa. 61:10; cf. 49:18).

John also has Ezekiel's vision of the restored Temple (Ezek. 40–48) in mind
as he pictures the new Jerusalem. Both prophets are taken by the spirit of God to
a mountain where they see a city (Ezek. 40:2; Rev. 21:10). Both are thinking of
Mount Zion, on which Jerusalem was built and which comes in Hebrew poetry
to stand metonymically for God's dwelling place. In Ezekiel's vision, the new
Jerusalem is a square, with three gates on each side, each named after the 12 tribes
of Israel (Ezek. 48:30–35). John's new Jerusalem too is a square with three gates
on each side, each named after the 12 tribes of Israel (Rev. 21:12–13). Ezekiel
sees an angelic figure with a measuring reed (Ezek. 40:3), who talks to him and
measures the new Temple's walls and gates; John sees an angel with a measuring
rod, who talks to him and measures the new Jerusalem's walls and gates (Rev.
21:15–17). Ezekiel sees a river flowing from the Temple, with trees on either bank,
which bears fruit every month and whose leaves are "for healing" (Ezek. 47:12);
John sees a river flowing from the throne of God and of the Lamb, with "the tree
of life" on either side, which bears fruit every month and whose leaves are "for
[...] healing" (Rev. 22:2). In Blount's words, "John is clearly channeling Ezekiel;
John's vision will serve as a prophetic reinterpretation" (385). John has studied
the Hebrew prophets' visions of the eschatological climax to sacred history, carefully and repeatedly, and they have fundamentally structured his own vision. His
Christian belief that Jesus is the Messiah prophesied in the Hebrew Scriptures leads
him to think that these visions need only a little reinterpretation to be understood
as having rightly proclaimed the ways in which the kingdom of God will come.

Ezekiel's new city was a square, of 4,500 cubits, or approximately 1.25 miles
(Ezek. 48:30–35). John's new city is enormous in comparison. It is 12,000 stadia in
length and breadth, so that its area is 144,000,000 square stadia, a thousand times
the 144,000 of those sealed for the Lamb (7:4; 14:1–5). Twelve thousand stadia is
approximately 1,500 miles. Furthermore, John's city is also 12,000 stadia (1,500
miles) in height (Rev. 21:16), so it is a gigantic cube in shape. Here is an example in
which John has brought his own thinking to the vision that he has shaped from his
knowledge of the prophets. Perhaps the first significance of the golden cube – "the
city is pure gold, clear as glass" (Rev. 21:18) – is that it picks up on the previous
golden cube in John's Scriptures, that is, the holy of holies in Solomon's Temple.
In the account of Solomon's building the Temple in 1 Kings, we read, "The interior
of the inner sanctuary was twenty cubits long, twenty cubits wide, and twenty

198   *The Bible as Literature*

cubits high; he overlaid it with pure gold" (1 Kings 6:20). The holy of holies in the Temple is where Yahweh dwells in the midst of Israel, specifically between the wings of the two cherubim cast on the lid of the Ark of the Covenant, which is itself his footstool. No one may enter the space because of its extreme holiness, with the one exception of the high priest once a year, on the Day of Atonement. In picturing the new Jerusalem as a golden cube like the holy of holies in the Temple, John clearly means to say that in the new Jerusalem to which the righteous can look forward, the presence of God will be everywhere. It will become universal rather than restricted, as during the old covenant, to one central point in Jerusalem. God will be everywhere and all in all. As Koester puts it, "Where God's glory once filled the holy of holies, it now fills the New Jerusalem [...] The massive size of the city exhibits holiness on a cosmic scale" (816).

The enormous size of the new Jerusalem, which John has invented for himself, speaks also to one of the most striking features of John's final vision. John seems to be a hard-liner by temperament, and from the very beginning of the Book of Revelation he has emphasized how important it is for the Christians to whom he is writing not to compromise in any way with the Satanic influence of Roman imperial society. They must not eat food sacrificed to idols (about which Paul is less uncompromising), practice fornication, or listen to the teachings of the Nicolaitans, Jezebel, or Balaam, who were probably Christian teachers who permitted compromise with Roman religious customs. For John, one either compromises with Satan, in the form of the religion and morals of the Roman Empire, or one is faithful to God. There is no middle ground. As Reddish comments, for John "a radical choice is demanded – either one lives in Babylon or one lives in Jerusalem; either one joins the whore or one joins the bride" (Reddish 411). However, in the final vision of the book John repeatedly hints at how many people, how many nations indeed, will enter the presence of God in the new Jerusalem. This seems to me to be part of the significance of the enormous size of the visionary city, which John adds to the prophetic tradition from which he has learned so much. As Boring writes, "Against everything we might have expected, [John] has modified his tradition in order to portray a radically inclusive city" (221). His new Jerusalem is big enough for everyone, for all the nations of the world, despite his own position as a member of a persecuted minority within that world. Its vast size suggests that, as the Hebrew prophets also said, everyone can enter.

John makes this point repeatedly throughout the vision. As he first sees the new Jerusalem coming down from heaven, he hears a voice saying of God, "He will dwell with [mortals] as their God; / they will be his peoples [*laoi*]" (Rev. 21:3). The prophets frequently use some version of the formula, "They will be my people [*laos*] and I will be their God" (cf. Jer. 24:7; Ezek. 37:23; Zech. 8:8, LXX). John develops this idea, saying that God will dwell with his people, that he will be their God and they will be his "peoples," in the plural. In one sense, John means that Jesus's sacrifice has opened the blessing of the covenant to all nations. Hence, he adds the names of Jesus's twelve apostles on the foundations of the city to Ezekiel's names of the twelve tribes of Israel on its gates (Rev. 21:14, 12; Ezek. 48:30–35). He also gives the strong impression in this final vision that this opening will be a very large, very inclusive, if not positively universal process. A vast number of people, nations, and kings will enter the new Jerusalem. "The nations will walk by its light, and the kings of the earth will bring their glory into it [...] People will bring into it the glory and the honor of the nations" (Rev. 21:24, 26). "The kings of the earth" is an especially surprising phrase here, since so much of the rest of the book has been about rejecting the great empires of the earth like Babylon and Rome. Reddish calls it "one of the most astounding passages in the Apocalypse" (409). Finally, John adds to Ezekiel's vision of the river of life from God's dwelling-place that the leaves of the tree of life which grows along the banks of the river are "for the healing of the nations [*therapeia tōn ethnōn*]" (Rev. 22:2). In Ezekiel's vision, they were "for healing [*teruphah*]" (Ezek. 47:12). John adds to this that they are specifically for the healing of the nations. The river of life that flows from God is not only for the restored Israel, for John, but for all nations. As Reddish comments, "John leaves open the possibility that God's mercy is wider than we might expect or even imagine" (420).

John does not seem to believe in universal salvation. The rest of the book has been too dualistic for that. But in the vision of the new Jerusalem it suddenly appears, as has not been the case previously in Revelation, that very many, and possibly all, are written in the Lamb's book of life. Suddenly it becomes clear that, at the very least, all are called to enter the new Jerusalem. All are invited. As Koester puts it, "The vision of redemption includes all humanity because this is the future to which all humanity is called" (806). John's previously clearly expressed view that there is faithfulness to God and faithlessness to God in the world does not exactly change in his last vision. Rather, the emphasis turns from the two ways to the individual who is faced with them. There is no one, not even the Roman emperor himself, who is not called to enter the new Jerusalem with joy and praise, like a "bride adorned for her husband." There is no one in the empire or beyond to whom God and the Lamb do not call today. The question is only what each person's response will be. The vision of the new Jerusalem suggests that the persecuted minority of Christians to whom John writes, and of whom he is one, might be surprised at how many will answer yes.

TEXT FOR DISCUSSION

Albrecht Dürer, *The Four Horsemen, from "The Apocalypse"*

The German painter, printmaker, and writer Albrecht Dürer (1471–1528) painted and published a series of 15 woodcuts illustrating the Book of Revelation in 1498. The book was entitled The Apocalypse, with Pictures. *Below is the fourth image, of the four horsemen John sees as the first four seals of the scroll in the hand of God are opened* (Rev. 6:1–8).

200 *The Bible as Literature*

Figure 9.1 Albrecht Dürer, *The Four Horsemen, from "The Apocalypse,"* 1498, woodcut. The Metropolitan Museum of Art, New York. Gift of Junius Spencer Morgan, 1919

QUESTIONS

1. Perhaps the first effect on the viewer of Dürer's picture is motion. Things seem to be moving fast and chaotically as the Lamb opens the first four seals of the scroll. Do you think this is a good representation of Revelation 6:1–8, and why (or why not)?
2. There are some aspects of the biblical vision that Dürer does not represent. He does not depict the Lamb who is opening the seals (6:1), nor the four living creatures who loudly summon the horsemen each time one is opened. These creatures are like a lion, ox, human, and eagle, each with six wings and covered in eyes (4:6–8). In place of these, Dürer depicts an angel, and the rays of the light at the top left indicating God's presence. Why do you think he made these changes to the biblical vision? Do they improve or impoverish his representation of the scene?
3. Dürer does not attempt to portray the four different colors of the horses – white, red, black, and pale green [*chlōros*; *pallidus* in Dürer's Latin Bible]. It would be possible to indicate white and black (and possibly even pale and a fourth shade) in a woodcut, but Dürer does not. The color symbolism is clearly important to John. Does Dürer's representation of the biblical scene suffer without it? Does he make any attempt to compensate for it?
4. In Revelation, the first rider comes out "conquering and to conquer" [*vincens ut vinceret*]; the second to unleash war; the third to make food impossibly expensive for the poor; and the fourth to kill one fourth of the earth. These effects are not clearly represented in the picture; rather, a mixed group of people are trampled down by the four horses. What is the effect of this difference from the biblical text? Does Dürer's picture adequately represent John's vision of the events with which the world will end?
5. In John's text, the fourth horseman, unlike the first three, has a name, "Death." Dürer depicts the horseman as a very emaciated man, carrying a trident (a detail Dürer has added to the biblical text), and riding an emaciated horse. How faithful is Dürer's portrayal of this character to John's vision?
6. The beast in the bottom left of the picture represents Hades, the world of the dead, which follows Death in Revelation 6:8. The first person Death is sending to Hades in Dürer's picture is a bishop. Why do you think Dürer adds this detail to the biblical scene? How well do you think it expresses the message of the scene or of the book of Revelation as whole?

Works Cited

Blount, Brian K. *Revelation: A Commentary*. Westminster John Knox Press, 2009.
Boring, M. Eugene. *Revelation*. Westminster John Knox Press, 1989.
Collins, John J. "Towards the Morphology of a Genre." *Semeia*, vol. 14, 1979, pp. 1–19.
Koester, Craig R. *Revelation: A New Translation with Introduction and Commentary*. Yale UP, 2014.
Reddish, Mitchell G. *Revelation*. Smyth and Helwys, 2001.

Index

Aaron 41–2
Abraham 9, 17–21, 93, 182
Acts, Book of 163, 164, 166, 179–80
Adam 12–15, 149, 182–5
Ahasuerus 68–72
Alexamenos graffito 169–70
Alexander the Great 192
Allen, Leslie 135
Alter, Robert 65, 112, 144
angel: Hebrew Bible 26, 27, 55; New
    Testament 164–5, 197, 201
Annunciation, the *see* Mary, mother of
    Jesus; annunciation to
apocalypse 190–1
apocrypha, Protestant 3, 69, 173–4
Ark of the Covenant 31, 62, 198
Aristophanes 71, 73
Assyria 7, 8, 127–9, 136
Astruc, Jean 7
Augustine, St. 29–30, 183–4
Austen, Jane 60

Babylon 15–16, 127, 136–9, 144–8, 189,
    191, 192, 198–9; poetry of 15–17, 90,
    117–18; wisdom literature of 102, 111
Babylonian exile 8, 15, 44, 51, 53, 94, 127,
    129–31, 133–4, 136–40, 143–9, 190
Bailey, Lloyd 37, 40, 41
Balentine, Samuel 34, 102, 105
Baruch 3, 136
Bathsheba 63–8
Bechtel, Carol 70, 71
Ben Sira 173
Berlin, Adele 69–73
Bernard of Clairvaux, St. 99–101
Bible, Eastern Orthodox 2–3, 69; *see also*
    Septuagint

Bible, Hebrew 2–3, 12, 16, 18, 31, 32, 57,
    61, 62, 66, 68, 78, 86–8, 94, 104, 112,
    114, 119, 131, 144, 158, 173, 174, 189,
    196; *see also* Masoretic Text
Bible, King James version 2, 12, 14, 16,
    17, 34, 39, 62, 66, 68, 90, 108, 113, 120,
    123, 132, 134, 163, 164, 167, 177, 183
Bible, New International Version 108, 113
Bible, Protestant 1–4, 32, 33, 68, 69, 183;
    see also apocrypha, Protestant
Bible, Roman Catholic 2–3, 32, 69;
    see also apocrypha, Protestant
Birch, Bruce 63, 64
Blake, William 149–51
Blenkinsopp, Joseph 126, 127
Block, Daniel 142, 144, 197
Blount, Brian 189, 194
Boaz 58–61
Boring, Eugene 159, 192, 194, 196, 198
Bovon, François 163, 164
Brown, Raymond 171
Brown, William 14, 77
Brueggemann, Walter 11, 13, 24, 27, 62–4,
    77, 82

Calvin, John 54
Campbell, Edward 58
Canaan 17–19, 23, 39, 40, 46, 52–5, 106
Cardenal, Ernesto 83–4
Carr, David 6, 9
Carroll, John 164–6, 168
Cartledge, Tony 62–5
cherem 52–4
Childs, Brevard 127, 131
Chronicles, Books of 58, 62, 68, 103, 104
Cicero 167
circumcision 9, 17, 182

204 *Index*

Clements, Ronald 31, 43, 44
Clifford, Richard 112
comedy 70–3
covenant: with Abraham 9, 17–19, 21; at
  Sinai 31–4, 38–40, 43, 45–7, 52, 55–7,
  65–6, 73, 79–86, 93, 97–9, 136–41, 144–8,
  166; *see also* new covenant
Creach, Jerome 54
Crenshaw, James 77, 105, 118
Cross, Frank Moore 51
crucifixion *see* Jesus, crucifixion of
Cyrus II, emperor of Persia 127
Culler, Jonathan 4
Culpepper, Alan 157, 169

Daniel, Book of 191–3
Darr, Katherine Pfisterer 143, 144
David, King 58, 61–8, 97–8, 111, 118, 129;
  as an artist 62–3; with Bathsheba and
  Uriah 63–8; in the Psalms 77–8, 85
Delilah 56–7
Dell, Kathleen 103
Deuteronomistic History 43–4, 51–2, 54–7,
  61–2, 68, 136, 137, 148
Deuteronomists 9–10, 32–4, 43–7,
  51–2, 54, 55, 65, 66, 136; *see also*
  Deuteronomistic History; Deuteronomy
Deuteronomy 6–10, 8, 22, 31–4, 41, 43–7,
  51–2, 58–9, 65–6, 81, 113, 119, 136,
  140, 160
de Wette, Wilhelm 7, 43
Dietrich, Walther 44, 51
Dinah 23
documentary hypothesis 7–10
Domitian 189, 192–4, 196
Douglas, Mary 36, 37
Dozeman, Thomas 40–2
Duhm, Bernard 126, 132
Dürer, Albrecht 199–201

Eagleton, Terry 3–4
Ecclesiastes, Book of 117–24; religious
  ideas of 121–2; on vanity 119–22,
  124
ecology 13–15, 142
Eden, garden of 13–15, 109, 149
Egypt 18, 40, 59, 136; Israelite slavery in
  18, 25–8, 31–3, 39–40, 46, 193; poetry
  of 90–1; religion of 112, 165; wisdom
  literature of 102, 111, 117
Elihu 103, 107
Enuma Elish 15–17
Epic of Gilgamesh 117–18
Esau 22–4

Eskenazi, Tamara 58
Esther, Book of 68–75; Greek additions
  to 73–5
Eve 12–15
Exodus, the 26–31, 39–41, 44, 45, 59
Exum, Cheryl 89–90, 92, 94–6
Ezekiel 142–51, 193, 196–9; school
  of 142–3; sign-acts of 146–7, 150–1;
  vision of divine chariot 143–6; vision
  of dry bones 147–8; vision of restored
  Temple 197–9; vision of river of life
  148–9, 197
Ezra 58, 68, 112

Fischer, Irmtraud 58
Fishbane, Michael 90
Fitzmeyer, Joseph 183, 184
Fontaine, Carol 112, 114
form-criticism 78
Fox, Michael 111, 112, 115, 119
Fretheim, Terence 10–12, 14, 18, 19, 22,
  26–8, 33, 135, 136
Freud, Sigmund 49

Gideon 57
Golden Calf 49
Goldingay, John 127, 129
Goodacre, Mark 153, 154
Green, Joel 164, 166, 167
Griesbach, Johann Jakob 153
Gunkel, Hermann 78, 82, 85

Habel, Norman 14
Hagar 17–19
Haman 67, 68, 71–3, 75
Handel, Georg Friedrich 134–5
Hannah: song of 165–7
Harding, Mark 181
Hellenistic period 68, 90, 112, 118;
  Hellenistic empire 192
Hemingway, Ernest 123–4
Herbert, George 169–70
Herodotus 69, 70
hevel see Ecclesiastes, Book of; on vanity
Hezekiah, King 128, 134
Holy Spirit 53, 164, 165, 185–7
Hopkins, Gerard Manley 141–2
Horeb, Mount 2, 26, 46–7; *see also*
  Sinai, Mount
Hunt, William Holman 175–7

Infancy Gospel of Thomas, the 161–2
Irenaeus, St. 164, 189
Isaac 17–21

Index 205

Isaiah, book of 17, 126–35, 142, 150–1, 157–8, 191, 196; composition history of 126–7; First Isaiah (1-39) 126–9, 133–5; Second Isaiah (40-55) 126–7, 129–33, 196–7; servant songs 132–3; Third Isaiah (56-66) 127, 133–4, 196–7
Ishmael 17–19

Jacob 21–4; and Esau 23–4; wrestling with God 22–3
Jehoiachin, King 136
Jehoiakim, King 136
Jephthah 57
Jeremiah 135–42; Book of Consolation in 138–41; composition history of 135–6
Jerome, St. 1, 3, 69, 132, 183
Jesus 99, 110, 134, 153, 156–72, 174–6, 179–86, 189, 195, 197, 198; crucifixion of 99–100, 110, 166–70; curses a fig tree 163; infancy narratives of 161–2, 164–7; parables of 156–61; resurrection of 166, 170–2
Jewett, Robert 183, 185
Job 17, 102–10, 117, 122, 175; companions of 105–7; composition history of book of 102–3; dialogue with God 107–9; God's test of 103–5
John, Gospel of 171–7; authorship of 171–2, 189; beloved disciple in 171–2; Word of God (*logos*) in 172–5
Johnstone, William 27, 28, 31, 33
Jonathan 62
Joseph, father of Jesus 161–2, 167
Josephus 168, 179
Joshua 46, 52–4
Josiah, King 7–8, 43–4, 51, 136
Joyce, Paul 142
Judges 54–8
Jung, C. G. 109–10
justification: Paul's thought on 182–5

Kant, Immanuel 21
Kierkegaard, Søren 19–21
King James Bible *see* Bible, King James version
Koester, Craig 193, 198, 199
Konradt, Matthias 159

LaCoque, André 72
Levenson, Jon 68–71
Levine, Baruch 39, 41
Leviticus 7, 22, 34–9, 55, 58–9, 61, 131, 147, 160; *see also* purity laws
Light of the World, The 175–7

logos see John, Gospel of; Word of God (*logos*) in
Luke, Gospel of 153, 163–70; author of 163–4; special Luke (L) 153–4
Luther, Martin 118

Marduk 15–17
Mark, Gospel of 153, 156–8, 163, 164, 168
marriage 12–13, 59–61, 69–72, 113–16; marriage between God and soul/Israel/ church 99–101, 114–16
Mary, mother of Jesus 99, 164–7; Annunciation to 164–7; song of (Magnificat) 165–7; virgin conception 164–5
mashal 111, 156–7
Masoretic Text 3, 11, 32, 62, 68–9, 73, 77, 85–8, 158; *see also* Bible, Hebrew
Matthew, Gospel of 153, 156–63; author of 156; special Matthew (M) 153–4
Mays, James 80
McCann, J. Clinton 57, 77, 81
McCarter, P. Kyle 65
Mein, Andrew 143
Messiah: Hebrew Bible 83–5, 97, 129–35; New Testament 165, 167, 172, 179, 197
Michelangelo 47–9
Milgrom, Jacob 37, 38, 41–2
Miller, Patrick 33, 45, 135–6, 138, 139
monarchy, Israelite 51, 52, 57–8, 66, 127–9, 136; in Psalms 84–5; *see also* David, King; Jehoiachin, King; Jehoiakim, King; Hezekiah, King; Josiah, King; Saul, King; Solomon, King; Zedekiah, King
Moses 26–34, 39–49
Murphy, Roland 105, 107
music 62–3, 78, 85–6

Nebuchadnezzar, King 136, 137, 139, 147
Nehemiah 58, 68
Nelson, Richard 44, 47
Nero 180, 186, 189–90, 192–3, 195–6
new covenant 140–1, 196
Newlyn, Lucy 116–17
Newsom, Carol 13–14, 102, 105, 107
Nielsen, Kirsten 60
non-Priestly writers of the Pentateuch (non-P) 9–13, 18, 19, 41, 43
Norton, David 4
Noth, Martin 43–4, 51–2, 61

O'Connor, Kathleen 11–13, 21, 23
Odell, Margaret 142, 145

206 *Index*

Olson, Dennis 39–42, 55
Origen 53

parables 156–61; the laborers in the
vineyard 160–1
Passover 27–30, 40, 167
patriarchy 12, 61, 95–6, 112
Paul 163, 164, 171, 179–87; apocryphal
letters of 182, 185–7; authorship of
letters of 180–2; life of 179–80, 192;
thought on Adam and Christ of 182–5;
see also Paul, letters of
Paul, letters of: Colossians
164, 181; 1 Corinthians 179–81, 185–7;
2 Corinthians 181, 185; Ephesians 181;
Galatians 179, 180, 185, 181; Philemon
164, 181; Philippians 181; Romans
181–5; 1 Thessalonians 181, 182, 186;
2 Thessalonians 181, 182; 1 Timothy
164, 181; 2 Timothy 181; Titus 181
Pelagius 183–4
Persia: Persian empire 68–73, 127, 192;
Persian loan-words 90; Persian period
58, 68, 112, 118, 127
1 Peter 191
Pharisees 159, 179–80
Philo of Alexandria 173, 179
philosophy 19, 21, 29–30, 112, 118, 119,
122, 172–3, 175; Stoic 172, 182, 185–7
Pisgah, Mount 41, 44–5
Pliny the Younger 190
Plutarch 165; life of Alexander 165; life of
Numa 165
poetry 11, 150–1
poetry, Ancient Near Eastern 90–1, 96
poetry, Biblical 11, 12, 79, 86–9, 91–2, 94,
96, 103, 113, 119, 135, 137, 139, 157,
165, 197; acrostic 114
Porter, Stanley 153
Priestly writers of the Pentateuch (P) 7–12,
14, 19, 28, 32, 34, 36, 39, 43, 45
promised land 17–19, 27, 28, 33, 39, 41,
44–6, 93; *see also* Canaan
Propp, William 27, 31
proverbs 111–17, 118, 173; modern-day
116–17; Wisdom in 173–4; women
figures in 113–16; woman of strength
in 114–16
Prothro, James 179, 180
Psalms 77–9; Psalm 1; 83–4, 86–8;
Psalm 2 84; Psalm 3 81, 83; Psalm
4 78–9; Psalm 6 80–1; Psalm 10 83, 84;
Psalm 12 84; Psalm 16 166; Psalm

18 62–3; Psalm 22 168; Psalm 30 81;
Psalm 31 168; Psalm 33 174; Psalm
35 81–2; Psalm 45 84; Psalm 54 85;
Psalm 56 81, 85; Psalm 63 79–80;
Psalm 66 86; Psalm 67 86; Psalm 69 85;
Psalm 72 83–5; Psalm 73 85; Psalm 86 85;
Psalm 88 81; Psalm 89 17; Psalm 95 86;
Psalm 96 86; Psalm 98 86; Psalm 110 84;
Psalm 121 12; Psalm 150 86
purity laws 34–9, 55–6

Q (Gospel source) 153–5
qohelet: meaning of 118–19

Reddish, Mitchell 194, 198, 199
redeemer (*go'el*) 59, 131
Rembrandt 66–8
Revelation, Book of 171, 176–7, 189–201;
author of 189–91; four horsemen of
the apocalypse 199–201; number of
the name of the beast 194–5; vision of
beast from the earth 193–4; vision of
beast from the sea 191–3; vision of new
Jerusalem 189, 196–9
Riesner, Rainer 181
Roetzel, Calvin 180, 181
Rogerson, John 15
Rome 169, 191; Roman empire 167–8, 180,
185, 189–96, 198, 199
Römer, Thomas 51–2
Ruth, Book of 57–61, 114, 131

Sabbath, the 32–4, 182
Sakenfeld, Katherine Doob 60
Samson 54–7
Samuel 66, 166
Sarah 17–20
Sarna, Nahum 12, 13, 17, 22, 23
Satan 103, 109–10, 191, 193–5, 198; in Job
as *ha-satan* 103–5, 110; in Zechariah 103
Saul, King 62, 63, 64, 85
Schmid, Konrad 9
Seesengood, Robert 182
Seitz, Christopher 132–3
Seneca 182, 185–7
Sennacherib 128
Seow, C. L. 118
Septuagint 2–3, 31, 58, 61, 62, 68–9, 72,
73–5, 77, 78, 113, 118, 156, 158, 163,
165–6, 174, 175, 179, 197
shalom 82, 83, 98
Sinai, Mount 23, 26, 31, 39, 40, 46, 47,
140; *see also* Horeb, Mount

sin, Paul's thought on 182–5
Smend, Rudolf 51
Solomon, King 77, 89, 90, 94, 98–9, 111–12, 118, 197
Song of Songs 89–101; nighttime searches 94–6; religious significance of 97–101; songs of description (*wasf*) 92–4
spiritual sense of Scripture 29–30, 53, 99–101
Synoptic Gospels 153–70; double tradition 153–4; Farrer Hypothesis 155; synoptic problem 153–6; triple tradition 153; Two Source Hypothesis 153–5; *see also* Luke, Gospel of; Mark, Gospel of; Matthew, Gospel of; Q (Gospel source)
Syro-Ephraimite war 127, 129

Tabernacle, the 26, 29, 31, 165, 175
Tacitus 192
Talbert, Charles 182, 184
Temple, Jerusalem 2, 7, 43, 62, 78, 89, 127, 136, 144, 145, 148–9, 156, 164, 179, 180, 189, 191, 192, 197–8
Ten Commandments, the 31–4, 39–41, 46–7, 49
Thatcher, Tom 171
Thompson, Marianne Meye 174
Tobin, Thomas 173
Towner, W. Sibley 118–19
Tull, Patricia 126, 127, 128, 134

Uriah 63–8

van Dijk-Hemmes, Fokkelien 58
van Leeuwen, Raymond 115
Van Seters, John 9
Vashti, Queen 69–71
Vulgate 2, 3, 48–9, 69, 132, 141; *see also* Bible, Roman Catholic

Weems, Renita 89
Weinfeld, Moshe 47
Wellhausen, Julius 7–8
White, Lynn Jr. 14
wilderness 18, 26, 31, 39–42, 44–7, 131, 165
wisdom 103, 105, 107, 111, 114–17, 119, 122, 173–4; personified as Woman Wisdom 112–14
wisdom literature, Ancient Near Eastern 102, 111, 117–18; "Babylonian Theodicy" 102; "Counsels of Wisdom" 111; "Instruction of Amen-em-Opet" 111
woman of strength: in Proverbs 114–16; in Ruth 58
word of the LORD, the 174; *see also* John, Gospel of; Word of God (*logos*) in
Wright, David 38–9
Wright, N. T. 183

Yahweh: meaning of name 26–7

Zechariah, annunciation to 164
Zedekiah, King 136
Zimmerli, Walther 142, 145, 148

Printed in the United States
by Baker & Taylor Publisher Services